The Developing World of the Child

department for
education and skills
creating opportunity, releasing potential, achieving excellence

The Open University

Royal Holloway
University of London

NSPCC
Cruelty to children must stop. FULL STOP.

The Developing World of the Child

Edited by Jane Aldgate, David Jones, Wendy Rose and Carole Jeffery

Foreword by Maria Eagle MP

Jessica Kingsley *Publishers*
London and Philadelphia

Figure 1.1 and Figure 2.1 are adapted from *Child Sexual Abuse: Informing Practice from Research* by D.P.H. Jones and P. Ramchandani (1999) by permission of Radcliffe Publishing Ltd.

Figure 3.1, Figure 3.2 and Table 3.3 are reproduced from 'The significance of genetic variation for abnormal behavioural development' by J. Stevenson in *Research and Innovation on the Road to Modern Psychiatry 1*, edited by J. Green and W. Yule (2001) by permission of Gaskell Publications.

Table 3.1 is reproduced from *A Neuropsychiatric Study in Childhood: Clinics in Developmental Medicine* by M. Rutter, P Graham and W. Yuke (1970) by permission of Elsevier and Michael Rutter.

Box 7.1 is Crown copyright material, reproduced from *Framework for the Assessment of Children in Need and their Families* by the Department of Health, Department for Education and Employment and Home Office (2000) by permission of the Controller of HMSO.

Table 8.1 is reproduced from *The Missing Side of the Triangle* by G. Jack and O. Gill (2003) by permission of Barnardo's.

'I feel' on p.294 by Ann aged 16, is reproduced from *Shout to be Heard* by Voice for the Child in Care (1998) by permission of VOICE, previously Voice for the Child in Care.

Extract on p.301 is reproduced from 'Please miss, can I have a detention?' by Jonathan Glancey from *G2*, 19 July 2004, by permission of the *Guardian*. Copyright © Guardian Newspapers Limited 2004.

First published in 2006
by Jessica Kingsley Publishers
73 Collier Street
London N1 9BE, UK
and
400 Market Street, Suite 400
Philadelphia, PA 19106, USA

www.jkp.com

Library of Congress Cataloging in Publication Data
The developing world of the child / edited by Jane Aldgate ... [et al.].
p. cm.
Includes bibliographical references and index.
ISBN-13: 978-1-84310-244-1 (pbk. : alk. paper)
ISBN-10: 1-84310-244-7 (pbk. : alk. paper) 1. Social work with children. 2. Child development. I. Aldgate, Jane, 1945-
HV713.D49 2006
305.231--dc22

2005029509

British Library Cataloguing in Publication Data
A CIP catalogue record for this book is available from the British Library

ISBN 978 1 84310 244 1
eISBN 978 1 84642 468 7

Contents

Foreword

The Government is committed to improving the lives of children, young people and their families. Every Child Matters sets out the five outcomes that we have acknowledged are key to well-being in childhood and later life – being healthy, staying safe, enjoying and achieving, making a positive contribution and achieving economic well-being.

We recognise that it will be hard to ensure the achievement of this ambition for some children because of their vulnerability and poor prospects for the future unless we can provide timely help. In order to give every child the opportunity to develop to the best of their potential, we need to ensure that all staff working with children fully understand the influences on children's development and the needs of those children whose development has been impaired or impeded in some way.

The Government has recognised that we require the development of a competent, confident and valued workforce, as a critical part of its reform agenda to improve children's outcomes.

A fundamental starting point for improvement is that all staff know how to assess, plan and provide services that will give vulnerable children the opportunity to become resilient adults.

It is evident that every step along the way in growing up is important for each individual child and young person. That is why the Department for Education and Skills commissioned The Open University and its partners to produce resource materials about children's development. It is intended that they should provide a robust understanding of child development to help staff wherever they may have responsibility for working with children and young people. This book should be an invaluable resource and I hope it will be an important building block in the continuing professional development of staff.

Maria Eagle MP, Parliamentary Under Secretary of State for Children, Young People and Families

Acknowledgements

This book was developed as part of a pack of resources commissioned by the Department for Education and Skills for use by practitioners working with children and families, their managers and trainers. The pack was produced in a partnership between the Faculty of Health and Social Care (The Open University), the NSPCC and Royal Holloway College, University of London.

The material, presented in a range of media, includes new perspectives on child development and looks at children in their varied and diverse contexts. It builds vital bridges between the need to understand children's development and the ways practitioners carry out their tasks when working with children and their families.

It is particularly relevant for staff working in social care, health and education, in both the statutory and independent sectors, who may be required to assess the developmental needs of children and young people and think about appropriate help.

The heartfelt thanks of the editors go to Jenny Gray of the Department for Education and Skills, who commissioned the project and expertly and patiently guided it to completion, and to Amy Lankester-Owen and Stephen Jones of Jessica Kingsley Publishers for their encouragement and enthusiasm throughout the project. The editors also extend their gratitude to members of the Project's Steering Group and Advisory Group listed at the end of the book, who collectively and individually contributed their expertise to the project, ensured we were fully informed of different professional perspectives, and tested out ideas and resources in their own agencies. There are many others who helped us with their advice and support. In particular we would wish to thank Lynne Murray, Peter Cooper and Oliver James for sharing their expertise on child development. Maureen Crouch, NSPCC Training Associate, who undertook a valuable training needs survey for us, Enid Henry and other NSPCC colleagues who participated in a developmental workshop at the start of the project and continued their support through the preparation of the book. Sheena Doyle and her colleagues in the Children's Society provided a practice seminar for the Steering Group, and members of the London Family Consultation Service advised us on resources for working with children. We are indebted to them all.

Special thanks go to Barnardo's for generously allowing us to reproduce the chart in Chapter 8, developed by Gordon Jack and Owen Gill.

The editors are immensely grateful to Linda Camborne-Paynter, course team assistant in the Faculty of Health and Social Care and secretary to the Project Team, for her painstaking work during the editing of the chapters and her contribution to the final preparation of this book, and to Dawn Tharpe, personal assistant to Jenny Gray, for her invaluable contribution throughout the life of the project.

Preface

Books about children reflect the time and context in which they are written. This is especially so with books on children's development which set out to explore the different influences on their growing up. Mercifully, we have travelled some distance from the time when the prevailing view was that children were inherently sinful by nature and required regular beating to civilise them, as advocated by Lewis Carroll's Duchess in *Alice in Wonderland*:

> Speak roughly to your little boy,
> And beat him when he sneezes:
> He only does it to annoy,
> Because he knows it teases.

Our book has been commissioned at a time when a number of powerful themes have come together in the public policy arena. Current government policy, now enshrined in the Children Act 2004, has for the first time been explicitly committed to children and young people achieving their full potential, ensuring their well-being is improved through the co-operation of the agencies with responsibility for them.

At the same time, another strand of national and international policy has been a commitment to children and young people's involvement and participation in the development of policies and services affecting them. It acknowledges children as active agents in their own lives and accepts the challenge of translating the rhetoric of children's rights into reality. Accompanying these themes has been a shift from focusing exclusively on parental responsibilities and competence in parents' relationships with their children to a more broadly based understanding of the impact of community and environment on children and their caregivers. Adopting such an ecological approach accepts there is a complex interplay of diverse factors which influence children's development. Parents bringing up children in circumstances of poverty and isolation will experience additional pressures and increased risk of exclusion from good quality community resources.

In order to achieve the desired improvements in the well-being of children and young people, it has been recognised that a more integrated approach between all agencies with responsibility for children is essential. Furthermore, underpinning closer interprofessional collaboration is the recognition that knowledge about and sensitivity to children's development are of fundamental importance to any staff working with children and families. Child development is, therefore, a core area of knowledge for all professionals working with children and young people, whether in health, education or social care, and across the spectrum of statutory, voluntary and private sectors (as required in *Common Core: Skills and Knowledge for the Children's Workforce*, Department for Education and Skills 2005a). Increasingly, concerns have been expressed about the level of knowledge and the capacity of staff to apply their understanding about child development in practice. These concerns have come from all quarters including practitioners themselves. As a result, the Government has commissioned a range of resources to assist professionals in their training, management, supervision and day to day practice, of which *The Developing World of the Child* is a key building block.

The contemporary policy themes reflect our own clinical and research experience, and the values and principles about children which have shaped us as professionals. We have had in mind when working on the book all those children who come into contact with professionals through the universal provision of health and education services, and also those children growing up in circumstances of maltreatment or with complex needs where they may require more specialist intervention, inluding social work. Our experience has reinforced for us the concept that we cannot make sense of children's development without adopting an ecological perspective which takes account of the enormous variety of influences there can be on children. The reasons supporting such an approach are explored by Jane Aldgate in Chapter 1 and Janet Seden in Chapter 2, and exemplified in subsequent chapters in Part 1. The central concept of attachment is discussed by Jane Aldgate and David Jones in Chapter 4, drawing on new thinking and research. David Quinton and Kwame Owusu-Bempah provide new insights as they examine the development of self and the sense of belonging in Chapters 5 and 6.

Trainers whom we consulted identified gaps for practitioners in their knowledge about developmental stages and milestones, and a particular desire for a practical checklist or framework which could be referred to as a baseline. Part 2 presents chapters about children developing from early childhood through to adolescence and beyond, together with an extended grid developed by David Jones identifying what might be expected in children's development at different ages. Applying our understanding of theory in practice is addressed in Part 3. How can we promote positive developmental outcomes for children? These issues are discussed in terms of the importance of direct work with children, communicating with children about adverse circumstances and then using what we know about children to make and implement effective plans for intervention. Finally, we listen to what children and young people have to tell us about what is important to them in their development.

We are grateful to all our contributing authors for their diverse perspectives and the enrichment they bring to our understanding of children's development.

During the course of editing the book, our friend and colleague from the University of Leicester, the remarkable Pauline Hardiker, died in August 2004. Writer, teacher, researcher and Honorary Doctor of The Open University, she was a tireless champion for improving the well-being of children, especially those whose development was disrupted in some way. This book is dedicated to her memory.

Jane Aldgate, David Jones,
Wendy Rose and Carole Jeffery

Part 1

Child Development: Frameworks, Theories and Influences

CHAPTER 1

Children, Development and Ecology

Jane Aldgate

> We cannot begin to improve the lives of disadvantaged and vulnerable children unless we identify their needs and understand what is happening to them in order to take appropriate action.
>
> *(Hutton 2000)*

Introduction

Core professional activity increasingly demands from the children's services workforce across different professions an evidence and research informed approach to practice, with an emphasis on helping vulnerable children achieve optimal developmental outcomes. The responsibility for improving the well-being of children is a duty within the Children Act 2004.

The legislative mandate for action enshrined in the Children Act 1989 also demands that professionals are able to define who are children in need of services. It is difficult to see how any professional can implement the primary legislation without knowing about, and understanding about, children's development. Furthermore, knowledge of the developing child is not just confined to responding to an individual. It permeates and underpins all the parts of the child welfare system.

> Child development is both a basic and an applied science. It is the study of how and why children develop perception, thought

processes, emotional reactions, and patterns of social behaviour. It also provides knowledge that is important for advising parents, forming educational programmes, creating and defending Government programmes for children, making legal policies affecting children, and devising treatments for problem behaviour. (Mussen *et al.* 1990, p.2)

No one could question how that understanding of a child's development is absolutely crucial in shaping assessments and professional judgements about appropriate services to meet children's developmental needs. Yet often, as Gray has pointed out, that knowledge and understanding 'has not always been easily available to practitioners and their managers' (Department of Health 2000, p.xi).

In this book, the authors want to look at the developing child in a way that builds bridges between the knowledge of the how, why and what develops in children with the application of that knowledge in direct practice. It is important that professionals not only have an understanding of child development but also are ready to use the evidence from that knowledge to promote the optimal development of each individual child with whom they are working. Accurate application is just as important as the knowledge itself. Such application might be within the Government's *Framework for the Assessment of Children in Need and their Families* (Department of Health, Department for Education and Employment and Home Office 2000b). Its use also informs policy and practice developments, such as early intervention programmes like Sure Start, family support programmes like Homestart and services for adolescents.

The fact that child development issues are germane to all child welfare practice is in itself justification for studying the developing child but what will be learned about children from studying their development? Mussen *et al.* (1990, p.5) believe there are three broad goals to be achieved from studying child development:

1. To understand changes that appear to be *universal* (those that occur in all children regardless of culture or personal experience).

2. To explain *individual differences* (why infants react in a particular way to their mother leaving the room while others play happily, or why some children learn mathematical concepts quicker than others, etc.).

3. To understand how children's behaviour is influenced by the environmental *context* or situation (in this sense the context is not the immediate situation but also attributed to the larger settings within which people live – families, neighbourhoods, cultural groups. Such settings are sometimes called the ecology of the child's behaviour).

This book on the developing child aims to provide a resource which is accessible to and relevant for practice. The first chapter introduces readers to what is meant by the term child development, and provides a theoretical framework for understanding the main influences on development. It also explores how special circumstances which cause concern to children's services professionals, such as child maltreatment, or traumatic separation and loss, may be seen in the context of their impact on the developing child. It takes a stance on development which seeks to acknowledge and promote the individuality and potential of all children, including those who are disabled and those who are in need because of factors within themselves or because of the circumstances and relationships which are part of their world.

Defining child development

The first question in considering the developing child is to ask: what actually is child development? Mussen and colleagues have produced a standard textbook used frequently by different children's services professionals (1990). They define child development as follows:

> Development is defined as orderly and relatively enduring changes over time in physical and neurological structures, thought processes, and behaviour. In the first 20 years of life these changes usually result in new, improved ways of reacting – that is in behaviour that is healthier, better organised, more complex, more stable, more competent or more efficient. We speak of advances from creeping to walking, from babbling to talking, or from concrete to abstract thinking as instances of development. In each such instance we judge the later-appearing state to be a more adequate way of functioning than the earlier one. (Mussen *et al.* 1990, p.4)

This definition implies several things:

- there are defined dimensions of development

- development is orderly

- the results of different stages of development lead to a more efficient way of functioning

- there are interactions between children and the context in which they grow up which will influence their development.

There is for every child a sense of progression and increasing complexity. The child becomes increasingly organised, integrated yet more complex as an individual as he or she grows up. We call this the *developmental perspective*.

Such a definition assumes that there are different interwoven areas of development, each of which contributes to the development of the whole child. In order to unpack the complex processes and interactions of development, writers often deconstruct development into different areas, such as physical, cognitive, emotional and psychosocial development. Later in this book, we will also use this device to look at children at different ages and stages of development. In spite of this artificial device, most writers on development agree that there are *interactions* between different aspects of development, as they also agree that all children have to progress systematically through different stages to become more competent, integrated and complex. These stages are broadly age related, although there can be considerable variation in the progression of individual children. These variations may have many causes, often resulting from a complex fusion of a child's inner world and external influences. As Mussen *et al.* (1990) suggest, 'Children may go through stages at different ages, but they all go through them in the same order' (p.10). This is a fundamental principle and one which can be applied to all children no matter whether they have the special circumstance of illness or disability or have been affected by abuse or neglect. Later in the chapter there will be discussion of child development relevant to the perspective of some of these special children, including those who have been abused or who are disabled but, initially, the focus will be on general principles.

How do children develop?

The next question to ask is: how do children develop? Writers on child development generally agree that there are developmental changes which can be termed *continuous* and *quantitative*. These continuing changes in development can be measured quite easily, for example, a child's gradual changes in height and weight. But children sometimes make leaps to a different level of development. When it comes to discussing *how* children develop between each stage, there is no universal agreement between developmentalists on all aspects of how changes take place. Some writers describe these as 'stages of development', believing any changes to be *discontinuous* or *qualitative*, for example, the leap that occurs when a child changes from a nonverbal baby to an individual who can talk or the child who develops abstract thinking. These changes represent a break with development that has already occurred to a new level which is of a different qualitative order. Others would say that all changes are cumulative, building on what went before.

Professionals cannot escape from confronting these different approaches because they are constantly asked to assess children against a normative level of attainment.

This is a good place to pause and think about the concept of milestones, in terms of physical and cognitive development.

Milestones

Milestones help identify two universal factors:

- As children grow, and assuming they have been given appropriate parenting and support from others, their competencies and, consequently, confidence in different areas of development will change.

- For all children, development will be sequential – all children will gain competence in certain developmental tasks, in the same order but not necessarily at the same rate.

The authors have strong views about the imperative to avoid stigmatising or 'pathologising' children and believe such an approach is unethical. We also believe that to do nothing where a child may be impaired on the grounds this will place the child apart from others is equally unethical. Accordingly, this book takes the stance that, in order to apply our vast fund of knowledge in a non-stigmatising way, we need to know what are, for want of a better phrase, the normative expectations. Using milestones, for example, to identify expected stages of development, is a useful tool in identifying impairments as early as possible, so that each child who has a developmental problem may be given the best possible opportunity to address that problem and reach his or her optimal potential as an individual. A good example is the importance of recognising language delay early on. There may be many causes, hearing impairment being the most obvious, but deprivation of social interaction could be another cause.

The authors are, however, fundamentally opposed to the use of such identification of difference as abnormal or defective, and believe that any assessment in relation to a normative level of attainment has to be set in a wider societal context that recognises difference and values individuals intrinsically. Any intervention should be seen in the context of acceptance of each child as an individual. Coleridge, for example, writing about dis-ability, liberation and development, suggests this starts from the point 'that integration is ultimately about removing barriers, not normalisation, cure, or care. Rehabilitation conducted within a comprehensive social framework is about the removal of barriers and attitudinal barriers in society at large' (Coleridge 1993, p.73).

Milestones and disability

Within this book, we look to apply the concept of milestones for disabled children along the lines spelt out by Marchant (2001). If a disability is iden-tified, then the milestones for that individual child would have to be carefully redefined as Marchant suggests. She says that 'professionals should assess whether a child is developing in line with what would be expected of a child with similar impairments at a similar level of develop-ment (not necessarily age)' (Marchant 2001, p.212). Taking such an approach maximises the possibilities of reaching optimal outcomes for indi-vidual children with impairments, recognising that some may reach different levels of development along different dimensions. For example, children who have cerebral palsy may have difficulty with mobility but achieve well academically.

There is a special group of children who are profoundly ill. Children with profound health problems, such as terminal cancer, will need special attention. For them, the achievement of 'optimal developmental outcomes' will place an emphasis on the best possible clinical treatment but equally on the quality of living in each day. In this way children's development is being addressed in terms of their current well-being as well as their future well-becoming (Ben-Arieh 2002). Adopting this approach to milestones is important. It recognises the responsibility of early identification of impairments but emphasises that recognition is necessary to promote the potential of each child, not simply to identify the fact the child is different or cannot achieve along some dimensions of development.

It is also important not to be seduced into thinking children's disability dominates the total experience of their development. As Marchant also suggests, it is necessary to differentiate the impact of a child's impairments from the impact of a child's total experiences. As the Children Act 1989 emphasises, disabled children are children first (Department of Health 1991b). This does not deny their needs but rather reiterates an inclusive approach to assessment and services set in the context of children's whole lives. Sometimes those services will include helping parents come to terms with their child's disability and ensuring that both practical and emotionally supportive services are offered. Indeed, what such an approach clearly shows is that development is more than what happens within the child. There are powerful external influences which will interact with the *developmental perspective*. These will now be considered.

Influences on development – a child's ecology

There are many influences that will shape the developing child and the outcome for an individual throughout and beyond childhood. Some are within the child, such as genetic factors. Others are from outside such as physical, psychological and family influences, as well as the wider neighbourhood and cultural influences. Traumatic events, such as abuse or separation, can lead to derailment or disruption in the developmental processes. Subsequent influences on a child can either be ameliorating or further potentiate the effect of early damage (Jones and Ramchandani 1999).

It is increasingly recognised that alongside a *developmental perspective*, there is an *ecological perspective* of children's development. This considers children within their environment. In the next chapter Janet Seden gives a detailed exposition of ecological theory and how it informs the debates on development. In this chapter, the concept of a child's ecology is introduced as part of the discussion of the underpinning theoretical framework of this book. Ecological theory suggests that children are surrounded by layers of successively larger and more complex social groupings which have an influence on them. These include family and extended family, friendship networks, school, neighbourhood and work influences, and the family's place within the community. Still wider is the influence of the culture within which the family live. Children across the world will experience childhood in many different ways.

One of the main criticisms of traditional approaches to child development has been that they take a very Western perspective of the influences of the child's ecology on development. This is an issue which confronts children's services professionals every day. The authors here take the view that maltreatment and its related developmental problems remain universal concepts across cultures, although different countries and cultures will at any one time construct the threshold for maltreatment according to the values of the day. What is at issue is understanding that there may be very different expectations of children's social development across cultures. It is now widely known through research that there are very different patterns of attachment behaviour in different cultures (Boyden, Ling and Myers 1998; Quinton 1994; Rashid 1996). These differences are discussed in Chapter 4.

In the West, there has been a strong emphasis on parent–child bonding being enhanced by eye contact and touch. In other cultures, such as Japan, for example, children are taught to avert their gaze from parents as a mark of respect (Rashid 1996). Another much quoted example relates to issues of identity. Writers such as Woodhead (1999) and Owusu-Bempah and Howitt (2000b) have suggested different cultures and societies place a different emphasis on the relationship between self and others. In Western cultures, ideas of self and autonomy are highly valued as part of identity. In some other cultures, the concept of self cannot be separated from the concept of belonging to the group and having an obligation to the group or community. In assessing the development of a young person's sense of self-esteem, for example, it is necessary to be aware of the impact of culture on the perception of what constitutes self-esteem.

In the UK, child welfare law acknowledges and values the differences which will be inevitable and desirable in a multi-cultural society and encourages cultural awareness.

> Although some basic needs are universal, there can be a variety of ways of meeting them. Patterns of family life differ according to culture, class and community and these differences should be respected and accepted. There is no perfect way to bring up children and care must be taken to avoid value judgements and stereotyping. (Department of Health 1990, p.7)

What the legislation does not do is to provide information on the relationship between family diversity and developmental outcomes. As reports following inquiries into the deaths of children have shown, stereotyping or racist attitudes can be as detrimental to a child's well-being as denial of difference. An example of this is to be found in the discussion in Chapter 13 (Cm 5730 2003).

The nature–nurture debate

There is another dimension which cuts across both the developmental and the ecological perspectives. For many years, there has existed a debate about the relative influences of 'nature and nurture' on children's development. Can we predict what the adult will be like from observing the child? Will an aggressive child grow to be an aggressive adult? Will early experience influence the course of a child's development irrevocably? Can children recover from adversity and abuse? Various theories have swung the pendulum one way or the other. Interpretation of the findings from studies of identical twins brought up apart from birth is an excellent example of pendulum swings in the nature–nurture debate (James 2002).

The contemporary view seems to be that the relationship between nature, of which one example is genetic factors, cannot be disengaged from the influence of nurture or external influences on development. Rutter (1992), for example, suggests that environment can influence genetic endowment, as in the case of height. The genes that influence height in the UK have changed little in the last century but nutrition has changed and the next generation is on average taller than their parents. Knowledge and intervention are able to mediate the effects of genetically carried metabolic diseases such as phenylketonuria. However, factors that affect one child in a family are more influential than family-wide factors that impinge on everyone in the family. This helps to explain why one child in a family may be singled out for abuse. This has important implications for the assessment of individual children who are being scapegoated. Conversely, infant irritability patterns may be influenced more by genetics than child rearing. Anti-social behaviour may run in families but be more as a result of environment than genes (Rutter 1992). These issues and the findings from research are discussed in more detail in Chapter 3.

These debates will continue and it is important that children's services professionals are aware of the discovery of new findings, if for no other reason than to learn how to balance knowledge about different kinds of factors that affect development. It is as important to know about genetic factors as it is to know about how far environmental input may modify these. This approach is justified by the fact that, overall, the research seems to come down on the side that environmental input can make a difference to children's lives in many areas of development (Rutter 1992). In the end, this provides us with what Schaffer has called 'a much more positive and optimistic view of childhood':

> We now know that whatever stresses an individual may have encountered in the early years, he or she need not be for ever more at the mercy of the past. There are survivors as well as victims; children's resilience must be acknowledged every bit as much as their vulnerability; single horrific experiences, however traumatic at the time, need not lead to permanent harm but can be modified and reversed by subsequent experiences; children who miss out on particular experiences at the usual time may well make up for them subsequently; and healthy development can occur under a far wider range of circumstances than was thought possible at one time. (Schaffer 1992, p.40)

Children influencing their own development

Schaffer's view of children's development links to the fact that there is an increasing body of knowledge that suggests children have a major part in shaping their own development. It used to be thought that children were 'blank slates' upon which the influence of those around them could be imprinted. Now it is recognised that there are *transactions* between each individual child and his or her environment. This can occur in several ways. Children will elicit positive or negative responses in adults. Children's individual temperament and their behaviour will shape the responses they elicit in those who influence their lives. Schaffer believes that children actively select and shape environments that are appropriate to their own characteristics.

> Children themselves, that is, seek out and construct compatible environments and in this way help to determine which settings will have an opportunity to influence their own development – surely a much more dynamic and truly reciprocal view of the social influence process. (Schaffer 1992, p.46)

Much work has been done in recent years on the concept of resilience as a protective factor in children's development. Resilience suggests that children can reach optimal potential even under stressful circumstances. Rutter (1985) cites three factors associated with resilience:

1. A sense of self-esteem and confidence.

2. A belief in own self efficacy and ability to deal with change and adaptation.

3. A repertoire of problem-solving approaches.

The children's rights and participation movements have also been instrumental in demonstrating that children may be capable of advanced social behaviour at ages earlier than standard textbooks would suggest. Murray and Andrews (2000) illustrate how the newborn child is an active actor in his or her world. Lansdown reinforces the idea of children influencing adults by suggesting that, 'far from being "in waiting" until they acquire adult competencies, children can, when empowered to do so, act as a source of expertise, skill and information for adults and contribute towards meeting their own needs' (2001, p.93). Further, de Winter (1997) provides a compelling discussion of a theoretical framework for the participation by children and young people as fellow citizens.

The relative weighting of influences on development

Not only has thinking changed on the dynamic transactions between children and their environment. Through the development of the ecological perspective, thinking is changing about the relative influence of different parts of children's ecosystems on their development. The idea that parents are directly and primarily to be held solely responsible for their children's development is now increasingly seen as too simplistic. Children are capable of forming multiple relationships. Fathers, siblings, extended family and peers will all influence a child's development from an early age, as will carers in their lives, such as childminders, day nursery staff, au pairs and nannies. Furthermore, Schaffer (1992) suggests that the research is now able to identify that the inhibition of impulsive behaviour takes place within the child surprisingly independently of the way in which parents treat their children and to blame parents for their children's drug addiction, for example, may be missing the developmental point.

Schaffer goes on to suggest that the cumulative influences of all the inputs into development will create a whole greater than the sum of the parts. Looking at mother–child or father–child relationships alone is not enough. The relationship will be affected by the relationship that each of these individuals has with the other two. The family environment is therefore as important as the individual parent–child relationship. Siblings, wider family, friends, teachers and community can all be specific influences but one has also to understand their combined impact.

The developmental–ecological model for the developing child

Contemporary thinking on children's development allows for a diversity of inputs, transactions and outcomes. In this book we are adopting a framework of development which attempts to acknowledge these different broad perspectives. We call this the *developmental–ecological* model of child development.

The essential features of this model have been outlined by Jones and Ramchandani (1999). There are several important implications which arise from combining a developmental and an ecological perspective. One is that dissimilar pathways can arrive at similar destinations in terms of the effect on the developing child, and conversely, similar pathways can have quite diverse outcomes. Second, the framework suggests that development is a process which involves interactions between the growing child and his or her social environment. Third, while experiences such as abuse or separation from loved ones in traumatic circumstances can affect a child's development negatively, change is still possible in many different ways. The outcome will be influenced by three factors:

1. the child's life experiences before a negative experience has occurred

2. the timing and duration of that experience

3. what happens afterwards.

The developmental–ecological model gives scope to identify and assess the range of positive and negative influences which may have an impact on outcome in terms of a child's development. Jones and Ramchandani (1999, pp.3–4) suggest that:

> the range of positive and negative influences are important to consider when examining the occurrence, or looking at the outcome, of an influence upon children, such a child sexual abuse.
>
> Once abuse has occurred there are a number of intervening factors which influence outcome. These include the individual child's coping skills and strategies, parental and family support, and societal influence including the impact of child protection procedures and, where offered, psychological treatment.

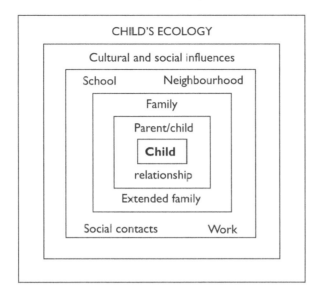

Figure 1.1: A developmental and ecological framework. A good example of how the developmental–ecological model can be applied in cases of child sexual abuse. (Adapted from Jones and Ramchandani 1999, p.3.)

It has to be accepted, however, that where there are severe developmental problems caused by child maltreatment, recovery, though not insurmountable, may be more difficult. Cicchetti and Lynch (1993), for example, assert that there are serious differences in developmental disadvantage between abused and non-abused children.

The concept of wellness

Schaffer's optimism about the dynamic nature of children's developmental experiences is now also present in newer approaches to children's development Lorion (2000). Kelly (1974) summarises the new perspective of 'wellness', which embraces both mental and physical health in children and adolescents.

> The work of psychologists is moving from an emphasis upon the troubles, the anxieties, the sickness of people, to an interest in how we acquire positive qualities, and how social influences contribute to perceptions of well-being, personal effectiveness, and even joy. There will be signs that, in the future, psychologists less and less will be viewing us as having diseases. Instead the psychological view will be one of persons in process over time and as participants in social settings. (Kelly 1974, p.1)

This approach is very helpful in moving away from a success/failure model of development. It allows for all sorts of permutations of wellness. Most of us will never achieve the ideal but that does not matter. The agenda here is 'to process' and, it could be argued, make progress, not to be labelled as ill or failed. This approach is in tune with the principles that underpin the Assessment Framework (Department of Health *et al.* 2000b) which stresses the promotion of strengths as well as the identification of developmental issues and presents an optimistic value base. It stresses the potential for change within a developmental–ecological approach.

Using research and knowledge about child development in practice

If professionals are going to take child development seriously and apply their knowledge in their assessments and interventions, they need to be sure that the knowledge they have is up to date and accurate. Research on child development is constantly evolving. It is inevitably going to be influenced by contemporary social values. Large institutions, for example, used to be acceptable for small babies. Today they are not, because we understand a lot more about how different types of care promote or hinder children's development. Conversely, carefully organised group living need not be detrimental to children provided it meets children's developmental needs, as many years of group living in Israel have shown. It is, therefore, unhelpful to believe there is a right or wrong way to bring up children. To carry out the professional role ethically and responsibly, it is more helpful to understand the meaning of the evidence about the developing child within his or her social and cultural environment.

According to Mussen *et al.* (1990), a good starting point to assist our understanding of the evidence is to recognise that there are two main sorts of research on child development:

1. applied research
2. basic research.

The applied research is often driven by the need to find answers to social issues. How is children's development affected by their parents' divorce? Will children's development be affected by frequent changes of care? What will be the effect on development of child abuse? Will the intervention I offer make any difference to a child's ability to achieve at school? These are questions not easily answered by a simple response but many of the research answers to these types of questions have influenced legislation and policy. The Children Act 1989, for example, advocates that in court cases, there should be as little delay as possible. This clause was included on the basis of child development research on the patterns of attachment in young children and the importance of time in a child's life being measured in terms of days and weeks, not years (Department of Health 1990). The Looking After Children System was developed in response to applied research that showed children leaving the care system to be disadvantaged developmentally along several dimensions, but particularly in their cognitive and social attainments in comparison to the general population (Department of Health 1985; Parker et al. 1991).

In contrast to applied research, basic research is concerned with understanding the developing child. A good example of such research which was later applied to help children with hearing impairments was research into whether young babies could discriminate between different speech sounds (Mussen et al. 1990). Much basic research into child development has been based on systematic observations of behaviour. Conclusions have been drawn from these observations which, in turn, have generated new research questions and sometimes have led to changes in policy. A vivid example emerged from the Robertsons' work in the 1950s (Robertson 1952) about the care of children in hospital, which led to the closer involvement of parents when children were admitted to hospital and throughout their stay. Another good example was the permanency planning movement in the late 1970s. This was a response to research which revealed developmental problems in self-esteem and attachment in children in temporary placements in the care system (Rowe and Lambert 1973).

Much of both the applied and basic research has generated tools which professionals may use to measure children's development. In some cases, these are universally applicable, but in other cases, the tools are considered to be too culturally specific and these have been much criticised. Traditional ideas of intelligence, for example, have concentrated on what can be measured through psychometric tests. These have tended to focus on verbal, visuo-spatial and mathematical abilities. They measure a certain type of ability which is closely related to education systems in the USA and the UK and other European countries. They are fine for the children who have grown up in those systems but have been shown to be flawed when applied to children in different cultures. Woodhead (1999), for example, points out that children who work as street vendors can perform complex mathematical calculations but will fail in classroom tests.

Alongside understanding the different types of research, professionals need to have some understanding of the relative usefulness of different methodologies in contributing to using research findings in practice. This subject warrants a book in its own right and all we can do here is to suggest further reading, such as Mussen *et al.* (1990); Davies, Brechin and Gomm (2000). No one method is necessarily better or worse than another but each will have a different contribution according to what it is trying to achieve. Being able to understand the differences between methodologies used in child development research will help professionals ensure they are acting on the best possible information available at the time and will avoid informing decisions with outdated information. Keeping up with the evidence is fundamental to being an ethical practitioner.

In more recent times, an important new dimension has entered the evaluation of research. This relates to the ethics of undertaking research with children. Questions are now being asked about whether children have given informed consent to participate in research. This new ethical dimension may well influence the direction of research with the developing child in the future (Fraser *et al.* 2003). Increasingly, importance is being laid on involving children in research, asking them about their well-being and other aspects of their lives (see for example, Department of Health 2001).

The key factors in the developmental–ecological model

In this chapter so far, many aspects of children's development have been discussed. The key points may be summarised as follows:

- Each child is an individual with individual potentialities.

- Children develop along different dimensions simultaneously.

- Milestones are an important concept but need to be used within a context that recognises each individual's potentialities.

- In relation to disabled children, milestones need to be used not to emphasise difference but inclusively to identify strengths and enable access to services that will promote children's full potential as soon as possible.

- Children themselves will have a part in influencing their development through their behaviour and dynamic transactions with others.

- Children can recover from abuse or other negative experiences but it is more difficult for those who have been seriously maltreated.

- Children's recovery will depend on the inputs of significant adults and the positive ecology of their environment.

- Cultural diversity is an important determinant in how individual children transact with the environment in which they live.

- Children's development is influenced by many factors, including internal factors such as their temperament, and external factors such as input from parents and others, so that the circumstances in which children grow up will interact with their intrinsic capabilities.

Connecting child development with practice

Many children's services professionals are likely to be dealing with children who have not reached developmental milestones or whose development is in question for some other reason, perhaps because they are ill, disabled or suffering from malnutrition. They may be living in households of conflict which affect their emotional wellness or they may have been put at risk of significant harm. There are many ways children in need may be in danger of not reaching their optimal development. This is recognised in the definition of children in need in section 17 of the Children Act 1989:

A child shall be taken to be in need if –

(a) he is unlikely to achieve or maintain, or to have the opportunity of achieving or maintaining, a reasonable standard of health or development without the provision for him of services by a local authority...

(b) his health or development is likely to be significantly impaired, or further impaired, without the provision for him of such services; or

(c) he is disabled.

>And 'family' in relation to such a child, includes any person who has parental responsibility for the child and any other person with whom he has been living. (Children Act 1989 s17(10))

This section of the Act is important because it links the promotion of children's optimal development with the provision of services.

Establishing why a particular child is in need requires assessment based on knowledge of children's developmental and ecological perspectives. Often agencies will only deal with one aspect of children's development. Schools will be looking at educational development, while social workers may be more concerned about the influence of family and environment on children's development. Research about social work intervention has suggested that parents are often very aware of the complexity of children's developmental needs. They want professionals to see their child as a whole child and would like services to work together much more (Tunstill and Aldgate 2000). Rose and Aldgate (2000) say that professionals should follow this parental view. Nothing can be taken for granted in looking at children's development and an approach to assessment that emphasises dimensions and intertwining influences from many sources is essential. The Assessment Framework (Department of Health *et al.* 2000b) is premised on the view that each practitioner needs to understand the language and concepts used by others so they can work together to provide the range of services to help children in need to reach their optimal developmental potential. An essential starting point for this joint voyage of discovery is to know about the developing child.

CHAPTER 2

Frameworks and Theories

Janet Seden

Introduction

Professionals who work with vulnerable children, young people and their carers need to be clear about how, when, where and why they intervene and to be able to explain and be accountable for their actions to service users, other professionals, managers, councillors, inspectors and ultimately to the public, government and the courts.

The ability to be clear about the basis for assessments and interventions is critical, first of all at the point where professionals are talking with children and their families about why they are involved in their lives, and then at all other levels of practice activity. As Robbins (2001, p.153) says:

> Confident and effective practice depends on workers being able to distinguish between:
>
> - the values that they and their agency support, combined in the philosophy which underpins their practice
> - the theoretical framework set by their agency and/or their background
> - the demands of legislation and guidance (which in turn will reflect values and theory).

In this chapter it is argued that the frameworks and theories of practice are not separate from the tasks of practice. They are the means by which professionals make sense of their roles and responsibilities and provide the best responses they can for the people who use services.

Professionals need to be able to reflect consciously how their internalised values and theories are influencing their practice. This includes judging what theoretical knowledge is relevant. Theory does not stand alone. All our actions and interventions are underpinned by some kind of theorising, so that understanding and articulating theory makes practice explicit and communicable. Jane Rowe (1980) issued a warning about developing practice in a theoretical vacuum when she wrote that fostering, for example, lacked a theoretical underpinning and that 'practice wisdom' was not enough to develop an integrated, professional service:

> From 1948 onwards fostering took its place in British social work textbooks, and a number of important and helpful studies were undertaken. Nevertheless, fostering practice in children's departments basically relied on shared experience and 'practice wisdom'… This laid bare the inadequate theoretical underpinning of fostering services. Practice wisdom is a useful, indeed an essential aid, but it is insufficient unless allied to a firmly based coherent body of knowledge. (pp.56–57)

Work with children and families does not start from a blank theoretical sheet. The legal contexts for the work and the legal mandate for the professional's agency role mean that frameworks and theories are already built into society's expectations of the professional's actions. An illustration of this is to be found from the history of practice in relation to safeguarding children (Corby 2000). In recent years the emphasis on practice-based evidence from research has provided a knowledge base from which professionals can identify how theories and frameworks affect practice outcomes (for example, Cleaver et al. 1999; Department of Health 1991a, 1995, 1996, 1998, 2001; Jones 1998; Quinton 2004).

This chapter outlines the different theoretical frameworks most commonly used to explain developmental processes, and provides an overview to underpin subsequent chapters. By the end of the chapter, the reader should have a general map of the theoretical landscape and be aware of the relevance of:

- the historical context of different theoretical frameworks
- the main models of development, including:
  - intrapersonal theories
  - interpersonal theories

- sociological perspectives and influences, including the children's rights movement, social constructionism, and its relevance to the presentation of the development of children in different cultures and disabled children

- psychosocial models of adversity and resilience in relation to children's development

and in particular:

- understand the usefulness of ecological theory to understanding how to analyse the complex cluster of influences on children's development.

Historically, professionals working with children and their families have drawn from the theories of a range of other disciplines and developed frameworks from them to apply to practice. In the beginnings of social work, for example, individual psychodynamic theories were the most useful, although a reliance on more behavioural approaches quickly followed. Alongside this, professionals working with children and families have always been concerned with social justice and combating social disadvantage. Political and sociological theories have informed this strand of theorising. The study of racism, gender inequality, disability, ageing and other aspects of human experience has also informed practice. Sociology has made a major contribution to the understanding of the social construction of childhood and of social problems. Professional social workers who are involved with children and their families have used group work theory and ideas from management to inform their work in teams and offices. Health care professionals use these bodies of theory as well as the most up-to-date medical knowledge, as they seek to work with the whole person. Education professionals work from a similar theoretical background of psychology, social and learning theories. From this shared knowledge, there are common understandings from which to work together in a collaborative way and to develop effective multi-disciplinary practice. What Hardiker and Barker suggest for social work is equally applicable for all professionals working with children and families, that it: 'requires a breadth of discipline knowledge (e.g. law, psychiatry and philosophy). Furthermore, social workers need to be sufficiently familiar with them to make informed choices, keep up to date with advances and to discard redundant theories' (1991, p.87).

The literature that offers theoretical knowledge for work with children and families, therefore, encompasses a diverse range of approaches (Compton and Galaway 1989; Coulshed 1991; Howe 1987; Lishman 1991; Payne 1992). Understanding those theories and frameworks which have an impact on the world of the developing child requires an awareness of a breadth of theory, with an ability to assess what is relevant at any given point. For this reason the chapter begins with a discussion of ecological theory because the theoretical thinking which underpins it and the resulting frameworks for practice provide an overarching model within which other theories and frameworks can nest.

Ecological thinking, theories, frameworks

Recent writing for professionals working with children and families has laid a great deal of emphasis on ecological thinking and theorising, and the analytical frameworks that come from this. This theory, first outlined by Bronfenbrenner (1979), has been developed by many others since (for example, Bilson and Ross 1989; Department of Health, Department for Education and Employment and Home Office 2000b; Jack 1997, 2001; Stevenson 1998). The ecological approach takes a holistic view of the person in his or her environment and has the capacity for incorporating other approaches (Allen-Meares and Lane 1987). Work on child maltreatment has brought the ecological perspective into the foreground as the multi-dimensional aspects of poverty, neglect and maltreatment have had a greater emphasis in research (Belsky 1993; Cicchetti and Lynch 1993). Jack (2001) says:

> A number of lessons for practitioners and managers emerge from an ecological approach to assessing children and their families. For practitioners and their immediate supervisors, an awareness of the cumulative effect of adverse family circumstances and their potential for negative impact on children's development to begin early and last through to adulthood is obviously important. It is for this reason that the third domain, family and environment is included in the Framework for the Assessment of Children in Need and their Families. Because of the positive potential of social support for families with children assessment should take into account the informal support already available... (p.68)

In this chapter, following Allen-Meares and Lane (1987), it is argued that an ecological approach to assessment and any subsequent intervention offers the capacity to provide a relevant organising framework for apparently competing theories. This provides a structure within which professionals can examine the extent to which they have considered relevant factors and variables that have an impact on individual children and their families (Jones and Ramchandani 1999). Such systems-thinking helps professionals to remember that several areas of influence have to be understood in relation to a child's situation. Also, intervention in one area may alter others, so holistic and analytical thinking is essential before intervening. How do professionals know that what they are doing is helpful rather than compounding harm or exchanging one kind of disadvantage for another? It is important to be able to consider possible outcomes across a range of areas before intervening, although of course no one can predict everything and unintended outcomes both helpful and unhelpful are always possible. Where practice is informed by evidence of what might be expected for children from theories, it is more open to scrutiny and informed adaptation.

In Figure 2.1 the framework offered by Jones and Ramchandani in *Child Sexual Abuse – Informing Practice from Research* (1999, p.3) illustrates the developmental and ecological factors associated with all children, not just those who have experienced maltreatment, as outlined by Aldgate in Chapter 1.

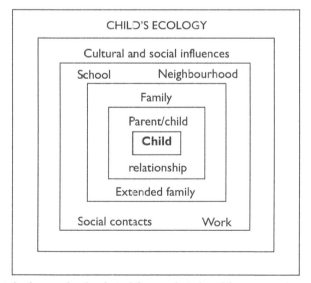

Figure 2.1: A developmental and ecological framework. (Adapted from Jones and Ramchandani 1999, p.3)

The chapter now takes an overview of relevant underpinning theories starting with cultural and social issues.

Theories of society

Sociology points to the social construction of experience. 'It can be argued that we live in a socially constructed world' (Stainton Rogers 1992, p.28). It can also be said of the world of families and children that what is considered a problem and what is not is decided by society (Dallos and McLaughlin 1993). Ideas about the family change over time, a clear example being the change between strict Victorian child rearing practices and the more liberal child-led ones of the 1960s in England. What may be regarded as a problem also changes, so that to be a single parent in the early 21st century is different from being labelled as an 'unmarried mother' in the 1960s or as in need of 'moral guidance' in the 1940s. Thus, what is considered a 'good outcome' in terms of a child's development does depend upon the way the child's society and the people in their immediate culture think about children, parents and the relationships between them and the wider social environment. There have been swings of fashion about 'how to bring up baby' and different generations have favoured different writers (for example, Jolly 1981; Leach 1991; Spock 1999) with some, like Spock, finding favour with a new generation after years of being unfashionable.

Furthermore, in any given society, different groups may experience childhood quite differently. As Foley, Roche and Tucker (2001) note:

> Children are differently positioned in society. Race, class, religion and disability shape their lives. These factors have an impact on their health, life chances and educational experiences. Positive and proactive action to combat prejudices and the disrespectful treatment of all children, whether by adults or other children, is an integral part of the commitment to promote children's welfare. (p.3)

For example, disabled children have been positioned by society in the UK in ways that discriminate and fail to recognise their needs and rights. This has resulted in segregation and poor services that do not recognise the unique circumstances of each child. An approach which recognises the way society contributes to dis-able by creating barriers and denying opportunities is a first step to seeing the individual child and working with them and their family in order to consider what social supports and resources are the most useful to them (Department of Health 2000; Marchant 2001; Middleton 1999; Morris 1999).

Starting with the outer square in Figure 2.1, theories about culture and social influences are very relevant. Different world views mean that there is more than one cultural approach to the developing child (Boyden *et al.* 1998; Rashid 1996). Attention must always be given to the impact of a child's cultural background, language, religion and gender when thinking about whether his or her development is progressing well enough. There has to be a full acknowledgement in thinking about society and culture of the pluralism of twenty-first century society (see Chapter 6). Another recent development is a politicised view of children as having rights and the ability to act upon the world and change it for themselves (UN Convention on the Rights of the Child, ratified in 1991 in the UK). The Children Act 1989 placed a new emphasis on children having their wishes and feelings heard and acted on in decisions affecting their lives. This requirement has been reinforced by amendments made to the Children Act 1989 by section 53 in the Children Act 2004.

The thinking that constructs or shapes childhood, therefore, includes and changes over time our understandings about the social construction of:

- the family and family policies (poverty, health, education)

- play, education, work and life opportunities

- gender, race, disability, age, sexuality and spirituality

- moral judgement.

All this is explored further in later chapters.

Professionals need to be aware of the changing nature of such historical constructions and the implications for particular assessments and interventions, in order to avoid stereotypical ideas and assumptions. The impact of Human Rights legislation and the children's rights movement will continue to change thinking about childhood and the power relations between children, their caretakers and society more widely. Keeping up with sociological perspectives and social policy research will enable an understanding of the developing world of culture and social influences (see Chapters 6 and 7). Children can find themselves living within overlapping or conflicting constructions of childhood. It can be important to be able to identify and work with such issues (Chapters 4 and 5).

School, neighbourhood, work, social contacts

Society for each child starts as a small world, the primary carer, and grows as D.W. Winnicott (1964) says to include the family, the wider family and the neighbourhood. The impact of nursery, playgroups and then school is very significant. During the early years when the child is perhaps attending nursery or day care and, subsequently, as the child is in school, some important developmental changes are happening. These will include conceptual changes, social and emotional developments and changes in self-concept and morality (Daniel, Wassell and Gilligan 1999, p.197).

Equally important are the range and quality of other social contacts with the birth of siblings, wider family, friends, neighbours and neighbourhood resources. A holistic picture of any child's situation will include an understanding of these factors. Theories about social inclusion and the consequences of exclusion (Moss and Petrie 1996) are relevant here. It is also clear that school, extended family and community resources are highly effective in helping to build resilience in children (Seden 2002b) and positive experiences contribute to the development of significant protective factors for children who are experiencing adversity (Gilligan 2001; Rutter 1985, 1990).

Conversely, however, there can be stresses for children created, for example, by the experience of being bullied in school, education pressures or the impact of living in a poor neighbourhood (Chapter 8). Each age brings its own potential for positive or negative developmental influences (Chapters 10, 11 and 12).

Family, extended family, significant others, parent and child relationships

It has already been said that ideas about the family, parents and children are socially constructed. Family and significant relationships are now constructed as consisting of much more than mother, father and child. The family is perhaps more socially than biologically constructed in developmental thinking. Genetic and biological influences play their part in the way a child develops (Chapter 3) but this is not the whole story. A range of significant people, such as teachers or parents' friends, can influence a child's developmental path. This includes biological parents, brothers, sisters (Dunn 1984), extended kin and also step-parents and the individuals that make up the 'blended' or 'reconstituted' families created by changing patterns of marriage, divorce and cohabitation. There are also families created through fostering or adoption (Dunn 1993). The social constructionist approach to the family, therefore, suggests a move away from pathologising from a norm of the 'nuclear family' to a theorising about shifting patterns and diversity which is inclusive and exists within an understanding of a pluralist society (Chapters 6 and 7).

The family

Whatever the shape of the child's immediate family, two bodies of theorising have been commonly used to understand the processes within it which have an impact on a child's development and his or her relationships with caregivers and others. Two main strands of psychological theory have, subject to revision, remained prevalent. They are psychodynamic and social learning theory. These ideas have been subject to much adaptation but none the less remain major organising ideas for thinking about processes in families and understanding people and their behaviours when they are in relationship with each other.

Psychodynamic theory

The ideas that psychodynamic theory contains about how personality is formed and developed are derived from Freudian psychoanalysis. Since its introduction into American and European thinking from the 1940s to the present, it has been used by caring professionals in health, education and social work as a way of understanding relationships between the self and significant others; past and present experience; and inner and outer experience (Brearley 1991). While such professionals are not practising psychodynamic psychotherapy (as counsellors and psychotherapists do), the theories have been highly influential in providing health and social care professionals with ways of understanding the people for whom they provide a service. The important idea of the use of the relationship as an agent of change, which permeates helping work, is essentially a psychodynamic one. Many of the key ideas about how children grow and develop emotionally are also psychodynamic in their origin.

Psychodynamic ideas have had a strong influence on studies of human growth and development across the disciplines which inform caring professionals (Bowlby 1988; Erikson 1965; Fairbairn 1952; Rutter, Taylor and Hersov 1994; Winnicott 1985). They underpin at a very fundamental level both past and current research and practice (Trowell and Bower 1996; Trowell, Hodges and Leighton-Lang 1977). They have influenced the way professionals understand people and groups, how they think about the way the past might be permeating the present, how they build relationships to achieve changes, how they understand children and their behaviour and how they understand and work with hostility, loss, change, transition, bereavement and defensiveness. They have also influenced the way professionals support and supervise each other (Hawkins and Shohet 2000; Kadushin 1997).

Psychodynamic theory is not the same as a psychosocial approach. Psychosocial understanding combines personal, social and practical elements when planning work with a particular service user. Developmental thinking about resilience, for example, can be said to be psychosocial in the sense that it draws from the inner understanding of the child's emotional development (personal qualities and experience) and an assessment of the child's outer world and environment for some protective factors.

Learning theory

Learning theory, as found in behaviour modification, behavioural therapy and behavioural social work, has been equally influential in caring work. As Hudson (1991) comments: 'Learning theories form a body of theory about how behaviour changes as a result of experience, how behaviour is learned, maintained and unlearned' (p.123).

Learning theory is based on scientific experiments and is consistently modified on the basis of new findings. The appeal of behavioural work is the way it can be measured. It begins with an assessment to establish a base line from which to plan goals for change. Behaviours are analysed and intervention techniques based on operant learning, and respondent conditioning. Social learning methods are then used as the tools for intervention. The techniques of behaviour therapy rely on selecting a specific area to change and then planning a step by step approach to changing the targeted area. Because society has placed a high value on the socialisation of children into the acceptable behaviours of the particular time and place, it has had specific roles in relation to children in nurseries, schools and residential homes. It has also been widely and successfully used in parenting classes and projects designed to help parents manage their child's behaviour.

Learning theory, by regarding behaviours as learned and subject to modification by means of new learning, takes an approach which prioritises nurture over nature. While this can be a very successful approach for particular kinds of behaviour, the relationship between nature and nurture is very complex (Rutter 1991) and not all behaviours can be targeted and changed in this way. Nonetheless Hudson and Macdonald (1986) describe some relevant applications for social care professionals including: anger control; child management with parents who abuse; helping foster carers manage children's behaviour; use in residential settings. Social learning theory has become a key perspective for assessing child and parent interactions with specific and focused frameworks that can be linked to outcomes. Such frameworks can be learned and used relatively easily by professionals working with children and their families (Herbert 1981, 1989, 1997). Parenting classes in family and other community projects often show parents how to use behavioural techniques with their children. The programmes which have resulted have given parents a sense of control and self esteem which in turn influences their child's behaviour (Webster-Stratton and Taylor 1998).

Cognitive-behavioural work has also developed from social learning theory (Sheldon 1995). Cognitive-behavioural approaches aim to change the ways people think about themselves and the difficulties this can cause (e.g. depression, misusing alcohol, self-harm) Professionals work on reinforcing positive behaviour and thinking, using contracts and activity-based, problem solving tasks. The aim is: to reduce negative self-perceptions; reduce irrational thoughts and thinking styles and promote positive self-talk and internal dialogue. This approach can be very helpful with children, young people and their families and has been found particularly effective in work with sexually abused children and their families (Jones and Ramchandani 1999).

Frameworks and theories for family work

Supporting families to raise their own children wherever possible is still the cornerstone of professional practice, when it is considered that allowing a child to stay at home is safe enough and the professional is not leaving them in a situation of maltreatment or danger of significant harm. This next section briefly considers other approaches which professionals might use to support families and help them to build their strengths and abilities. The areas considered are: crisis intervention, task-centred work, family therapy and strengths and solution-focused approaches. All of these can be utilised to solve problems, build on strengths and enhance coping strategies.

Crisis intervention

Crisis intervention can be described as a theoretical framework drawn from psychodynamic theory but using some cognitive understandings (Caplan 1964; Coulshed 1991; Coulshed and Orme 1998; Golan 1981). Many families come to the attention of agencies through a crisis or unexpected event which requires a focused, brief form of assistance. Often those who seek help are in a state of distress. A change or a traumatic event may have caused a temporary period of upset and disorganisation, where the person's usual abilities to manage are temporarily immobilised. Writers on crisis suggest it has identifiable phases, which are the:

- precipitating event and perception

- upset

- inability to use previously tried coping methods and disequilibrium

- potential for hope

- intervention which links current difficulties to past coping strategies

- resolution or homeostasis restored within a few weeks.

The professional who works with this framework alongside the family can support people to find the abilities they already possess for handling crises. They can also support families to find new strategies and resources to manage in future. This approach requires only the necessary intervention to build on strengths and aims to restore families to better functioning.

Task-centred practice

Task-centred work is another framework for practice, drawing from psychological theory. It is a focused way of supporting children and families to resolve identified key areas in their lives that are difficult. The origins of the method can be found in American literature in the 1960s and 1970s (Epstein 1988; Reid and Epstein 1976; Reid and Shyne 1969). The framework is based on the idea that a task-centred approach in partnership with service users can solve problems quickly. It requires:

- service user agreement

- an open agenda about service user and worker activities

- specificity about concrete goals and tasks

- allocation of tasks

- time limits

- review and evaluation

- reciprocal accountability (both worker and service user taking responsibility for outcomes).

This approach emphasises that tasks selected must be achievable and structured. It is an approach that works with someone's personal resources and strengths. It is in itself a systematic model moving from assessment through intervention to review. It embodies an empowering partnership approach (Coulshed and Orme 1998; Doel and Marsh 1992; Payne 1992).

Family therapy

Frontline workers do not often practise family therapy, although they might refer families to specialist agencies. These are most usually found in child psychiatry and child and adolescent mental health settings, some voluntary sector agencies, family courts and conciliation teams. Family therapy is not a unified approach since family therapists work diversely from a range of psychological theories. However, it has some key identifying elements which are: to observe family interactions; to consider problems in the context of intimate relationships and the wider social network of which the family is a part; and to bring about a change in interactions between poorly connected parts of the family and the social system (Gorell Barnes 1994). The defining feature of family therapy is that the therapist targets the family system, rather than the individual, for intervention. This is a specific application of a systems approach. The family is worked with as a group by the therapist who assesses the functioning of the family and intervenes in relation to family interactions and styles. By changing the family system, the roles of the individuals can be changed towards more satisfying ways of relating.

There is a range of approaches (Bentovim, Gorell Barnes and Cooklin 1982; Erickson and Hogan 1972; Gorell Barnes 1994; Lau 1984; Walrond-Skinner 1976). Family therapy writing has been useful in helping professionals to understand family dynamics and their impact on the developing child. Treating the family as a unit for intervention can be more effective and far reaching than treating the individual alone. It has relevance to any worker facilitating family meetings or family group conferences. Information gained directly by observing and listening to all family members together can result in working out joint solutions (Barnardo's 2002; Marsh and Crow 1997).

Strengths and solution-focused approaches

The strengths perspective and solution-focused methods are an essential underpinning for the assessment of children and their families and also for subsequent intervention and partnership work with service users. Saleebey (1997) argues for the advantages of a strengths approach to helping individuals, groups and communities to 'meet the challenges of their lives' (p.xvii). This approach to practice seeks to identify and assess possibilities rather than problems. Saleebey (1997) argues for working collaboratively with people who can use their own resilience to achieve change. Solution-focused methods derived from brief therapy (de Shazer 1985) detail how this may be achieved, working with service users to externalise problems, building on existing successful coping strategies, and working towards jointly owned and realistic goals.

Working with families from their strengths is an approach which is frequently practised in family centres and family therapy groups, and is transferable to professional practice in communities. Turnell and Edwards (1999), for example, show how such practice can be effective for social workers who are involved with families where child maltreatment is an issue and the safety of children a critical concern in the casework and planning. They argue that partnership approaches using a solution-focused model of work are still possible even where coercive action to safeguard children may be a necessary part of what happens. They set out applied practice principles (p.51) illustrated by case examples.

Parent and child relationships

It was Winnicott (1960) who argued that 'there is no such thing as an infant' meaning that a child is always in a relationship with the principal carers. Recent research from the Winnicott Centre at Reading University would suggest that the baby is an actor in this process and by no means a passive party in the interaction with carers (Murray and Andrews 2002). Throughout life children are powerfully shaped and influenced by their immediate carers, although this is not the whole story (Schaffer 1977). Work with the family and with relationships between parents and children requires a professional to draw from several strands of thinking about development and the child's contribution to the process. The child begins with biological and genetic traits that will influence development (Chapter 3). Family, parents and others will have a key role in shaping the developmental experiences of children and these are explored in Chapter 7.

The child

An ecological model places each child, rightly, at the centre of his or her own world. Each child is a unique individual in relationship to parents, wider family, school, neighbourhood and society, and development will depend on the relationships between the individual's temperament, genetic endowment and other elements. As Jones (1998) has argued, a developmental approach allows professionals to develop a model that illustrates the multi-faceted nature of the key influences upon a child's development. A 'developmental ecological perspective' (Jones and Ramchandani 1999, p.2) reflects the understanding that development is a 'process which involves interactions between the growing child and his or her social environment'. Thus knowing about a range of theoretical knowledge enables professionals better to untangle the threads when something is amiss or help is needed. This is in order to intervene in the most effective way to achieve the best possible developmental outcomes for the child concerned.

Parents with several children will often be very aware of the differences between them. One might have been a slow feeder; one might have cried a lot; another may have been very active. Some children talk by one year. Others may speak as late as three years old. Some of these matters are not significant in the long run, and others indicate delay that can lead to later disadvantage. This is where understanding the theoretical range of stages at which children do certain things is helpful, as was discussed in Chapter 1. Biological and genetic factors certainly have an influence on the course and rate of a child's development (Chapter 3). Some of these are significant. As well as the matter of temperament (Schaffer 1990), there are also physical factors to take into account, such as disease, disorder or impairment.

Individual development brings a sense of self and with it a sense of identity and a level of self-esteem which can range from being quite poor to very positive and buoyant (discussed in detail in Chapter 5). The place of theory is to help the professional to know whether a child's behaviour is appropriate to his or her age and circumstances. This calls for a sound knowledge of child development along the key dimensions of cognitive, social and emotional development, and the interaction between children and significant others (attachment). Professional assessment is normally concerned with identifying when children's developmental needs are not being met. This is reflected in the definition of a child in need in the Children Act 1989, quoted in our opening chapter:

Under the Act (s17.10) a child is identified as being in need if:

(a) he is unlikely to achieve or maintain, or have the opportunity for achieving or maintaining, a reasonable standard of health or development without the provision for him of services by a local authority...

(b) his health or development is likely to be significantly impaired, or further impaired without the provision for him of such services; or

(c) he is disabled.

Development means physical, intellectual, emotional, social or behavioural development, and health means physical or mental health.

The needs of children

Research into the needs of children has produced several useful frameworks (Black 1990; Maslow 1943; Pringle 1980). Jones (2001, p.260), for example, lists the following as being the dimensions of parenting capacity which are required to ensure children's healthy development:

- basic care
- ensuring safety
- emotional warmth
- stimulation
- guidance and boundaries
- stability.

Beyond being clear about the basic minimum needs, the developmental approach to thinking about each child can draw from a wealth of established and current research. This discusses what appears to be universal to children; how to explain individual differences; how to understand the relationship of behaviour to context; the influence of neighbourhood, cultural background, social and economic situations. This can help professionals to balance genetic and environmental factors in their thinking, as they work to assess, plan and intervene. A holistic approach will consider the transaction between biological and environmental determinants and this will be further explored in the chapters that follow.

The spiritual and moral needs of children

It can be argued that all children have an inherent spirituality which should be considered to achieve a truly holistic picture of developmental needs. As Bradford (1995) puts it:

> For a human being, especially a child or young person, to have a full quality of life, spirituality in all its aspects must be nurtured and affirmed. For children or young people who have been marginalised or who have suffered deprivation in every way, the need for such nurture and affirmation in human spirituality is all the more pronounced. (p.72)

Children's spiritual needs can be considered in terms of what may be universal (or innate) and what might be expressed through religious persuasion or affiliation to a faith community. Children appear to have inbuilt curiosity about the world, which expresses itself in wonder and questions about their origins and the meaning of death. Children also experience extreme terror and fear. Children's literature enables them to confront and accommodate fear and monsters from within and without. Bettelheim (1951) analyses this process, which is also seen in the story *Where the Wild Things Are* (Sendak 1963). Bettleheim's ideas are developed by Rustin and Rustin (2001) and others. The runaway success of the Harry Potter books by J.K. Rowling may also indicate the way children need to engage with magic, mystery, terror and fantasy (Seden 2002a).

Hay (1995) and Nye (1996), educational researchers, suggest that spirituality is innate in children. The features they identify in children's spirituality are presented by Crompton (1996) as: sensing a changed quality in awareness; sensing values, ideas about good and evil or what matters;

sensing mystery, wonder and awe; sensing meaning or insight or connectedness. This ties in closely with humanistic concepts of spirituality which according to Crompton (1996) embrace:

> aspirations, moral sensibility, creativity, love and friendship, response to natural and human beauty, scientific and artistic endeavour, appreciation and wonder at the natural world, intellectual achievement, physical activity, surmounting suffering and persecution, selfless love, the quest for meaning and values by which to live. (p.100)

Thus there appears to be an expression of spirituality which might be appreciated and nurtured in every child. This includes their need for creative expression through music, and art. Pullman (2004) argues that 'children need the arts as much as they need fresh air. Otherwise they perish in the inside'. Children have spiritual rights as expressed in the UN Convention on the Rights of the Child (articles 17, 23, 27, 32). Religious rights are expressed in articles 2, 14, 20, 30. They include the right to freedom from discrimination in respect of status or beliefs; the right to freedom of thought, conscience and religion. Children can expect adults to meet responsibilities towards them to promote their physical, mental, emotional, and social development, including their spiritual needs, according to their developmental ages and understanding and the relevant cultural expression of those within their faith communities (Seden 1995, 1998).

Spirituality and morality are linked concepts. Winnicott (1985) argued that all children have a capacity for forming moral judgements. Piaget (1965) and Kohlberg (1981) suggest this capacity develops in the growing child. Rogers (1961) believed that children and adults are self-actualising, if they are fortunate in the care that they receive, and it is characterised by the core conditions of warmth, empathy and unconditional positive regard. This perhaps suggests that children's spirituality and moral development can be nurtured by empathic adults.

Most religious belief systems have concerns about the sanctity of life, respect and care for the family, community and others. This may be enshrined in a moral code, or practices connected with food or dress or festivals. Much of this practice will be positive for a child, giving meaning to births, coming of age, marriages or deaths in the family and community. Many people turn to religious beliefs and rituals to help them through stress or to celebrate a transition. Children who belong to faith communities need to have such practices continued when away from home. While the abuses of religion and the strife caused by sectarianism cannot be denied, a religious belief or affiliation can provide support and/or inner resilience in times of difficulty.

Summary

Understanding child development is complex. As Cicchetti and Rizley (1981) write: 'the empirical study of child development is a perplexing scientific problem for which we have no ready answers or simple solutions' (p.34). Complexity has to be acknowledged but there are some well-evidenced trends on which to rely (Bee 1995). Much is established about the long-term outcomes of early deprivation (Rutter *et al.* 1994) or the importance of understanding a child's attachments (Daniel, Wassell and Gilligan 1999; Howe 1995). There are some sure foundations to rely upon in thinking about children and their families. Many such theories have been developed and tested over time. They still need to be understood and applied in the context of the circumstances with which children and families have to grapple in the twenty-first century. Such theories, however, still provide a firm basis for the development of practice.

Back to the ecological approach

This chapter has viewed the ecological perspective – with the individual child at the heart of the model – as a comprehensive unifying framework, for understanding the factors which have an impact on the developing child and which can be used in assessment and for planning intervention. In so doing, this chapter reflects the emphasis of the Framework for the Assessment of Children in Need and their Families (Department of Health, Department for Education and Employment and Home Office 2000b). The strength of this approach is based on a set of key ideas about which apply to the developing child and throughout adulthood:

- the person–environment relationship is continuous
- person, behaviour and environment are mutually inter-dependent
- systems theory is useful to analyse the ecology of the person in the situation
- behaviour is site specific

- assessment and evaluation are through direct observation of the person–environment system

- behaviour is the outcome of transactions between the person and the environment

- behavioural science should seek to understand and analyse these interactions. (Allen-Meares and Lane 1987, pp.518–519)

The ecological approach therefore takes a holistic view of the person in his or her environment and has the capacity for incorporating other approaches. It can provide an organising framework for the professional theorising in practice. As Stevenson (1998) says: 'though it is theoretical it is very practical, it provides a kind of map to guide us through very confusing terrain' (p.19).

CHAPTER 3

Genetic and Biological Influences

Marian Perkins

At a personal and professional level, it is often striking to see the individual differences between children raised by the same parents and ostensibly in the same environment. These observed differences have fuelled a long-standing debate about the role of nature and nurture in child development that was enlarged on in Chapter 1. Whilst previously there has been an implicit recognition that genetic and biological influences must play some part in a child's overall development such as cognition, language and physical characteristics, the details of this have remained elusive. Not only has this applied to normal child development, but more specifically to the relative contribution of biological and genetic factors versus social factors, when a child's development goes awry.

Due to many technological advances, we are now in a position to specify the genetic and environmental risk factors in much greater detail. However, whilst most aspects of abnormal development in children are influenced to some extent by genetic variation, the ways in which genes and environments interact are very complex. It is likely to be extremely rare that any childhood psychological difficulty is caused by a single major gene effect. Most of the information that we have regarding the contribution of genes and the environment to any difficulty is known only at the population level. Hence we cannot extrapolate to what extent an individual's problems may be determined by these relative factors. Even when these factors are identified, the complexity with which they interact and other moderating forces along the child's life course will make the application of this knowledge to any particular child very difficult. In this chapter selected biological and genetic influences on the child's development are discussed, in order to illustrate general principles about the impact of these on an individual child.

The early work of Thomas and Chess (Thomas *et al.* 1963; Thomas, Chess and Birch 1968; Thomas and Chess 1977), who formulated ideas about the temperament of a child in biological terms, led to the burgeoning of research as to how biological aspects of the child's development could interact with parental child rearing practices and how this may affect the child's later psychological functioning. Indeed, in Rutter's early seminal papers (Rutter, Korn and Birch 1963) concerning genetic and environmental influences on temperament, he noted that children presenting with psychiatric problems often had parents who also suffered from some form of mental disorder. He commented that, because parental mental disorder was so often accompanied by serious family difficulties and disturbance, it was not surprising that most of the attention had been focused on the environmental risk factors. The conclusions from these early investigations were hampered by methodological problems.

The Isle of Wight study (Rutter 1976) was therefore a crucial landmark, using stringent epidemiological methods, in determining some important parameters of children's development and factors that may adversely affect it. The data from this study, undertaken in the 1960s, elucidated some powerful risk factors for later child psychiatric problems; in particular, brain disorders (see Table 3.1).

Table 3.1: The Isle of Wight neuropsychiatric study

Type of disorder	Proportion of children with psychiatric disorder (%)
No physical disorder	7
Physical disorder not affecting the brain	12
Idiopathic epilepsy	29
Cerebral palsy and allied disorders, IQ >50	44

Source: *Rutter et al. 1970.*

The particularly high rate of later psychiatric difficulties associated with brain damage is over and above any difficulties that may arise, for example from the degree of disability or stigmatisation. Many of the problems suffered by children with brain disorders are similar to those of other children with mental health difficulties, for example conduct, emotional and mixed disorders. However, there appear to be some exceptions to this. Whilst all psychiatric disorders are more common in children with neurological problems, autistic spectrum disorders and hyperactivity disorders are over-represented. For example, in the Isle of Wight study, hyperkinesis accounted for 19 per cent of psychiatric disorders among children with cerebral palsy but only 1 per cent of psychiatric disorders among neurologically intact children.

These previous studies identified certain risks. The design, however, did not allow the relative contribution of genetic factors in the aetiology to be disentangled. More recently powerful new sets of methodologies have allowed the presence of genetic or biological markers to be identified. This information can be used to quantify the genetic risk carried by an individual child.

Genetic effects

Recent genetic research can be broadly divided into molecular genetic investigations that attempt to identify specific genes which may affect a child's development, or quantitative statistical procedures that try to identify the relative contributions of environmental and genetic influences on an individual. The main tool for quantitative genetic research has been the study of twins, which has allowed us to identify the 'basic heritability' of different kinds of conditions. By comparing the outcome of twins who share all their genes (identical or monozygotic) with twins who share on average 50 per cent of their genes (fraternal or dizygotic), the relative contribution of genetic and environmental inferences can be estimated. The estimate that emerges from this type of analysis is referred to as 'heritability'. This figure gives us a feel about how observable characteristics within a population (phenotype) may be due to genetic differences. It is important to recognise, however, that this does not tell us anything about a particular child. In general, the higher the heritability the more important the genetic contribution for a particular difficulty. For example, the most 'heritable' condition identified within the broad range of childhood difficulties is autism. Other problems show a less robust heritability, such as hyperactivity, anorexia nervosa, obsessive compulsive disorder, or Tourette's syndrome. In these latter conditions there is a stronger environmental influence affecting the child's ultimate course and outcome.

Other lines of evidence have come from the study of children who are now known to have specific genetic defects, for example Fragile X syndrome, Angelman's syndrome, and Prader-Willi syndrome. In each of these conditions the genetic defect is now delineated and the syndromes associated with a set of specific physical difficulties. It is, however, the information regarding these children's psychological and behavioural difficulties, i.e. the behavioural phenotype (a specific characteristic behaviour repertoire exhibited by people with a genetic or chromosomal disorder) that has provided other windows of knowledge about the child's ultimate functioning. In Fragile X it is known that this syndrome arises from a mutation that is located at the bottom of the X chromosome. The physical characteristics include particular facial features such as prominent ears with a cupping of the upper part of the ear. The behavioural difficulties vary from language delay and hyperactivity in early life developing to a more autistic-like picture with poor eye contact, sensitivity to touch, hand flapping and particular communication difficulties later in childhood. Angelman's syndrome and Prader-Willi syndrome are two distinct neurodevelopmental disorders that are linked genetically because they are both caused by deletion in the 15q11-q13 region. In Angelman's syndrome the distinguishing clinical features are severe learning difficulties, a small head size, lack of language, incoordination and seizures. In Prader-Willi syndrome the clinical features are different, including severe muscle floppiness in infancy, hyperphagia (overeating with a lack of normal association) and rapid weight gain after the first year, obsessive compulsive behaviour, mild to moderate developmental delay and small sex organs. Although there are genetic similarities, interestingly the behaviour problems are somewhat different. In Angelman's syndrome, for example, there tends to be severe hyperactivity in childhood, with poor attention span, impulsive behaviour and sleep problems. In comparison, children with Prader-Willi syndrome are said to be more stubborn and irritable, often with temper tantrums or rages particularly associated with food restriction. Also, affected children can show skin picking and other obsessive compulsive behaviour such as counting or symmetry compulsions, handwashing and cleaning compulsions.

Whilst these studies have elucidated interesting facts about the relative genetic basis for many childhood difficulties, the process of a child's development is not static. It has long been recognised that a child's eventual outcome will reflect a process of interplay between genetic and environmental risk factors and subsequent events that happen during the child's life. A simple model of how these risk factors may operate is shown in Figure 3.1.

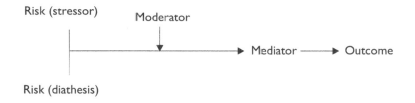

Figure 3.1: Model of realisation of risk (from Stevenson 2001, p.31)

This traditional model would conceptualise an interaction of factors: a diathesis risk factor (usually thought of as biological or genetic) interacting with an environmental factor (stressor) to affect outcome. The child's eventual development is affected by moderating factors, that may increase the possibility of an adverse outcome (vulnerability factor), or those that are likely to have a positive effect (protective factor). Protective factors may be consistent parenting or a relatively high IQ, whilst vulnerability factors may be aspects of temperament or poor peer relations. Mediating influences include such factors as the degree to which the child learns to contain and manage his or her own impulses.

In Figure 3.2 Stevenson (2001) uses the paradigm of attention deficit hyperactivity disorder to highlight the complex possibility of varying contributions of genetic and environmental effects and their interplay, leading to one observable outcome, namely ADHD.

For many other difficulties the past decade has witnessed a rapid growth in research on the genetic underpinnings of psychological disorders. Language difficulties are a very common problem for young children. Whilst there is a huge range of language difficulties in children, there are certain genetic syndromes that are associated with language impairment (Tager-Flusberg 1999). Examples include Down's syndrome, which is characterised by deficits in phonology and pragmatics, and Fragile X syndrome, which is associated with deficits in expressive language, speech and pragmatics. Other twin and family studies have provided evidence for

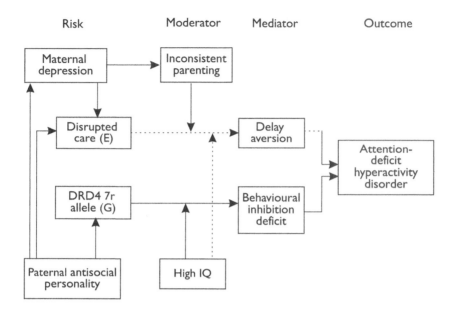

Figure 3.2: Two routes leading to attention deficit hyperactivity disorder (broken line indicates environmental transmission). E, environmental; G, genetic. (from Stevenson 2001, p.32)

familial aggregation of speech and language impairment (Bishop, North and Donlan 1995). More recently there has been a suggestion from a molecular genetic study that has postulated a specific chromosome that *may* be responsible for aspects of language development (Grigorenko *et al.* 1997). Studies have shown that the children at greatest risk of later psychological problems are those with receptive language impairments and language impairments secondary to general cognitive delay. Interestingly, psychiatric disorder, which is diagnosed in roughly half of the children with a specific language impairment, tends to increase over time. A particular association has been noted with anxiety disorder, especially social phobia (Beitchman *et al.* 2001).

Similar genetic contributions have been implicated with reading difficulties, another very common childhood problem. If one looks at first degree relatives of children with reading difficulties, between 35 and 40 per cent will have similar problems (Sheppard and Uhry 1993). Interestingly, children with specific reading difficulties are more likely than other children to have neurodevelopmental and neuropsychological impairments, including left/right confusion, poor coordination, poor constructional abilities and clumsiness. These children seem at particular risk for the later development of conduct disorder and delinquency. More recently it has been suggested that this association may be brought about by earlier hyperactivity rather than a direct link between specific reading difficulties and later conduct problems.

Biological influences

Whilst genetic contribution can be seen to be very important to the development of later child psychiatric difficulties, there are many other biological influences that can be shown to have a significant impact on a child's later development. The biological assaults that children suffer at different times in their lives have produced crucial information about the links between disorders of the brain and later behavioural difficulties.

Prenatal and perinatal influences

Exposure prenatally to harmful substances such as alcohol is known to have permanent adverse effects on the child's ultimate physical attributes and a complex pattern of behavioural and cognitive abnormalities that are inconsistent with the child's developmental level and cannot be fully explained by adverse family background or environment (Stratton, Howe and Battaglia 1996). The exposure of the infant to alcohol in utero is known to disrupt many of the normal processes of brain maturation. The ultimate extent and severity of the child's condition depends on many factors including how much, how often, and during what period of pregnancy the mother consumed alcohol (Hagerman 1999).

Other biological assaults also correlate with later problems. For example, interesting data have resulted from longitudinal studies that have followed up infants from neonatal intensive care units. Early studies on the long term prognosis of extremely low birth weight babies showed that many of the children continued to have a combination of cognitive, perceptual and motor deficits combined with behavioural problems. These behavioural problems encompassed a wide range of problems such as psychosomatic symptoms, overactivity and poor concentration (Weisglas-Kuperus et al. 1993). More recent follow-up studies of low birth weight babies (less than or equal to 1500 grams) found that even in early adolescence the young people had a persistence of a significantly higher prevalence of behavioural problems as reported both by their parents and their teachers. These findings of an increased prevalence of conduct and emotional problems in low birth weight children at this stage highlight our ignorance in many of these areas. Whilst one could impute a significant contribution from the biological difficulties that these children have faced, undoubtedly the experience of long periods of stay in the neonatal intensive care may also have affected aspects of the mother/child relationship which could have contributed to the higher prevalence of behavioural problems seen later (Stevenson, Blackburn and Pharoah 1999).

Physical conditions

Various types of physical conditions are known to be associated with increased risk for later psychological problems.

CEREBRAL PALSY

Cerebral palsy (CP) is the single largest cause of severe physical disability in childhood. Cerebral palsy is an 'umbrella' term for a heterogeneous group of congenital and early acquired brain disorders. These children can have a range of motor difficulties, for example stiffness and weakness of the affected muscles, which tend to be the predominant motor difficulty. Whilst the cause is largely unknown, there are some recognised associations, for example severe jaundice in the newborn period or prematurity. Congenitally hemiplegic children whose brain disorder dates back to pregnancy, birth or a few weeks after, account for about 80 per cent of the children. Acquired hemiplegia, i.e. children whose brain disorder occurs later in development, typically between one and sixty months of age, has a range of origins, for example from brain infection such as meningitis or encephalitis to child abuse, strokes or road traffic accidents. Recent studies of the frequency of psychological problems in hemiplegic cerebral palsied children have highlighted these children's difficulties (Goodman and Graham 1996). Careful follow up of these children suggested a high rate of psychiatric disorder throughout childhood. Common types of disorder included anxiety and depression in 25 per cent of the children; conduct disorder involving disruptive behaviour in 24 per cent; severe hyperactivity and inattention in 10 per cent; and autistic disorder in 3 per cent. Hence it appears that the overall rate of psychiatric difficulties in these children was at least three times higher than in children without physical disability. It also appeared that hyperactivity and autistic disorders were particularly over-represented (Goodman 1998).

HEAD INJURIES

Head injuries similarly have a variety of causes and mild head injuries are very common in childhood. It is not clear to what extent mild head injuries have long-term adverse psychiatric consequences. Serious cognitive and psychiatric sequelae undoubtedly occur, however, after severe head injuries (e.g. closed head injuries resulting in at least two weeks of post traumatic amnesia). In general the difficulties suffered by these children are those comparable to those suffered by other children, i.e. ordinary child psychiatric difficulties such as emotional and conduct problems predominate. It does appear, however, that severe closed head injury (i.e., where the skull is not penetrated, but the brain is injured by sudden acceleration or deceleration) may sometimes result in a specific range of difficulties with impulsivity, irritability and social disinhibition. This constellation of difficulties may be associated with difficulties in the frontal lobe of the brain. This part of the brain is responsible for many organisational and executive functions that influence these aspects of our behaviour (Middleton 2001).

OTHER CHRONIC PHYSICAL DISORDERS

A large body of studies on other chronic physical disorders, such as severe asthma, diabetes and cystic fibrosis for example, demonstrate that both children and their mothers, as groups, are at increased risk of psychosocial adjustment problems compared with their peers. It is notable that there is considerable individual variation in outcome. As with the theoretical model regarding moderating and ameliorating factors for attention deficit hyperactivity disorder, similar models have been proposed to identify risk and resilience factors associated with differences in adjustment for these families (see Table 3.2). For example, factors about the disease itself such as severity, chronicity and likelihood of early death, are known to be important, as are personal factors in the child such as temperament, competence and problem solving ability. Other psychosocial factors such as handicap-related problems, major life events or other social factors such as the family environment and social support have an important part to play in the child's adjustment (Wallander and Varni 1998).

Brain and environment

Throughout this chapter we have emphasised the complex nature of the interplay between genetic and environmental risk factors. There has been recent interest in the potentially damaging effects of child abuse and neglect

Table 3.2: Examples of risks and moderating and mediating factors for attention deficit hyperactivity disorder

Factor	Basis		
	Genetic		Environmental
Risk	7-repeat DRD4 allele		Disrupted care
Moderators			
Vulnerability	Temperament		Poor peer relationships
Protective	High IQ		Consistent parenting
Mediators		Delay aversion	
		Behavioural inhibition	

Source: Stevenson 2001.

upon the young child's developing brain (see Glaser 2000 for a review). This has led in some quarters to a somewhat deterministic view that the impact of maltreatment may have direct physical effects on the brain and that these are immutable to future change. However, the relationships between abuse and the brain are far from straightforward.

There are general effects of early adverse circumstances on cognitive function, lasting into adult life (Richards and Wadsworth 2004). Against this background some children are then probably relatively more vulnerable to the effects of added abuse and neglect. Abuse and neglect in early life, including prenatally, increase hormones associated with stress, which in turn have an effect on brain development. They may do this in a number of ways; partly through affecting how the brain is organised and develops, but also through how the child's genes are expressed within the individual. Such changes then in turn have further effects on just how the child copes with and responds to further environmental influences (Rutter 2005). Thus the relationships between child abuse and neglect, the child's genetic make-up and inherent vulnerability and the biology of his or her brain's development are extremely complex, with influences in multiple directions.

Additionally, and most importantly, we have very little evidence on what happens if a child's circumstances improve. There is insufficient information about this but, based on research on children removed from appalling conditions and subsequently adopted, many of whom show remarkable capacity for change and recovery (O'Connor *et al.* 2000), it seems reasonable to assume that biological change is also possible.

Overall, these lines of research remind us of the biological effects of significant harm, and paradoxically the remarkable capacity of children to adapt and change. It should also caution us to avoid linear, deterministic thinking when considering genetic, biological and environmental risk factors – the relationship is far from straightforward.

Future developments

As with genetic research, recent developments in other areas of technology are potentially advancing our knowledge regarding normal brain development in children but also children with difficulties. The relatively recent development in neuroimaging of magnetic resonance imaging has made an important contribution. As no exposure to radiation is necessitated with this type of scan, it is particularly well suited to the study of children. These studies have shown that there are changes in the brain morphology that happen over many years. In the first few years there are significant decreases in certain areas of the brain and the overall stability in brain size does not occur until later in childhood and adolescence. These regional changes in brain volume throughout childhood and adolescence may be relevant in relation to the question as to why certain difficulties or clinical disorders emerge at different stages of a child's development.

There are also interesting differences between the developing male and female brain, possibly attributable to hormonal variations, that may account for differences in the susceptibility of males to many of the childhood psychopathologies. Whilst these imaging techniques have identified some non-specific neuro-anatomical changes, for example increased brain volume in autism, there are some other more specific anatomical differences that have been noted in certain disorders that may be pertinent to the clinical picture. An example is a correlation between the size of a particular part of the brain in children with ADHD, when compared with controls, that is known to be critical in executing control and the speed with which children switch to different topics.

The advent of functional magnetic resonance imaging holds great promise for further delineation of particular tasks and behaviours and linking these to quantitative differences in brain activity.

Hence it is clear not only how important the genetic and biological influences on a child's development can be, but also that it is a most exciting time regarding the rapid increase in our knowledge in these areas. As this knowledge becomes greater and more specific, it is hoped that this will allow more specific and appropriately targeted therapeutic interventions to improve children and young people's outcomes.

CHAPTER 4

The Place of Attachment in Children's Development

Jane Aldgate and David Jones

This chapter is about attachment and loss and the significance of these two concepts for children's development. Attachment theory has long been seen as significant in children's emotional development. Trying to make sense of the theory is not easy partly because of its complexity, and partly because it has seen many interpretations. In this chapter, we have taken a line which tries to draw together the different strands of the theory espoused by different disciplines. We have consciously adopted a stance which we see as representing the most common usage in contemporary texts and which will be useful to a multi-disciplinary readership of professionals working with children.

We begin with a definition of attachment and an exposition of some of the common terms used in discussing attachment. Attachment theory is explored from the separate perspectives of children and their caregivers. We then go on to look at how attachment develops and to explain the classification of attachment which is commonly used by a range of practitioners. Attachment is placed in the context of family styles which include multiple carers, incorporating material from cross-cultural studies. Finally we examine the application of attachment theory in practice, including using classifications of attachment in children and adults for purposes of assessment. We explore the relevance of the application of attachment across cultures and end by asking whether patterns of attachment established in childhood can be modified.

Where did attachment come from?

It is impossible to talk about attachment in human relationships without reference to John Bowlby. As Howe suggests: 'Under the creative genius of John Bowlby, insights garnered from evolutionary theory, ethology, systems theory and developmental psychology were fashioned over a number of years into what is today known as attachment theory' (2001, p.194). Bowlby's thesis (for example, Bowlby 1958), which still holds today, is based on the idea that attachment behaviour is a biological response which arises from a desire of an individual, either adult or child, to seek security and protection from harm through proximity to an attachment figure who is seen as stronger and wiser, with the ultimate aim of survival from predators and thereby preservation of the species. This biological approach to attachment is in Bowlby's view an evolutionary adaptation to self-preservation. It can be compared to the evolutionary development of other adaptations, such as camouflage, among all species. As Cassidy (1999) suggests, 'within this framework, attachment is considered a normal and healthy characteristic of humans throughout the life span, rather than a sign of immaturity that needs to be outgrown' (p.5). Attachments, therefore, can last over time and can be formed at any stage of the life cycle, although it is generally recognised that attachments between peers in adulthood are of a more reciprocal nature than those between children and their parents.

Bowlby has been much quoted and misquoted. He has been accused of being too mother-focused, and thereby neglecting fathers and significant other parenting figures. He has been called Eurocentric, not accounting for different styles of parenting in other cultures, and misinterpreted in saying that children were capable of only forming one attachment – to their mothers. In his earliest writing (Bowlby 1951) Bowlby used the term principal attachment figure or mothering figure rather than the term mother. He recognised that it is the nature and behaviour of that figure which is more important than its designated status. From early on he also suggested that children could have multiple attachment figures (Bowlby 1969/1982). Many contemporary writers on attachment have re-evaluated Bowlby and recognised that his original theory still holds within today's range of lifestyles that embrace family and cultural diversity. Bowlby provides for us today the foundation of our understanding of children's behaviours when they are stressed or frightened. Attachment theory also tells us how the developing child's view of the world will be influenced by the responses to those fears and anxieties from adults whom children have come to see as their attachment figures.

What is attachment?

Sometimes attachment is talked about as if it encompassed the whole of the relationship between child and parent. One hears children described as being attached to their parents or carers as though this represents the entirety of the relationship between them. To describe attachment in this broad way is confusing and mistaken. As Green suggests, 'attachment describes a crucial part of the parent–child relationship but is not the whole' (2003, p.1). While attachment behaviours are important to children's development and well-being, they are only one part, albeit an important part, of the whole range of children's developing behaviours and emotions. Children, for example, also develop sociable and affectional relationships, many of which will not be attachment relationships. Parents feed, clothe, play with and educate their children. These activities contribute to children's development but they are not part of attachment.

As Green suggests, 'Attachment applies to a specific aspect of parent–child relationship and the child's representation of this' (2003, p.3). Attachment is concerned with the behaviour and emotions that occur in particular situations where a child is stressed or fearful of perceived danger and seeks the proximity of another who is seen as stronger and wiser. As will be shown, attachment behaviour needs to be seen alongside the development of children's curiosity and exploration of their environment on the one hand and to the development of fear on the other. When fear is activated in a young child, curiosity and exploration will be suppressed. Feeling safe allows children to activate their exploratory system.

The aim in this chapter is to demystify the terms and to help professionals working with children see where attachment theory is relevant in their assessments and interventions. Let us start by giving a glossary of some of the most commonly used terms related to attachment. The first is attachment theory.

Attachment theory

This refers to the ideas and principles outlined by Bowlby, Ainsworth and others since. In this chapter we will draw on the work of contemporary child developmentalists like Cassidy and Shaver, Green and Howe. We will also look at the work of those who have approached attachment from a cultural perspective, such as Quinton and Rashid. In a later chapter, Owusu-Bempah complements this chapter by taking forward a new strand of theory related to attachment, children's socio-geneological connections, which is highly relevant for children living away from their families.

Attachment system

Another term widely used is the attachment system. Writers have used this in different ways. In all cases the attachment system includes all the behaviours and developing emotions involved in proximity seeking and seeking security.

The attachment system is also used to describe how children internalise the response they get from those with whom they seek safety into the organisation of a variety of mental processes, called the *internal working model*. We will examine this model in some detail later in the chapter. On one issue researchers agree: the way children's attachment is organised will have a strong association with other aspects of children's development and especially the development of their relationships with others (Howe *et al*. 1999; Solomon and George 1996). There is also an important debate to be had about how much childhood attachment patterns can have an impact on the development of later parenting styles.

Some writers also include in the attachment system the extent to which children's behaviour is embedded in the responses of their caregivers. Though the responses of caregivers to children's attachment behaviour will affect children's subsequent attachment patterns, in trying to make sense of attachment in this chapter, the path of developmentalists like Cassidy and Shaver (1999) has been followed. They look at the child and the caregiver from two separate perspectives. Such an approach distinguishes the main facets of attachment and caregiving behaviours.

Attachment behaviour

This refers to a range of behaviours which children display towards chosen individuals in specific circumstances of being frightened. Such behaviours are triggered by a child feeling stressed or fearful and wishing to seek safety. The range of behaviours includes proximity seeking, exploration, signalling and approach behaviours, which are designed to promote proximity. Some of these behaviours will be culturally determined but their aim is universal – to seek safety. An important point to remember is that the goal of attachment behaviour is not the individual with whom the child seeks proximity but the attainment through proximity to that individual of a state of equilibrium or homeostasis.

Attachment behaviour is closely related to the exploratory behaviour system and the fear behavioural system in such a way that produces something of a paradox. In other words, children are likely to feel secure enough to explore the world around them when they feel safe and they do not need to seek safety and proximity to adults. When the child feels safe to explore the immediate environment, attachment behaviour will not be activated. Conversely, if a child is frightened there will be a concentration on attachment behaviour, with curiosity temporarily extinguished.

Two sets of factors will activate attachment behaviour. Both indicate to the child that he or she is stressed or in danger. The first is the conditions within the child, such as hunger or pain. The other relates to the environment. Something triggers fear in the child who then seeks the protection of the attachment figure.

It is important to recognise that attachment behaviour is not the same as the development of a child's sociability. Interacting with others socially is a normal expectation in every culture. Children may show affectionate behaviour to each other and to a range of adults but this is not necessarily attachment behaviour. As with the exploratory behaviour system, the 'sociable behaviour system' is likely to be activated when the attachment system is not activated (Cassidy 1999, p.9).

Developmental theorists suggest that attachment behaviour begins to develop from around 7 months onwards. That is not to say babies cannot have affectional relationships with their carers but that behaviour which is related to attachment will not develop until after this time. However, its roots may be evident earlier.

Attachment figures

These are the individuals whom the children see as stronger and wiser than themselves, with whom they have a relationship that is beyond that of other affectional relationships because it specifically relates to seeking safety.

Usually, they will be parental figures but not necessarily so. As we will see later, it is possible for children to have multiple attachments but contemporary thinking is divided on whether children have a hierarchy of attachments or whether they can have equal but different attachment figures at the same time.

The development of different patterns of attachment behaviour will be influenced by the response of attachment figures, also known as the caregivers. Although the caregiving system will influence the development of different patterns of attachment, and the way a child internalises these, it is separate from the attachment system. Parents are not attached to their children – they have sensitive, affectional relationships with them. The sensitivity of these relationships will influence children's patterns of attachment. Looking at the two parts of the attachment system separately also helps to clarify what may be termed the 'attachment relationship'.

Attachment relationship

Contemporary writers tend to use the term attachment relationship only to describe the child's attachment relationship with adults. In the past, some writers have defined this as a two-way relationship between child and attachment figure. We take the line that it is helpful to separate the child's behaviour and feelings from that of the adult, and so confine the attachment relationship to a one-way relationship from child to adult (calling the other direction the 'caregiver relationship').

Attachment behaviour will change according to children's age and stage of development. Nevertheless, writers agree that the aim of attachment behaviour will remain the same across the lifespan. There is a plethora of research that shows that the attachment relationship is an important contributing factor to other aspects of development, such as children's social relations with peers, their sense of self-esteem and their educational progress (see George and Solomon 1999).

Attachment bond

The term attachment relationship has often been interchanged with the attachment bond. This is misleading because there are subtle differences. The attachment bond is generally held to be of an enduring nature over time whereas the attachment relationship could have been in existence for only a short time. Second, the attachment bond is dependent on the presence of a wider relationship between child and attachment figure. It refers to an *affectional* tie between child and adult as perceived by the child, and evolved over time, which has as part of it, *an attachment relationship.* One normally thinks of a bond being mutually recognised between two or more people. This is not so with the attachment bond. The bond is one way only from the individual seeking an affectional relationship with an attachment figure. As Cassidy (1999) suggests, an attachment bond

> is not one between two people: it is instead a bond that one individual has to another individual who is perceived to be stronger and wiser (e.g. the bond of an infant to the mother). A person can be attached to another who is not, in turn, attached to him or her... this is usually the case with infants and their parents. (p.12)

Such a view might well apply to a situation where a child is in foster or residential care.

Although some writers talk of ' bonding' being from parent to child, we reject this view in the light of the consensus from contemporary developmentalists. We also reject a now discredited view, which emanated from a misunderstanding of the work of Bowlby and Ainsworth, that there is a critical period in which a reciprocal bond develops between baby and mother. This is not to deny that the early relationship between infant and parents is not important. Indeed, it is a fundamental part of establishing affectional relationships of each towards the other, of which an attachment relationship is one element, but not the sole one.

For a child to have an *attachment bond* to another person, the child must look to the other person for security and comfort and perceive that person to be stronger and wiser. At the same time, an attachment bond cannot exist by itself; it must be part of a *wider affectional bond* between that child and another person. Affectional bonds can exist between children and a whole range of individuals who are significant in their lives. There are many circumstances when such affectional bonds exist between individuals throughout life. Such affectional bonds exist between friends, partners and relatives in many different circumstances.

Cassidy (1999) suggests there are certain preconditions for such an affectional bond to exist:

1. The bond is not transitory but exists over time.

2. It involves a specific person who cannot be substituted by another.

3. The relationship is emotionally significant to the individual.

4. The individual wishes to remain in proximity or contact with the person. The definition of proximity will change over time and will be influenced by a range of factors such as the individual's age and what is going on in their environment.

5. A child will feel distressed when separated from the individual with whom they are bonded involuntarily. They will be very distressed when they cannot reach a person they wish to be near.

To turn an affectional bond into an attachment bond, all five criteria must exist but there must also be the additional criterion: the fact that the individual seeks security and comfort from fear or stress from a person who is considered to be stronger and wiser. Seeing the *attachment bond* in these terms is helpful because it explains how attachment behaviour fits into the context of the whole relationship between child and adult.

Caution has to be exercised in inferring that an attachment bond exists in every circumstance where a child displays attachment behaviour. Some babies will stop crying when comforted by a stranger or adult whom they trust, say a playgroup leader, but this does not mean they are *attached* to that person. If, for example, a child displays attachment behaviour to a relative stranger, say a foster parent, this does not imply an attachment bond. When the child has lived with those foster parents for several years, it is then likely that there will be an attachment bond, hopefully reciprocated by a sensitive, affectional, caregiver relationship.

If a child does have an attachment bond, this will endure over time, even when the adult is absent. This has important implications for children separated from parental attachment figures, as Owusu-Bempah discusses in Chapter 6. The fact that most children will develop attachment bonds to selected adults over time, even if these attachments are insecure, helps to explain why children who have been abused by their attachment figures are still devastated at being separated from them.

Caregiver relationship

How children's patterns of attachment develop will be influenced by the behaviour of their caregivers. The *caregiving* relationship refers to those aspects of the caregiver's behaviour that promotes the development and maintenance of attachment behaviour within the child. This includes the provision of nurturance and emotional availability, sensitivity, affection and other behaviours, which promote the child's security (Ainsworth *et al.* 1978). Such responses may have a cultural element but will, ideally, all have the same aim of being sensitive to the child's stress and fear. We also take the view of writers such as Cassidy that caregiving behaviour is not confined to promoting the child's attachment.

Parents and carers can be also be teachers, people who play with the child or, sometimes, those who set boundaries. A child trying to gain a parent's attention to play is not engaging in attachment behaviour. Discriminating about the context of a child seeking proximity to a parent is important in assessing the relationship between them in all its many facets. 'A behaviour may serve different behavioural systems at different times, even when directed to the same individual' (Cassidy 1999, p.13).

The caregiving system needs to be seen as working in parallel with the child's attachment system. It describes behaviour on the part of the caregiver that ideally responds to and preempts the child's attempts to gain safety. A lot less is known about the caregiver behavioural systems than is known about the attachment behavioural systems in children (Solomon and George 1996). It is known that the environment in which parents live can affect their caregiving capacity. Parents who are substance misusers can behave erratically and unpredictably causing children to be frightened and insecure in their attachments (Cleaver, Unell and Aldgate 1999). Research in Japan, the USA and England has suggested that there may be associations between the positive quality of partnership relationships and the sensitivity of parental responses to children's attachment needs (George and Solomon 1999). Conversely, negative partner relationships can also inhibit good caregiving, as research from domestic violence has shown (Cleaver *et al.* 1999). How far childhood experiences of attachment influence adult caregiving behaviour is a debatable matter, as will be discussed later in the chapter.

Attachment theory stresses the importance of caregivers' sensitive response to children's attachment behaviour. The importance of early sensitivity between parent and infant is seen as a rehearsal for responses to children's attachment. Parents of premature babies, for example, often find it difficult not to be able to be physically close to their infants and to respond by holding the baby. They may worry this will affect the child's attachment to them. However, it is important to stress that there is little relationship between early physical contact and later caregiving behaviour in relation to the quality of children's attachment (see George and Solomon 1999). Nevertheless, the early months of a child's life do provide most parents with the opportunity to learn how to be sensitive to their children, which in itself is preparation for responding to children's attachment behaviour when this develops several months later. The importance of this sensitivity cannot be emphasised too much. It is the critical factor that will influence children's representations of how they see their relationships with others in their world. Specifically, the degree of sensitivity or lack of it in caregivers over the first years of children's development will influence the development of children's internal organisation of their attachment behaviour. Solomon and George (1996), for example, distinguish between three groups of parents:

- those who provide a secure base

- those who reject and thereby de-activate the infants' attachment behaviours

- uncertain and helpless parents who provide disorganised caregiving.

These parenting styles seems to be universal across cultures and are present in societies where children have multiple carers, as much as in those where they spend their days with only one or two individuals (George and Solomon 1999).

Sensitivity of caregivers can also be seen in relation to the individual temperament of children in the same household. A sensitive parent will be able to respond to the individual temperaments of siblings and recognise that each child needs an individually sensitive and appropriate response to his or her attachment behaviour. This idea helps to make connections between attachment and children's individual temperaments. As Green suggests:

> parental sensitivity buffers the individual differences in children. The essence of parental sensitivity is flexibility to adjust to child individual difference: if this is successful, then arguably individual differences within the child will not determine the final attachment relationship. In other words, a good relationship is possible with many different kinds and types of children if the parent is able to adapt to the child's specific needs. (2003, p.5)

Dimensions of caregiving behaviour

Observation of parents' reactions to their children led Ainsworth and her colleagues to develop four dimensions of caregiving: sensitivity, acceptance/rejection, cooperation/interference and accessibility/ignoring.

These are summarised by Howe (2001, p.199):

1. Caregiving can be more or less sensitive and attuned to the physical and psychological condition of the baby. For example, insensitive carers might be very poor at reading and responding to children's signals of need and distress.

2. Degrees of acceptance or rejection may also be recognised. For example, some parents accept their babies, whatever the child's mood or behaviour. They also acknowledge that parenthood involves constraints on one's lifestyle. In contrast, rejecting caregivers often resent the demands that children make on them emotionally.

3. Caregiver–child relationship can be mapped in terms of levels of parental cooperation and interference. Carers who recognise, support and respect babies' autonomy appear able to cooperate with their children's needs and accomplishments. Interfering and rejecting parents are less able to recognise, respect or enjoy the full range of their children's needs and behaviours.

4. Along the accessibility-ignoring scale, accessible carers remain alert and available to their infants. Carers who are prone to ignore their children continue to be absorbed in their own needs and pursuits, only engaging with their children when it suits them as adults.

Howe points out that no parent is expected to be perfect within all these dimensions but only to be, as Winnicott suggested, 'good enough'.

How does attachment develop?

Earlier in the chapter, it was suggested that attachment behaviour is part of a cycle related to fear and exploration. The core hypothesis of the theory relates to a sequence of internal arousal; proximity seeking behaviour; assuagement of arousal; and return to exploration. Attachment theorists such as Bowlby (1958) and Ainsworth *et al.* (1978) suggest that, as infants develop and experience sensitive or insensitive caregiving, they come to represent those patterns of care in response to attachment behaviour in terms of mental representations of how the world responds to them. These patterns of thinking and feeling will be activated in new situations which provoke anxiety because the child has learned that adults will react in certain ways to their attachment behaviour. This internal organisation of a child's experience of caregiving in response to their attachment behaviour is known as the *internal working model.*

According to the response he or she has received to his or her attachment behaviour, the child learns to develop a strategy to gain the caregiver's attention and thereby reduce distress. Ideally, when a child seeks comfort and security, the caregiver will respond sensitively and the child will learn that he or she can trust the caregiver to provide safety. If caregivers respond negatively, with abusing, ignoring or rejecting behaviour, children will try to find alternative strategies to gain the caregiver's attention. This explains why children who have been abused will still show attachment behaviour towards their caregivers, although this will be of an insecure nature. In extreme cases, where children have not been able to find any comfort from their caregivers, as happens in some cases when caregiving behavior is influenced by substance misuse or serious mental health problems, children come to see adults as unreliable or even dangerous. Such children learn that the world is a dangerous place and learn to trust no one, not even themselves. Children who turn to themselves for safety are in fact, in the context of their experience, reacting logically to defend themselves from fear. The fact that such responses will be inappropriate in terms of children's developing social behaviour is an issue of which the child knows nothing. Such a child is simply fighting to overcome anxiety in the only way available to him or her. They have learnt that adults do not respond positively to them. This is in complete contrast to the securely attached child whose caregiver has responded to and often preempted their stress or fear. These children will turn to adults for safety because they have learned from their experiences of caregiving that adults can be trusted.

In other words, through the development of the internal working model, children learn that they can or cannot trust others to protect them and have to develop appropriate defensive strategies for dealing with caregivers' behaviour. In so doing, they begin to construct a view of the world around them that reflects how they have experienced adults' responses to their need to find proximity and security when attachment behaviour has been aroused. The consequence of this learning process, triggered by attachment behaviour, is that children learn to incorporate within themselves, through the internal working model, expectations and beliefs about their own and other people's behaviour. The internal working model creates for the child a sense of self, other people, and the relationship between self and others. In this respect, 'internal working models then begin to organise expectations and behaviours in all other significant relationships' (Howe *et al.* 1999, p.23).

Green (2003) suggests that a child is an active participant in constructing his or her representations of attachment from 'the materials of their experience' and consequently also 'an active participant in understanding and interpreting their world' (p.3).

> A child who has received a sensitive response to their attachment behaviour learns that 'attachment relationships are in this sense a primary social experience – confirming the value of others to my own life. I – as a child – also learn that the circle of familiar others is generally helpful and trustworthy, and to differentiate this from a healthy awareness of strangers. I – as a child am generally trusting and motivated to be social because it is in my interest to be so. I want to invest in others and maintain my social relationships. (pp.2–3)

Why the development of the internal working model is so important, therefore, is because it is the means by which children learn to develop a perception of their self worth, how much they are accepted by adults and how much they are loved. Not surprisingly, children who believe they are unloved will behave towards others in a way which reflects their experience. At its worst, this behaviour will be inappropriately controlling or aggressive and will increase the internalised perception by creating new responses of rejection.

Patterns of attachment

As a result of studying different styles of caregiving and children's reactions to stress when removed temporarily from their attachment figures and then returned to them, both in Uganda and subsequently in the USA, Ainsworth developed a threefold classification of attachment patterns to which a fourth pattern was added (see Howe 1995; Main 1991). The following descriptions summarise the patterns:

1. Secure attachment: children use their caregiver as a secure base for exploration. They miss him/her on separation, but are easily soothed on reunion, greeting the caregiver with smiles, words or gesture.

2. Ambivalent or resistant: children are either excessively fretful, or passive, and fail to explore their surroundings. They are distressed at separation and on reunion are not comforted, alternating bids for contact with angry rejection, or become passive.

3. Avoidant: children explore readily; are minimally responsive to separation, actively avoiding the caregiver on reunion, sometimes arching away and seeking comfort in toys.

4. Disorganised: children lack any coherent style of response to separation or reunion, showing incomplete or contradictory behaviours, including fear, depression, confusion, stilling/freezing.

These patterns are classified as:

- Avoidant (A)

- Secure (B)

- Ambivalent or resistant (C)

- Disorganised (D)

Each pattern of attachment results from the child's attempt to respond to the caregiving behaviour he or she has experienced. Here we provide a brief overview of the links between children's attachment, their socio-emotional development and the caretaking behaviour which they have experienced. More detail can be found in the following: Crittenden 1995; Howe 1995, 2001; Howe et al. 1999, Solomon and George 1999.

Children who have learnt attachment behaviour which is avoidant (A) may often be very compliant. They are typically the children whom foster carers describe as 'no trouble'. They have learnt to suppress their anger and be watchful, to seize the opportunity for proximity to attachment figures if it occurs, but have learnt such proximity is unreliable and will not be gained by demanding attention. Their caretakers tend to be rejecting, aggressive, ignoring or overly intrusive.

Children whose attachment patterns might be described as ambivalent or resistant (C) will have experienced inconsistently responsive caregiving which leaves them displaying behaviours which include aggression, helplessness and seeking attention, angrily focussing on their caregiver when the situation calls for play or exploration.

Children whose attachment behaviour is most extreme (Disorganised, D) will have learnt that no adult attachment figure in their lives was trustworthy and have often suffered abuse or neglect. They have had to rely on themselves for protection to survive emotionally. They are children who have learnt how to be in control but also perceive themselves as unlovable. Consequently, they often behave in a way that makes them unloved by other adults and children. Sometimes, such children will have difficulty both understanding their own emotions and responding to others. They are children who may show serious conduct disorders, are low achievers educationally, and generally are very difficult to live with. Green suggests that, sometimes, if these children are in foster and adoptive placements, it used to be thought that they were avoiding new relationships because of unresolved conflicts in relation to previous attachments but current thinking suggests their behaviour may be more influenced by the fact that they 'have impairments in the basic understanding of social relationships or social communication' (2003). Such children present a challenge to professionals because of their attitudes and behaviour (Howe *et al.* 1999).

In contrast, children who are securely attached to caregivers (pattern B) will learn that they can trust adults; they can explore the world around them but know they can seek the safety of caregivers if they are in distress. This positive mode of thinking will transfer itself to other relationships.

First, it seems from the research that children's internal working models of attachment are likely to have an association with a developing child's relationships with siblings and friends. The more securely attached child is likely to have more harmonious sibling relationships and have good relationships with friends, and make more friends in middle childhood, than children who were judged to have insecure attachments to their parental attachment figure. So children's attachment to their parents may have an influence on the quality and quantity of their friendships (see Berlin and Cassidy 1999). Second, children's attachment to their primary caregivers are likely to influence their relationships with other adults, such as teachers and playgroup leaders.

Multiple attachments

One of the criticisms laid at the door of early attachment theorists was that they focused too heavily on one primary attachment figure, usually the mother, at the expense of other significant adults in children's lives who may also be attachment figures. Many children in the UK and beyond spend their days within a network of caring adults. This has led developmentalists in the USA, like Howes (1999), to suggest that it may be useful to look at a child's *network* of attachment relationships rather than concentrating on a primary attachment figure.

Howes and her colleagues (1999, p.674) propose that attachment figures in multiple carer situations can be identified by asking the following questions:

1. Does this person provide physical and emotional care?

2. Is this person a consistent presence in the child's social network?

3. Is this person emotionally invested in the child?

These criteria are meant to apply to specific attachment figures for a particular child. It is easy to see how fathers, step-parents, grandparents, and other close relatives, as well as mothers, may all meet the criteria.

There are different pathways in the development of attachment relationships for three groups of children who may experience multiple attachments:

- children who from early infant childhood experience two or more attachment relationships

- children who have formed an attachment relationship with one or more attachment figure and who then subsequently establish a relationship with an alternative figure

- children who have established attachment relationships who may then lose their attachment figures and have them replaced by others.

There is a large body of literature asserting that, where two parents are actively involved in caregiving relating to attachment from the outset, there may be little difference between child–mother and child–father attachment relationships (Parke and Asher 1983). There are, however, many complexities, including the fact that the quality of time spent with children may be as important as the quantity of time spent together. Grandparents, for example, who spend only short periods of time with a child may have to exhibit very responsive caregiving behaviour to ensure the child is securely attached to them.

Where children begin to spend a substantial part of their days with alternative carers, such as childminders and nursery school teachers, subsequent to their having made attachment relationships with one or two primary attachment figures, it is suggested that these new relationships will reflect those the child has already established. This means that if children are secure in their attachment, they will develop secure attachments with other caregiving adults. If, however, children come to their alternative carers with insecure attachment patterns, it will call for extreme sensitivity on the part of the alternative caregiver to win children's trust.

Then, there is the situation where children are separated from attachment figures. This may be through death or separation. Three fundamental principles obtain in all cases:

1. Children will react to their loss in the light of their previous experiences of attachment.

2. Children should to be allowed to express their feelings about loss.

3. Children need sensitive caregiving to help them through experiences of loss.

Loss is the mirror image of attachment. Loss of an attachment figure means that children cannot turn to that adult to protect them. At the same time, the loss brings a heightened sense of fear and the need to respond to this through attachment behaviour. The normal source of protection has been removed so the child is placed in a very vulnerable state. If the response to this is not dealt with sensitively, children may be exposed to developmental harm.

Responding to loss

Children separated from adult attachment figures will go through a process of protest, despair and detachment (Bowlby 1958). How children recover from such loss will depend on what happens next. A short parental absence may cause distress but trust and positive attachments can be restored if the child is returned quickly to sensitive caregivers. The most enduring images of such experiences come from the films made by the Robertsons in the 1950s (see, for example, Robertson 1952) which showed graphically the strength of children's emotions on separation and the mixture of equally strong emotions on return, including anger, clinging and ignoring the parents.

Where children have a permanent loss of an attachment figure through death, they need to be allowed to grieve that loss in an age appropriate way. Above all they need to have very sensitive caregiving which allows them to express their grief and to find a replacement attachment figure (see Aldgate 1992; Jewett 1984).

Children who come into the care system are very much at risk of harm. As Stevenson suggested in the 1960s (Stevenson 1968), such an event will break the lifeline of the developing child. Given that many children who are looked after in foster or residential care will have had insecure experiences of attachment and caregiving, sensitive caregiving and continuity at this time are paramount to the preservation of children's emotional health. If such children are subject to further separations, which may easily happen, since children with disorganised patterns of attachment are likely to test the staying power of the majority of carers, this will only increase children's sense of being unlovable. These children need experienced caregivers who are themselves secure in their adult attachments and have living circumstances where children can be given the attention and consistent response they need. In some cases, children will have to learn how to be social beings almost from scratch.

Knowledge about how children view their attachment relationships in a multiple carer situation, where they have different experiences with different caregivers, is still developing and has been much influenced by studies from different cultural perspectives. There are three schools of thought.

One is the traditional Western view that children have a hierarchy of attachment figures with the main caregiver being the most influential. This model suggests that a child's first and most influential attachment figure will set the pattern for any subsequent attachments.

The second model suggests that children integrate all their attachment relationships into an internal representation. Therefore, children's internal perceptions of attachments will relate to the quality of all attachment relationships in a child's network (Howes 1999). One attachment relationship does not become more influential than another. However, two secure relationships are thought to be better in predicting positive developmental outcomes than one secure and one insecure.

A third model suggests that each attachment relationship is independent in its quality and influence. This model argues that different attachment relationships will have an affect predominantly on one domain of development. Thus mother–child attachment, for example, may influence a child's sense of competence, while father–child attachment may influence how a child deals with conflicts with others. It is possible to see this model fitting well across cultures, and especially in environments where different adults are ascribed special roles in relation to one aspect of a child's development (see Howes 1999).

Research in this area is just developing and is not yet conclusive. The current state of affairs seems to be that the outcome in terms of a child's development is related to what one is trying to predict or measure at any one time. For example, studies which try to predict children's competence have suggested that a hierarchy of attachments model or the independent model are relevant. Other studies that have looked at the relationship between security of attachment to a child care provider (beyond parents) suggest that good networks of attachment relationships predict children's ability to socialise with peers. There are implications of these relatively new ways of thinking about attachments for practitioners. Developments about thinking in terms of a network of attachments suggest a more creative approach to viewing attachments. Further developments in this area deserve a watching brief. As the research develops, we shall begin to be more certain about the impact of different experiences on children. Whatever the final outcomes are, one thing is certain, multiple attachments are very much part of the lives of many children and should be taken into account in assessing a child's attachment behaviour.

Assessing attachment patterns

Attachment today is just as important for children as it was when Bowlby and Ainsworth carried out their pioneering work. For this reason, practitioners in different disciplines need to be able to assess attachment in order to safeguard the welfare of the developing child. It is also recognised that attachment patterns in adulthood may affect the caregiving ability of individuals. Consequently, the assessment of attachment remains an important feature of working with children and their caregivers.

Ainsworth's standardised assessment of parent–infant reactions which led to her classifications described above is still used to assess the attachment of small children, while other tests have been developed with older children. The assessment test for small children is called the Strange Situation Test (see Box 4.1).

Box 4.1: The Strange Situation Test

The Strange Situation Test works as follows:

1. First, the attachment figure (mother) and infant are together while the child plays with toys and the adult watches.

2. Then a stranger enters the room and after a while she talks with the mother first and then plays with the child.

3. Mother leaves the room while the stranger remains and plays with the child.

4. Mother returns after a short period, approximately 30 seconds or as soon as the child shows heightened distress. She then settles the child and then the stranger leaves the room (this is the first reunion).

5. Mother exits the room and leaves the child on his or her own.

6. Stranger then enters and attempts to play with and comfort the child.

7. Mother returns after a short while and settles the child. Stranger leaves (second reunion).

The entire test takes about 20 minutes.

When mothers leave the room, most children stop playing and some degree of separation anxiety normally triggers attachment behaviour. Most important is what the infant does when the mother comes back into the room. The focus needs to be on this rather than on the child's reactions on separation from the caregiver.

The Strange Situation has been tested in homes within the USA with surprisingly similar results. Van IJzendoorn *et al.* (1992) undertook a meta-analysis of Strange Situation classifications of mother– child pairs, and found the following patterns:

Avoidant (A)	23%
Secure (B)	55%
Ambivalent (C)	8%
Disorganised (D)	15%

This shows that around half of children will be securely attached, around a quarter will be classed as avoidant, just under one tenth ambivalent and one sixth disorganised (see section on Patterns of Attachment above for further details on the interpretation of the four categories). Reporting on a later meta-analysis of Strange Situation classification between mothers and infants across different countries and cultures, van IJzendoorn and Sagi (1999) suggest the different types of attachment can be observed universally and that this could be measured in different cultures. As will be discussed later in the chapter, there is, however, recognition that variations in the proportion of children securely attached may be culturally determined, and therefore may be different in different cultures.

The concern remains for practitioners in children's services in relation to children who display disorganised patterns of attachment and serious attention should be given to their attachment needs from an early age to avoid major behaviour difficulties at a later stage of childhood.

Ainsworth's test is suitable for infants and small children aged between two and four but other tests have been developed for older children. Notable among these is the story stem completions technique (for example, Green *et al.* 2000). Children are asked to respond to a set of story stems where they are given the beginning of a story highlighting everyday family scenarios, each of which contains an inherent dilemma. Children are asked to describe or draw what happens next. This technique is useful because it avoids any threat children may feel from being asked direct questions about their families. It also allows for children to communicate verbally and non-verbally. The stems are designed to draw out themes about children's expectations of relationships with caregivers. This includes areas such as giving affection, setting boundaries and children's expectations of whether caregivers will be sensitive to their need for comfort or protection. The children's responses can be scored on a range of dimensions, including themes about how aggression is used, whether adults are represented as endangered or endangering, how conflict is overcome and on how children respond to the stories by being engaged with them (Hodges *et al.* 2003; Steele 2003). For further use of stem stories see Howe *et al.* (1999, pp.35–36).

Assessing adult attachment

It is generally agreed that there will be some continuities in attachment between childhood and adulthood, although with the important caveat that attachment is a dynamic concept which will change over time and can be influenced by intervening life events and relationships. Nevertheless, there have been important developments in the measurement of development of attachment in adults. These have been pioneered by Mary Main in the USA. It is very important to stress that the Adult Attachment Interview (AAI) developed by Main and Goldwyn (1984–94) relates to the adult's current state of mind. This interview, though relying on the recollections of individuals about their early attachment experience, is a measure of an individual's 'current state of mind with respect to attachment' (Berlin and Cassidy 1999, p.692). It is looking for the coherence or sense the individual has made of earlier experiences, i.e. how the adult feels about earlier experiences now. As Howe *et al.* (1999) suggest, the interview shows how adults organise attachment-related thoughts, feelings and memories. The way in which the individual relates memories of attachment is counted towards the classification of their current state. Concepts such as coherence and collaboration influence the way in which the adult participating in the interview handles attachment-related thoughts and memories.

The AAI is essentially a form of discourse analysis, because the semi-structured interview, which takes about an hour, is transcribed and then rated according to the types outlined in Box 4.2.

Main's interview has been tested in different non-clinical situations. Table 4.1 shows the categories derived from a meta-analysis based on over 2000 AAIs across 33 studies (van IJzendoorn and Bakermans-Kranenburg 1996).

Box 4.2: Adult attachment types

Secure – autonomous (F)
These persons are free to evaluate and are internally consistent in relation to the presentation and evaluation of their experiences. Their responses are clear, relevant and succinct. Such adults are able to reflect on and realistically evaluate their life experiences and can think about, reflect and appraise their own behaviour.

Dismissing adults (D)
These persons can be compared to avoidant infants, grown up. They make globally positive statements about parents and others which are not supported by specific examples or perhaps at other times are contradicted elsewhere in the interview. Attachment-related issues or emotionally charged memories are quickly glossed over and set to one side as unimportant or irrelevant.

Preoccupied – entangled (E)
These persons can be compared to ambivalent infants. They are over-absorbed with attachment-related events from childhood and talk about them in a confused, angry and ambivalent fashion. They are preoccupied with such relationships and with who was loved and who was not loved in their experience.

Unresolved – disorganised (U)
These persons can be compared with infant disorganised patterns. During their answers, these adults lose the thread of what they are saying as they become lost in past difficult traumatic memories. There are lapses or great gaps in monitoring what is being asked and what is being responded to.

Table 4.1: Distribution of adult attachment styles

Attachment types	Mothers	Fathers
Secure (F)	55%	57%
Dismissing (D)	16%	15%
Preoccupied – entangled (E)	9%	11%
Unresolved (U)	19%	17%

Other researchers have refined Main's AAI (see Hesse 1999; Howe *et al.* 1999), but the principle of evaluating past experiences in the context of present reflections remains the same.

This classification is useful in so far as it indicates adults' current feelings in relation to attachment. It has been used in studies of adoptions to see if there are relationships between caregivers' attachment measures on AAI and children's attachment patterns, as measured through stem story work described earlier. Steele (2003), for example, reports associations between children's stem stories and parents' measures on the AAI. In other words, adoptive parents who had unresolved issues of childhood attachment found it more difficult and less rewarding to manage their children's behaviour. Nevertheless, the research found that placements were able to endure, thus providing permanence for the children. This finding has implications for practice. It suggests that, in assessing foster and adoptive parents, the sense they have made of their attachment experiences may be a contributing factor to their responses and coping mechanisms in relation to the children in their care. As Steele suggests,

> Specifically, we found that if we look at individuals who suffered from deprivation in their childhoods and yet showed a capacity to reflect upon these experiences there was a strong likelihood that despite the adversity they would develop a secure parent-child attachment relationship with their own child. (2003, p.9)

In relation to the meta-analysis of the Adult Attachment Interview, there are some striking similarities in the assessment of mothers and fathers which suggest a relatively high level of secure attachments among adults. This knowledge can be used to advantage for children. Practitioners might wish to think about building any interventions on the strengths of these individuals. By contrast, just under one fifth of adults may have unresolved or lost memories of their childhood attachments. If practitioners are working with these adults, they may need to ensure unresolved feelings can be minimised to promote secure attachments in children. In the van IJzendoorn and Bakermans-Kranenburg analysis (1996, see above), over a quarter of both mothers and fathers were still struggling with over-preoccupation with or dismissing as irrelevant their early relationships. If practitioners are working with these individuals, awareness of these attitudes needs to be part of the equation of assessing both caregivers and supporting families.

How far does attachment apply across different cultures?

Critics of attachment theory in the 1980s and 1990s accused attachment theorists of promoting a model of attachment that was developed and applied in a Western culture but which was irrelevant in other cultures where there were different expectations of children's behaviour and roles in adulthood (see, for example, Rashid 1996; Woodhead 1999). Such critiques have inspired much research in this field which has come to some interesting conclusions. Although studies have tended to be small, meta-analyses, for example such as those reported by van IJzendoorn and Sagi (1999), have been able to identify commonalities and to give more validity to findings in different parts of the world. Quinton (1994) sums up the current thinking:

> it seems clear that many features of parent-child relationships have similar outcomes in widely different cultural settings and that within-culture variation on these features can be as great, if not greater, than cross-cultural variations. ... Because these developmental consistencies can be identified, the argument that cross-cultural studies of development are essentially flawed through ethnocentric bias is clearly wrong. (p.178)

The developmental consistencies which Quinton identifies include the evidence that attachment relationships will be established in any known culture. This is summarised by van IJzendoorn and Sagi (1999), who have studied patterns of attachment across different countries extensively. They conclude:

> Not only the attachment phenomenon itself but also the different types of attachment appear to be present in various western and non-western cultures. Avoidant, secure and resistant attachments have been observed in the African, Chinese and Japanese studies;

even in the extremely diverging child-rearing context of the Israeli kibbutzim, the differentiation between secure and insecure attachments could be made. (p.728)

In spite of this common ground which confirms the universality of attachment, there can be striking differences in the proportions of children who are in the different categories identified by Ainsworth. This is where cultural differences can be identified. This does not undermine the case for the universal application for attachment but rather strengthens it in recognising that attachment behaviours will be influenced by expectations of what is 'the ideal child' in different cultures and by expectations of adult parenting behaviour within a given society.

A well-known example of this is the study of children in Gusii society in Kenya. These children are brought up among a network of caregivers. There is an expectation that Gusii children will not be individualistic since this is against the norms of their culture, which the Gusii see as contributing to a supremely cooperative society. In relation to attachment behaviours, Gusii children are expected not to hug their caregivers but to shake their hands. When observed in the equivalent of a Strange Situation Test, securely attached Gusii infants did put up their hands when caregivers returned to them and received the positive handshake they were looking for from sensitive caregivers. The more insecurely attached child turned away and did not seek proximity with the parent (Kemonian and Leiderman 1986). As Quinton (1994) points out, even within similar cultures, there can be differences which reflect expectations of child behaviour. Work in Germany, for example, has suggested that German children are expected to be more independent at an earlier age than their US or UK counterparts. Therefore, in attachment situations, German children appear to show less distress when separated from parents, which is attributed to the fact they have been taught not to show their feelings and to trust their parents' behaviour (Howe 1995).

Cross-cultural research on attachment is extremely important because it has confirmed the universality of attachment. At the same time it has made researchers and practitioners sensitive to looking at children's attachment relationships. It has opened up the field of study in relation to networks of multiple caregivers through providing what Rashid (1996) has called 'a cultural lens'. Far from discrediting the idea of attachment, cross-cultural research has confirmed the richness of its variations within the universal principles of attachment theory. The common thread is that all children need to feel secure in their attachments and that, to achieve this, in all cultures, caregivers develop a sensitive response which is culturally appropriate.

Modification of the internal model

One major question remains. How far can patterns of attachment be modified through the lifespan? It is important to ask these questions because of the knowledge of how attachment patterns can affect behaviour in childhood and adulthood. The body of research on this area, albeit mostly from Europe and North America, suggests a complex picture.

First, attachment relationships are by their nature dynamic. A child and caregiver will constantly negotiate different patterns of behaviour as the child grows up. Many battles in adolescence in our culture between parents and children derive from differing stances on what constitutes sensitive caregiving. An adolescent may wish to push back the boundaries of safety beyond the limits of what caregivers still define as part of their sensitive and responsive caregiving role designed to keep children safe. A classic example is how long children may stay out at night. There is constantly a renegotiation of what is termed 'goal directed' behaviour between caregiver and child. The representations of behaviour which secure safety will change as the child develops.

Second, experiences within childhood can alter internal working models for good or ill. It is possible for a child who has been moved from an environment of insecure attachments to one which is secure to change their perception of the world but this will take very sensitive and purposive caregiving. Studies of adoption and fostering of children placed between 4 and 8 years show that children can improve their internal working model positively, although younger children show more change than older children (Steele 2003). Conversely, in the context of change which is negative, such as where children have experienced the stressful separation of parents and find themselves living with one parent whose caregiving capacity is diminished, children may move from secure to insecure attachments (Butler *et al.* 2003).

Third, there is some evidence of the influence of attachments on relationships across different generations. For example, in one study, mothers and fathers who were rated as having had loving parents were also observed to interact more positively with each other (Berlin and Cassidy 1999; Howe 1995). More significantly, some developmentalists have suggested that caregivers' own childhood experiences of attachment may influence their caregiving behaviour (see for example George and Solomon 1999; Howe *et al.* 1999; Schofield 1998a). It is suggested by these writers that early attachments tend to predict later styles in caregiving relationships. However, the research evidence is moving away from this rather deterministic view to a more dynamic mode. This newer approach stresses the line taken by the Main AAI – it is what individuals have made of experiences of attachment rather than the experiences themselves which are important. Further, attachment is a dynamic concept, and new experiences and relationships can have an impact on internal working models throughout the life cycle (Rutter and Quinton 1984).

Research in Japan, the US and England has suggested that there may be associations between the quality of partnership relationships and parental responses to children's attachment needs. This view recognises that life events and adult relationships can act as mediating factors. Consequently, experiences of poor quality attachments in one part of childhood may not preclude the development of secure attachments in later childhood or between adult partners which, in turn, are passed on to the next generation in the form of sensitive caregiving (see Berlin and Cassidy 1999). Even if internal working models do not change substantially, there can be protective factors within adult partnerships which improve caregiving to children. A partner who has a secure sense of adult attachment may act as a buffer for a parent who has an insecure internal representation of attachment. In summary, therefore, many intervening experiences, including relationships with therapists as well as with partners (Berlin and Cassidy 1999; Bowlby 1953; Rutter 1985) can influence individuals' working models and their adult state of mind.

Increasingly, in the light of this more dynamic approach to attachment, research is providing more and more evidence for the importance of understanding *discontinuity* rather than *continuity* in the shaping of adult patterns of caregiving and attachments in both children and adults. Such evidence comes from studies which have compared the caregiving behaviour of parents who had *continuous secure* attachments in childhood with those who had insecure attachments which were modified by later experiences. This second group, who were termed the *earned secure* group, showed equally positive parenting to their pre-school children (Pearson, Cohn, Cowan and Cowan 1994, reported in Berlin and Cassidy 1999, p.694). Similar findings come from research by Phelps *et al.* (1998)

observing parenting under conditions of high stress. They found that both *continuously secure* and *earned secure* parents displayed equally positive parenting.

The recent research and reappraisal of theory on attachment does provide a more optimistic view of the potential for change and growth within individuals across the lifespan. The implications of contemporary thinking are that the role of the professional is significant in contributing to the development of a secure sense of self, provided that there are timely and effective interventions. Where issues about attachment are identified, subsequent interventions should concentrate on building parenting capacity and helping to promote the securely attached developing child.

Conclusion

So, in the end, we can return to Bowlby's original arguments (Bowlby 1958): internal working models established in early childhood can have effects into adulthood but changes can occur through other influences which can alter the course of the early experience. This view gives cause for optimism in relation to the impact of poor early attachment experience, and has important implications for practice. It can no longer be taken for granted that a child will have the same internal working model throughout childhood. However, the most significant factor in any modification will be caregivers who become children's attachment figures.

Given the interconnections between attachment behaviour and caregiving behaviour, practitioners need to pay attention to both children and caregivers. It is not enough to assess attachment patterns in children but these need to be matched by assessment of adults' current state in relation to attachment. There needs to be a recognition that caregiving behaviour will be influenced by adult attachment behaviour. This suggests that, when assessing parenting capacity, for example, along the lines of the Assessment Framework (Department of Health, Department for Education and Employment and Home Office 2000b), in-depth attention should be given to assessing the sense caregivers have made of their earlier attachment experiences. Knowledge of the caregiving system is still evolving.

Only when the drivers behind caregiving behaviour are more fully understood can there be a complete picture of the attachment system which directly affects the developing child's emotional growth. As Steele (2003) concludes: 'The current applications of his seminal contributions to understanding the complexities of parent–child attachment relationships re-echo a sentiment Bowlby expressed in 1951, and frequently included in his later writings "if a society values its children, it must cherish their parents'" (p.17).

CHAPTER 5

Self-development

David Quinton

It is common nowadays to say that we are more 'self-something' than we used to be (self-centred, self-ish, self-preoccupied, self-indulgent etc.), and that these 'selves' are at risk of becoming fragmented because we have to present ourselves differently in many different social situations. As part of this discussion many things that affect us are judged in the light of what they do to our 'self-esteem' or 'sense of identity'. In this plethora of 'selves' how can we keep a hold on who we 'really' are?

It is worth trying to disentangle some of these meaning of the terms 'self' and 'identity' before discussing how they develop. The task of this chapter is to explore how these 'self' words are used, to set out some ideas that help in thinking about the self and to give an account of how the sense of self develops, what influences its stability and consistency and our feelings about ourselves, and what might be done to help children and young people. But, first, how have the words 'self' and 'identity' been used? What do people mean by them?

Definitions and issues

Unfortunately the use of the terms 'self' and 'identity' is not consistent. Sometimes they are used interchangeably, especially when people refer to a '*sense* of self' or a '*sense* of identity'. Is it worth keeping the two ideas separate? I shall risk a broad generalisation. This is that the 'self' is the broader concept and that our identity is part of our 'self' but not all of it. Our 'self' is everything we think and feel about what and who we are, our good points and our bad ones, what makes us different from other people and what makes us similar to them.

Our 'identity' is more like a *story of ourselves*, where we come from, where we fit into social life, to whom we are related and things like that. This 'identity' is *part* of our idea of our self, but it is not the whole of it. If, however, we do not feel we have a coherent story, then our sense of ourselves as individuals is likely to be compromised. For most of this chapter the word 'self' will be taken to cover both ideas but, before getting on to how the self develops, some important aspects of 'identity' will be discussed.

Identity

The word 'identity' is used in two different ways. The first involves those things that society 'outside of us' seems to think are important such as our names, date of birth, gender and other things that 'identify' us. These 'big descriptors' also include those things that we think society sees as important, such as who our parents are and what we do or are good at. The second involves what we mean by a 'sense of identity'. That is, how securely do we feel able to place ourselves in the world; how sure we are about our personal history; and how certain are we that we know 'who are we'? These are the things you ask or are asked when you meet someone new and the judgements you make of each other based on appearance and behaviour. But beyond this *social placing*, you are also likely to talk about what makes both of you *different* or interesting, such as your tastes or *identifications*, like the teams you support or the music you like. It is still worth reading Irving Goffman's classic *The Presentation of Self in Everyday Life* on these issues (Goffman 1959).

Of course, our tastes and identifications change over time and place and so does the importance of these big descriptors. Consider how gender defines people in different cultural groups or the changes in the meaning of illegitimacy over the past hundred years. Some aspects of our identity, like being a child or an adult, get left behind and others surprise us when we are forced to take them on. Their importance to our sense of ourselves depends on how important we think they are in defining us – that is, to use the jargon term, their *salience*.

Studying the self

The diversity of 'self' words in the academic literature – self-concept, self-perception, self-image, self-worth, self-representations, self-schemas, self-efficacy, self-monitoring and, of course, self-esteem, to name but a few (Harter 1999) – suggest that studying the self is difficult. Many researchers, like Susan Harter, restrict their *enquiries* to 'attributes or characteristics…that are consciously acknowledged…through language – that is, how one describes oneself' (Harter 1999, p.3; see also Siegler, Deloache and Eisenberg 2003).

This does not necessarily mean that we are aware of what may underpin what we say about ourselves. For example, the internal working models of relationships posited by attachment theory, as discussed in the previous chapter, are not things we are aware of in this way. Indeed, very sophisticated techniques have been devised to get at them for adults (Hesse 1999) as well as children (Solomon and George 1999). It usually takes time for therapists to uncover these representations and the feelings associated with them (Brinich and Shelley 2002). It follows that the conscious account of why we feel strongly about something may be wrong, a conclusion highlighted by the notion of 'defences' discussed below.

Some key ideas

I and me

A good place to start in thinking about *the* self is to think about *you*rself. What does all this talk about identity and the self mean to you? If you do this you are likely to discover a principle first set out by William James in 1890 when he made a distinction between the self as knower and the self as all those things I know about myself (James 1890). He called these the 'I-self' and the 'me-self'. Nearly all of us have a continuous sense of ourselves that is not dependent on the things we know about ourselves. There is debate about what the 'I-self' is, but it is generally seen as an organiser and linker of experience. Thus, the I-self allows us to look at ourselves as an 'object' (Rosenberg 1979) and decide on the importance of the information we are given about ourselves.

The looking-glass and the other

Other early theorists discussed where the things we know about ourselves come from. They concluded that they came from what we think others *think* about us. Cooley (1902) called this the 'looking-glass self'. This idea is important because it sees the self not as mechanically put together from the opinions and behaviours of others but constructed through our *interpretations* of these.

Two other theorists suggested how these interpretations might become part of who we think we are. Mead (1934) thought this happened through a process in which we try on roles and behaviours and come to conclusions based on the responses we get. These responses become combined into a 'generalised other'. Baldwin (1897) concluded that we learn what is approved through imitation and take these values into our 'habitual self'. That is, we 'internalise' them as an idea of who and what we are.

These early theorists have given us a number of key ideas that have stood the test of time: the *'I' and the 'me'*, the importance of *what we take from others and how we interpret this*, and an *internalising process* through which relatively enduring feelings about and attitudes towards the self develop.

Three other ideas that are helpful in thinking about the development of the self are worth outlining.

Distinctness and inclusion

These ideas crop up in many accounts in words like 'individuation', 'integration' and the like. They describe two contrasting needs that drive self-development. The first is the desire to be yourself or your own person, the other is the need to feel included in the family and the social group. This begins with the separation of the infant from the symbiotic relationship with the mother (in very early infancy) along with seeing oneself as distinct from the world of objects (Lovinger 1976). The assertion of this new self is a priority notably in the 'terrible twos' and in adolescence. At other times, feeling included leads to an emphasis on learning rules and appreciating differences. The point is that these two motives – to be one's own person and to find a place in social life – are in a regular dialogue and sometimes tension throughout life.

In some theories these developments are seen as *stages* – an idea we are used to in phrases like 'It's just a stage he's going through'. Erikson (1950), for example, argued that each stage has developmental tasks that need to be mastered before a child can move on to the next one. Thus, the task in early childhood is to resolve the problem of the shame and doubt associated with self-assertion and autonomy in a way that allows comfort with oneself. Stage theories often see later psychological problems as arising because these stage-related tasks or crises are not resolved, resulting in people getting 'stuck'.

Defences

The idea of defences comes from psychoanalysis (Freud 1966) but it is often used nowadays to refer to ways through which we project a positive view of ourselves. Rosenberg called this 'the self-esteem preservation motive' (Rosenberg 1979). Defences involve, for example, things like putting a positive gloss on our behaviour (*rationalisation*), overcoming failure in one area by trying to excel in another (*compensation*), attributing to others undesirable parts of ourselves (*projection*), and keeping in our subconscious impulses we do not wish to acknowledge (*repression*). We all use these strategies to some extent to maintain positive feelings about ourselves but they can lead to 'false selves' in which bad experiences are split off into an inaccessible part of the self, as can happen following sexual abuse.

Self-theories, scripts and schemata

These are a set of ideas that help in thinking about the link between self-attitudes and motives and actions. *Schemata* are an 'elaborate...organised system of internal cues regarding ourselves...' (Sternberg 1999, p.164). They are like routine *scripts* that provide us with explanations of how we behave and feel and influence what we do. The point is that they may not be correct. We can develop mistaken ideas about ourselves and act on them (Beck and Weishaar 1989). Correcting these misperceptions is one of the objectives of cognitive therapy.

Another way of thinking about this comes from Adlerian psychology (see Brinich and Shelley 2002) which argues that these mistaken ideas usually arise in childhood because we are trying to understand our place in the world when we are not equipped to interpret our experiences. These childhood ideas become the basis of a *style of life* through which we try to maintain a consistency of self. *Early memories* act as metaphors through which this approach to life can be uncovered and misperceptions worked with.

Finally, Dweck has explored the *self-theories* underlying children's approaches to learning and found that these depended on the theories children had about their capabilities, not on their ability, success, or confidence (Dweck 1999). Those who wanted to look smart focused on getting things right so they liked to do what they could already do. Those who had learning as their goal wanted to increase their competence. To put it another way the first group had an *entity theory* of intelligence: you either had it or you didn't. The second had an *incremental theory* of intelligence: effort enables you to fulfil your potential. Children who focus on getting things right and being reassured about their competence are much more likely to develop feeling of low self-worth and depression in the face of failure.

The development of self

There is little disagreement that a sense of self arises through interactions with others, its *content* is arrived at through the conclusions we draw from these interactions, and its *coherence* or *continuity* is largely determined by whether these conclusions are reaffirmed in interactions over time. We are active agents in this process whether we are newborn infants or pensioners, although our capacity to organise and judge our conclusions increases dramatically with age and cognitive sophistication.

There is also evidence that we develop both a baseline self-concept (like a global view) and a barometric self-concept, which varies depending on what happens from day to day (Demo and Savin-Williams 1992). Baseline self-concepts are acquired earlier and are harder to alter. The barometric self fluctuates wildly in adolescence and also for some more than others throughout life. This seems related to how sensitive people are to others' views and behaviour, perhaps as a consequence of parenting experiences in which approval *as a person* depended on what the child did.

Infancy and childhood

A child is engaged in the process of differentiation and self-building from the beginning (see for example, Berger 1999; Siegler *et al.* 2003; or, most engagingly, Gopnick, Meltzoff and Kuhl 1999). By age 2 to 4 months, infants have a sense of their ability to control objects outside themselves and by 3 to 5 months have some understanding of their control over their bodily movements. By age 1, they can check with adults that they have got something right – for example that they are looking at something at which the adult is pointing (Harter 1999) – and look for help in interpreting what they see or do. By 18–20 months, they know that the person they are looking at in a mirror is them and that what they see is a *reflection* of themselves (Lewis and Brooks-Gunn 1979).

During their third year self-awareness is shown through embarrassment and shame, emotions concerned with how others see us and the crucial glue in social integration (Lindsay-Hartz, De Rivera and Mascolo 1995). This development goes along with the self-assertion of the 'terrible twos', frustration and anger when thwarted and claims that things and people belong to them. Language makes it possible for them to organise information into categories and to begin to construct a story of themselves and their lives. The world adds evaluative labels to what they do and who they are – 'you're a clever girl', 'well done' – and they hear adults reporting their successes and failures to other adults. Parents' and other adults' roles in helping children build up this 'autobiographical memory' are extremely important (Snow 1990) and lay the foundations for a life story or 'sense of identity'.

At age 3 to 4, children describe themselves in terms of *observable characteristics* ('I have brown eyes', 'I can run fast'), *their social world* ('I have a sister and a brother'), or by *traits and temperament* ('nothing scares me!'). At this stage these characteristics are not grouped into broader notions – like being good at sport – but remain specific ('I am very strong, I can lift a chair') and self-evaluations are often unrealistically positive and resistant to counter-evidence. Even if they fail at something several times, they are likely to think they will succeed next time.

Around about age 4, children develop a *theory of mind*, that is, the ability to understand that others have thoughts in their own heads and may see things from a different perspective or know different things from the child him or herself (Baron-Cohen 1994).

The widening social world of nursery or school brings *social comparison* into play. Through this children begin to form ideas on what they think they can and can't do. At this time their descriptions of themselves often have a pronounced social element and focus on personal traits and characteristics (Damon and Hart 1988). Comparison with others makes it possible for them to develop views of themselves as adequate or of failing in one thing or another – that is the possibility of developing low 'self-esteem'.

With proper help and encouragement, they can make sense of these comparisons and learn to see themselves as good at some things and not so good at others *at the moment* rather than forever. They also become able to organise their knowledge of the social world into broader concepts like 'sport' or 'popularity' or 'maths' and to learn the signs that show how they are doing in these areas. For example, that a popular' child will be nice to others, ideally, will keep secrets and will stick up for their friends.

This ability to organise experiences and attributes within more general concepts makes it possible to have a global view of 'myself'. The benefits of this are the capacity to comprehend and anticipate events and relationships and to see that it is possible to have contradictory characteristics at the same time – that they can be both smart and dumb in different areas and at different times. The downside is an increased capacity to think about themselves globally – as a good or bad *person*, as a success or a failure, or as liked and not liked.

Self in adolescence

The ability to see one's self in abstract and global categories develops rapidly in adolescence alongside very rapid physical changes, the development of sexual interests and the process of separating from the safety of the parental home and the move towards adulthood and an adult 'self' (Coleman and Hendry 1999). This move is marked symbolically by clothing and cultural preferences that assert the young person's difference from their parents' generation, although these symbols often involve a pronounced conformity to the style of the friends and the peer cultures with which they identify. Despite this, studies regularly show the importance of the family as a secure reference point and a key help to young people in interpreting their experiences (Noller and Callan 1991).

The construction of the new 'self' needs a lot of reflection, attention and experiment. Adolescents are notably 'self-conscious' and develop a *personal fable* that emphasises the uniqueness of their experiences ('my parents don't understand what it's like to be a teenager'). The also see their friends and families as an *audience* that is constantly watching and commenting on what they are up to (Elkind 1967). However, as Cairns and Cairns (1994) have argued, the highest priority for thoughts about the self is to maintain a sense of personal integrity and balance. There is a general bias through development, including adolescence, to view oneself in a benign and positive light. Adolescents develop the ability to rationalise, reconstruct and compartmentalise their thinking and beliefs and develop normal defences for the self, an ability that will serve them for the rest of their lives.

In Erikson's theory the task for adolescents is to establish a coherent identity from the 'crises' in intimacy, thinking about the future, working and studying consistently, and differentiating from the family. He called this crisis 'identity diffusion'. From this idea, Marcia described three identity statuses leading, ideally, to *identity-achievement*, a coherent identit reached by one's own efforts. On the way young people may have no clear idea of who they are and not be looking for answers (*identity diffusion*); they may be experimenting (*moratorium*): or they may have come to decisions based on other people's views (*foreclosure*). Most young people get through all this but some tend to stick where they are, especially if their behaviour takes them away from exposure to different opportunities and ways of doing things (see Kroeger 1996 for an account of Eriksons and Marcia's ideas).

Coleman (1978) presents a different perspective that is not dependent on the idea of stages, which he called the *focal model*. He shows that adolescents tend to deal with, or focus on, one issue at a time and not necessarily in the same order. Problems tend to arise when young people have to cope with more than one issue at a time or when life changes, such as the age at which they transfer to secondary school, or when they are not ready to do so.

What is needed for the normal development of the self?

Whatever their theoretical perspective, most authorities agree that the self arises through social interactions and our own active interpretations of what we see and are told, depending on the cognitive capacities we have at different times of our lives. Luckily, this development is part of our biology so, given an 'average expectable environment' (Hartmann 1958), a good enough self will develop. Stable and predictable caregiving is the key element in this. This is usually provided by parents, supported by the wider family and friends, but it is the characteristics of the caregiving rather than who does it that is critical. If children are to develop a positive view of themselves, they need a predictable world that helps them make sense of what they come across, build their self-story and tells them how they and what they are doing is valued. (See Pugh, De'Ath and Smith 1994; Quinton 2004, for summaries of positive parenting.)

Positive caregiving

- provides a *secure base* from which a child can explore the world and to which he or she can return at times of anxiety, stress or tiredness

- is *sensitive to the child's experience of the world* – what he or she is puzzled, worried or scared about – and helps him or her make sense of it

- tells the child that he or she is *loved and valued for what he or she is, not for what he or she does*

- provides *boundaries and teaches what is and is not acceptable* in a firm but non-aggressive way – clear boundaries make children feel safe

- works to *provide new experiences and opportunities* for learning and for social relationships

- helps the child *build his or her self-story or biographical memory* through contacts with family and friends and the culture of which he or she is part, and through talking about experiences and linking them with what has happened in the past and what may be going to happen.

In short, caregiving should work towards valuing uniqueness or distinctness and fostering inclusion. These processes are central to the development and maintenance of a sense of self from infancy to old age. Adlerian psychologists have a useful formulation for this. They speak of the 'crucial Cs': that we need to feel we *count*; are *connected*; are *capable*: and that we have *courage*, especially the courage to be imperfect (Bettner and Lew 1990).

This is not to say that we are best off in a world that only says good things about us. Kohn has called this being 'punished by rewards' (Kohn 1993). Praising children whatever they do is a recipe for problems, because it does not challenge their view of themself and their entitlements – it does not provide 'reality testing' or help them develop and mature through change and challenge.

What can go wrong?

The conditions that lead to problems with a sense of self are, rather obviously, the opposite of the ones that facilitate a secure sense: frequent changes of caregiver; very unresponsive and/or markedly inconsistent – sometimes called aggressive-indulgent – parenting; sexual and physical abuse; and a pronounced lack of understandable connections with a personal history. These adversities underlie most of the serious distortions of the sense of self, as reflected in self-harm, eating disorders or even multiple personality disorders. Even so, a surprisingly large number of people with these experiences do not have these outcomes. For example, most children raised in long-stay children's homes do not (Quinton and Rutter 1998) neither do maltreated children (Gibbons *et al.* 1995; Nelson *et al.* 2002).

This is not to say that we do not need to worry unless caregiving environments are severely inadequate. Children are remarkably sensitive to the feedback they get and need consistent help in turning experiences into opportunities for development rather than threats to self-worth. The timing of moves through the educational system is a good example of this. The month of birth affects the point at which a child enters compulsory education and this affects his or her ability to cope with it (Goodman, Gledhill and Ford 2003). Sensitive parents are all too aware of the fine nuances of a child's responses to these changes and that support and interpretation are needed to help turn them into points of personal growth.

What can be done?

In trying to help, we can try to improve the contexts that influence the development of the self or we can work directly with children and young people. In either case, is it better to try to raise overall self-worth or to work on skills and perceptions?

Raising global self-esteem

Self-esteem is a very over-used term. It usually refers to some enduring overall or 'global' evaluation of ourselves: whether we feel good about who we are and what we do or whether we are beset by self-doubt and anxieties.

It is often assumed that low global self-esteem underlies all sorts of social problems and thus that raising it is the answer to those problems. This assumption has had some bizarre consequences, including a policy decision by the state of California in 1986 to set up a task force with the purpose of raising the self-esteem of the *entire population* (see Emler 2001, for an outline of some of the issues). In practice, most people maintain a positive view of themselves. Even those who are only a bit positive about themselves tend simply to be realistic and cautious, if slightly pessimistic (Baumeister, Tice and Hutton 1989). In fact, there is very little support for the idea that low self-esteem is the cause of social malaise or that high self-esteem is a good thing. Indeed, people with very high self-esteem are often very unrealistic, highly defended, rigid and authoritarian.

Low self-esteem measured on standard instruments is not related to: crime, racial prejudice and child maltreatment; it is only slightly connected with: educational attainment and alcohol and drug misuse; but it does increase the risk of: teenage pregnancy, eating disorders, suicide attempts and male unemployment, although only as one of many predictors. We know little about how these connections arise. For example, although low self-esteem predicts teenage pregnancy, it is not associated with contraceptive use, age at first intercourse or sexual activity generally. Indeed, higher self-esteem in girls tends to predict more sex, earlier first sex and propositioning boys more (Emler 2001).

However, although there is no case for trying to raise *global* self-esteem as the best way to tackle the problems associated with it, it must be good to help children, young people and, indeed, adults, feel happier and more positive about themselves to make their lives more satisfying, but that is a different question.

As Harter (1999) and others have pointed out, we do not just judge ourselves overall, we also judge ourselves differently in different areas – or 'domains', for example as good at sports but not so good at cooking; as not especially physically attractive but popular nevertheless. One way of maintaining a positive view of ourselves is to downplay the importance of those areas that do not make us feel good and to concentrate on those that do. Domain-related evaluations provide one way into helping children and young people change their views of themselves, so let us turn to what we might do.

Working with the context
STABILISING CONTEXTS

The first requirement is to work to provide the stability, predictability and responsive parenting or caregiving that are so important to a coherent and positive view of the self. At the extremes this means stopping abuse and breaking the contact between the child and the abusing adult (Sinclair, Gibbs and Wilson 2000). Even if we do this, we should not expect transformations in the sense of self of children who have suffered very poor early experiences. Their difficulties can prove extremely resistant to change, providing evidence for the substantial impacts of distorted early caregiving on self-development.

Increasing stability also means reducing to a minimum the number of changes of caretakers in children's and young people's lives. The frequency of children's problems rises rapidly with the number of changes they experience, even if one caregiver remains the same (Smith *et al.* 2002). Stabilising the context also means stabilising other key areas such as the number of school moves and disruptions in friendships. Sometimes this may mean moving children away from schools and peers that give them negative messages about themselves, as well as keeping them where they are. If you think about how much time parents and children usually spend talking and worrying about these matters, it will make it clear how important they are.

Even then, increasing stability is not enough, we also address the need for children to develop a sense of themselves as valued individuals as well as ensuring that they feel included. For example, recent research makes it clear how sensitive fostered children are to whether they are included within the foster family and how keenly they feel it if they are not (Sinclair *et al.* 2003).

PARENT TRAINING

The second way of working with the context is working on parenting skills and behaviours more directly. There is now ample evidence that doing this can be effective in moving parenting towards the positive characteristics mentioned earlier and that children's behaviour can change so that they are diverted from routes into antisocial behaviour and its consequences.

WORKING WITH CHILDREN AND YOUNG PEOPLE

I have stressed the active role of children and young people in constructing their sense of self and the role of adults, and later their friends, in helping to interpret their experiences so that they can do this. Service professionals have an important role beyond that of helping stabilise and improve developmental contexts. First they should see themselves as part of the caregiving environment and help children interpret their experiences and structure these in a way that gives their lives meaning. This role is as important in 'normal' circumstances, like teaching, as it is for special ones, like helping looked after children.

There are many programmes working with children around issues of 'self': such as self-esteem, self-confidence and self-presentation (Emler 2001; Harter 1999). It is not possible to review these different approaches here. Rather, it is useful to try to draw out some principles for interventions, bearing in mind the general contextual conditions for positive self-development set out earlier. A number of strategies have been suggested. Help should always include an assessment of what is important to the *individual child* as well as 'what works' generally.

1. *Work on skills and specific perceptions, not on global self-worth.* Research shows that, even if the aim is to improve the global sense of self, it is more profitable to focus on the skills and domains relevant to the child than to try to change views of the self directly (Harter 1999). The latter is likely to benefit from the former.

2. *Work with the gap between aspiration and perceived adequacy.* If the self-assessment is poor, work on the areas about which the child feels reasonably positive and try to diminish the importance of those where he or she does not. If the self-assessment is a serious over-estimate of capabilities, you may need to increase the gap, for example where unacceptable behaviour is valued or where there is a gross over-estimate of academic worth. In short, work towards a positive but realistic self-evaluation and sustain those contexts that reflect good messages about personal self-worth (Harter *et al.* 1998).

3. *Try to understand the child's 'self-theories'.* Can you uncover the central ideas and misperceptions that are driving behaviour and feelings? You may need specialist help or training to do this but uncovering the self-theory is likely to be helpful in working with individual children. Are their ideas about themselves driven by the views of others ('external attributions') or by some persisting misperception about their worth, perhaps focused on specific domains or experiences? You may be able to resolve contradictions in self-theories by uniting a perceived contradiction within a higher order concept, for example by pointing out that being moody and cheerful is part of being 'emotionally responsive'.

4. *Help to construct meaningful self-stories.* Meaningful stories are central to a coherent 'sense of identity' and therefore of the self (Gergen and Gergen 1988). Constructing or reconstructing these is especially important when early lives have been difficult and/or when there have been frequent changes in caregivers and contexts, but linking experiences is important to all children.

Conclusions

It has only been possible in this chapter to introduce some of the concepts and discussion of what we mean by the 'self' and 'identity'. The majority of the references have been chosen to be easily readable and informative, but the topic is necessarily complicated because it touches on everything we think and feel about ourselves and our place in social life. Nevertheless, the key features of what we need to do to foster a positive and coherent sense of self in our children and young people, and for that matter in ourselves as well, are well established. We need to feel we are distinctive and unique and valued for this and also to feel included in social life. Fortunately, most of us develop a good enough sense of self, but we need to make sure that the social contexts necessary for this are in place. We also need to help children and young people interpret their experiences and give the encouragement necessary to help them arrive at a positive and socially connected view of themselves.

Further reading

Rosenberg, M. (1965) *Society and the Adolescent Self Image.* Princeton, NJ: Princeton University Press.

Siegel, D. (1999) *The Developing Mind: Towards a Neurobiology of Interpersonal Experiences.* New York: The Guilford Press.

Wetherell, M. (ed.) (1996) *Identities, Groups and Social Issues.* Milton Keynes: The Open University Press.

CHAPTER 6

Socio-genealogical Connectedness: Knowledge and Identity

Kwame Owusu-Bempah

Introduction

> Relationships are the basis of social support – one of the main sources of happiness, and of mental and physical health.

> *(Argyle 1992, p.38)*

Interpersonal relationships begin at birth and develop throughout life. Through the development of the internal working model (discussed in Chapter 4), an infant's first relationships with significant caregivers form the prototype for his or her later relationships, not only with the social, but also with the child's spiritual and physical environments. As such, the following discussion of interpersonal relationships would be incomplete without consideration of Bowlby's (1969) notion of attachment. In 1951, Bowlby averred that it was essential for mental health that infants and young children should experience a warm, intimate and continuous relationship with their 'mother'; a mothering figure (see Chapter 4). Bowlby (1969) noted that the type of relationship an infant or a child experiences within the family forms the bedrock upon which future relationships are founded. As discussed in Chapter 4, Bowlby laid special emphasis on the need for consistent and continuous primary relationships;

he saw disruption or loss of continuity as particularly damaging to a child's development.

Attachment theory: separation and loss

For over a half of a century now, Bowlby's notion of human attachment, his emphasis on separation and loss, has been integral to understanding children's development and has influenced child-care policy, practice and child-rearing practices world-wide. Research based upon this notion continues to stress the need for positive interpersonal relationships in infancy, childhood and adolescence. It suggests that, for healthy development, a child needs to experience warm and consistent relationships within the family. Such research underscores the detrimental consequences of negative early experiences, such as neglect, rejection, abuse and separation, for the child's development. It reinforces Bowlby's concern about the long-lasting damaging effects of disruption in or loss of attachments on a child's emotional, intellectual and social development.

The clinical literature indicates that, relative to other children, separated children – those who have suffered loss of attachment-figures through adoption, fostering, parental divorce or death – display greater adjustment problems (for example, Amato and Keith 1991a; Ingersoll 1997; Johnson, Wilkinson and McNeil 1995; Shants 1964). These include emotional, behavioural, social and educational difficulties. In other words, as suggested in Chapter 4, separation in childhood often results in undesirable developmental outcomes. In adulthood, manifestations of the detrimental effects of separation in childhood, if not addressed, may lead to mental health problems such as depression, anxiety and other psychiatric problems, alcoholism, employment difficulties, relationship problems and parenting problems (Ainsworth and Eichberg 1991; Amato and Keith 1991b; Byng-Hall 1991; Harris and Bifulco 1991 Ross and Mirowsky 1999). These and other writers stress also the generational transmission of these negative experiences. Thus, now that child–parent separation, due to increasing divorce, adoption and fostering through natural and human disasters, has virtually become a way of life for many children throughout the world (Freundlich 1998; Goode 1992; Haskey 1990; Roll 1992; Simons et al. 1999), it remains a significant concern not only for separated children and their families, but also for children's services professionals. Regarding inter-country adoption, for example, Triseliotis (2000) estimates that each year around 35,000 children come into industrialised countries to be adopted. Quarles and Brodie (1998) report that, in the US alone, about 13,000 children are adopted from abroad annually, adding to the rising number of children separated from their parents through divorce, death and domestic adoptions and fostering.

Socio-genealogical connectedness

Research has traditionally highlighted attachment as a key explanatory factor in children's adjustment to family disruption. However, it needs stressing that factors, including cultural influences, affecting the nature, intensity and duration of children's reaction to separation and loss are complex. Reviews of the literature examining the impact of separation through parental divorce, for example, indicate that the negative consequences of family disruption for children vary. We must acknowledge the complexity of the psychosocial mechanisms involved in children's adjustment to separation and loss (Owusu-Bempah 1995). In this section, I discuss socio-genealogical connectedness as one of the possible psychosocial mechanisms mediating children's adjustment to separation or a loss of continuity. It is a theoretical framework for studying and understanding children, particularly separated children. It is also intended for consideration as a basis for developing new children's services interventions.

Socio-genealogical connectedness refers to the extent to which children integrate into their inner world their birth parents' biological and social backgrounds; the extent to which a child sees her or himself as an offshoot of his or her parents' backgrounds, biologically as well as socially. The following assumptions derive from this theory:

- The amount and/or quality of information children possess about their birth parents determines the degree to which they integrate the parents' backgrounds.

- Children who possess adequate and favourable information about their birth parents have a deeper sense of connectedness.

- Conversely, children who possess no, inadequate, or damaging information about their parents are less likely to integrate it and, therefore, have a shallower sense of connectedness.

- Children who have a deep sense of connectedness are better adjusted than those who have no or a shallow sense of connectedness.

Obviously, the first two assumptions are not entirely dependent upon actual or direct contact with the parents. The amount and quality of socio-genealogical knowledge does not have to be provided directly by the parent(s). For example, in an extended family or a small-scale collective community where linkage may be to the whole group rather than to birth parents, the information required to achieve a sense of connectedness is readily available throughout the community. In such a context, the child's interpersonal relationship extends beyond the immediate family; the child's sense of continuity is nourished by the whole community rather than the individual parent or family. So, it can be argued that the theory of socio-genealogical connectedness may be seen as culture- or even class-free.

The main aim of the studies that were guided by these assumptions has been to examine the relationship between socio-genealogical knowledge and the general well-being of separated children. These studies have, so far, involved community samples, and compared children separated through parental divorce/separation, death, and those whose mothers never married (see Owusu-Bempah 1995 for a detailed report). As Owusu-Bempah (1995) reports, one of the consistent findings is that children who possess adequate and favourable information about the absent parent fare better on measures of behaviour, academic achievement and emotional well-being than those who either have no information or possess inadequate or damaging information about the absent parent. Understandably, many of the problems associated with loss and separation are found to be prevalent amongst this group of children (Owusu-Bempah 1993, 1995; Owusu-Bempah and Howitt 1997, 2000a). In the studies on genealogical connectedness, therefore, information about parents has been found to be a major influence on children's overall development and well-being.

The studies suggest that the long-term psychological effects of separation may lie more in parental information than mere physical separation or loss. The essential factor, nonetheless, appears to be the quality of the information; it needs to be favourable in order to have positive developmental outcomes. Bowlby (1973) would endorse this suggestion. Derdeyn (1977) also suggests that knowledge about parents, even those who have abused their children, has a psychological value to a child. This, though, assumes a cognitive ability on the child's part to separate the parent as a person from his or her abusive behaviour. This means the child can still value the parent whilst obviously disapproving of his or her abuse.

Some children who have been abused may actively seek to disown socio-genealogical connectedness in circumstances where they feel they cannot value their parents. However, the consequences of such denial for the child are often ill-fated, especially in terms of identity-development (Owusu-Bempah and Howitt 1997). Socio-genealogical connectedness would hypothesise that a lack of a sense of connectedness may result in identity problems (Owusu-Bempah and Howitt 2000a).

Research involving fostered and adopted children lends support to this view. It indicates that a sense of connectedness is essential to psychosocial development and functioning (for example, see Brodzinsky 1987; Cleaver 2000; Pannor, Sorosky and Baran 1974; Schechter and Bertocci 1990; Triseliotis 1973; Walby and Symons 1990). It suggests that the loss of genealogical history caused by separation has major implications for the development of identity and self-esteem. More recently, in connection with adoption, Lifton (1994) has reiterated that the desire to attain a more cohesive identity is a predominant motivating factor in searching for birth parents. In the area of fostering, many writers have stressed the importance of contact or links (actual or symbolic) with biological parents (e.g. Cantos, Gries and Slis 1997; Cleaver 2000; Grigsby 1994; Littner 1975; McWey 2000). Just as attachment or interpersonal relationships are seen as a biological imperative (Bowlby 1969, 1973; see also Chapter 4), so there seems to exist a deeply rooted psychological need to experience connectedness. This, in turn, suggests that separated children have a need to maintain some kind of relationship to their 'lost' parents, rather than wanting to let go. Research with adult adoptees, for example, sees willingness to be found by biological parents as a confirmation of the need to be connected to their biological roots (Roche and Perlesz 2000; Triseliotis et al. 1997). This need may manifest itself in memories, feelings, and behaviours that the children believe bring them closer to their lost parents (Cleaver 2000; McWey 2000). It would, therefore, be beneficial to incorporate, where necessary, symbolic contact into therapeutic work with separated children.

Implications

The preceding discussion clearly indicates the importance of socio-genealogical connectedness to the development and overall functioning of children and, hence, the need to consider its place alongside other developmental theories and in children's services policy and practice.

What is the place of socio-genealogical connectedness in the context of attachment theory and what are its implications for professional children's services work? As previously indicated, research guided by socio-genealogical connectedness seeks to complement our understanding of the dynamics of a child's primary relationships, to update and increase our understanding of child development and the problems facing children of today's world. This is without implying socio-genealogical connectedness as an alternative to attachment theory. Nevertheless, the latter is, in certain subtle ways, distinct from the former theory. Initially, socio-genealogical connectedness extends our understanding of the concept of self-identity, its genesis and development (Owusu-Bempah and Howitt 2000a). As with contemporary thinking on attachment (see Chapter 4), socio-genealogical connectedness acknowledges that cultural practices influence the experience of separation. Moreover, it does not construe actual caregiver–child contact (or its absence) as such as the core of attachment behaviour. It may be argued, therefore, that its assumptions fit the broad diversity of modern family structure, lone-parent (male or female headed), nuclear and extended families. It also allows children's services work to embrace contemporary applications of attachment theory by extending the range of interventions to focus on wider child–parent/caregiver relationships.

There is a rationale for the integration of attachment theory and socio-geneological connectedness. Both make similar assumptions, although socio-genealogical connectedness de-emphasises physical proximity or actual contact as *sine qua non*. Instead, it places a special emphasis on the amount and quality of parental information. As such, its main function may be described as one of promoting psychological (as opposed to physical) proximity to a child's biological roots, and thereby promoting mental and emotional health.

Socio-genealogical connectedness and family work

Research suggests that socio-genealogical connectedness has a favourable influence on a child's development and overall functioning (e.g. Auer 1983; Lifton 1994; Triseliotis 1973). Auer (1983), for example, believes that favourable information about one's parents has a positive influence on a child's sense of trust, self-concept and overall adjustment. Conversely, Roche and Perlesz (2000) suggest that the loss of genealogical history has major implications for the development of identity and self-esteem. The ramifications of these suggestions for policy and practice in areas such as adoption, looked after children and issues of residence and contact are obvious. They argue for the importance that professionals should attach to enabling children to make such connections (Cleaver 2000; Masson *et al.* 1999).

Few would deny that, in adoption and divorce situations, for instance, the provision of parental knowledge through unhindered contact with non-resident parents ought to be facilitated. This, nevertheless, can prove very difficult. Where such contact is already severed or restricted, in the child's interest, professionals involved must emphasise to the parties concerned the developmental benefits of contact (which does not only mean face-to-face, as discussed earlier), and encourage them to facilitate the availability of undamaging socio-genealogical knowledge both of parents and extended family. Ideally children need not only two parents but an extended family as well to have a balanced view of their whole family (Owusu-Bempah 1993). Professional intervention could involve helping parents to achieve this for their children in practical ways. This applies equally to all categories of separated children, including those resulting from donor insemination (Walby and Symons 1990). The well-established technique of life story work, where children are helped to construct their autobiographies, is a good example of how socio-genealogical connectedness can be applied in practice. This and other examples of helping children confirm their identity are discussed further in Chapter 13.

Bowlby's (1973, 1988) notion of internal working models acknowledges the cognitive-affective component of attachment in humans. As discussed in Chapter 4, internal working models are a mental map that children construct about their relationship experiences and use to negotiate their social environment. Bowlby saw this map as modifiable through open and accurate communication between sensitive caregivers and the child. Thus, children who have adopted maladaptive internal working models, owing to their negative early experiences, may be helped to assimilate and accommodate new information about themselves and their early relationships. In this respect, socio-genealogical connectedness shares Bowlby's belief. For example, practice based upon socio-genealogical connectedness theory shares much with attachment theory. Both aim to identify and bring into conscious awareness, for the purpose of modification, an internal representation of the self and earlier caregivers in an attempt to increase children's potential to deal with their emotional, interpersonal and behavioural problems. The importance of helping children to construct meaningful self stories in circumstances where early lives have been disrupted was discussed in the previous chapter. Using socio-genealogical connectedness in practice provides a useful framework for such work.

As a knowledge-based approach, intervention informed by socio-genealogical connectedness would try to modify children's self-belief or self-knowledge and behaviour through the provision of resources and opportunities to help them develop a sense of connectedness or psychological wholeness. For example, the adverse psychological effects of the death or absence of a parent in childhood, according to socio-genealogical connectedness theory, may be mitigated through the provision of appropriate information gleaned from living relatives (especially grandparents) or other sources. This information, if favourable, is likely to be incorporated into the individual's sense of identity.

Socio-genealogical connectedness is conceptualised as a socio-psychological need to bridge chronological gaps. That is, a satisfactory sense of connectedness may be achieved in spite of long-term separation, due to, for example, adoption or death. In this connection, some writers (see, for example, Leitch 1986; Triseliotis 1973) have observed that longing for lost birth parents largely involves a need to know about and feel connected to heritage and biological roots, rather than to a persisting yearning for the return of the 'lost' parent(s). Still, the process cannot be completely emotionally neutral; the emotions involved in a child's or adult's wanting to know his or her roots must not be dismissed or ignored. Likewise, Safran and Segal (1990) propose an interpersonal relatedness approach to therapeutic family work. They see therapy or counselling as a congenial setting for exploring cognitive-affective processes and challenging or modifying the family's interpersonal schemata or models for relating to each other. The notion of socio-genealogical connectedness has an important role in this process; it postulates that such schemata are incomplete without a sense of continuity. Approaches such as Safran and Segal's could, therefore, profitably incorporate the exploration of a family's sense of socio-genealogical continuity.

Acknowledging the value of this concept is likely to lead to a deeper insight into childhood and adolescent emotional, intellectual and social needs. So far, this factor has been missing in theorising, research and practice concerning child development and welfare. This may be due, at least in part, to writers' and practitioners' over-concern regarding parent/ carer–child interactions to the virtual exclusion of other broader cultural influences in the child's ecology. Nevertheless, many parents and carers of separated children appreciate the importance of ecological factors to their children's well-being. In research with lone-parent families (Owusu-Bempah 1995), regardless of the nature of their relationships with their estranged partners, many parents acknowledged the important role of cultural influences, typically the extended family, in their children's well-being. They accepted contact with the absent parents' close relatives, especially grandparents, as a major factor in developmental outcomes. Practice that seeks to maintain or strengthen any emotional ties that children may have by facilitating the provision of parental information to them is likely to enhance their sense of connectedness or continuity, and consequently their well-being.

Of course, the factors which inhibit or facilitate a satisfactory sense of continuity and connectedness will differ not only from one family to another, but also from one culture to another. Different cultures perceive and treat separation differently; cultural practices influence the experience of separation and loss (Owusu-Bempah and Howitt 2000b). In the case of bereaved children, for instance, Courtney (2000) has suggested that these may involve symbolic contact with the dead parent, reverence for the deceased, and understanding the part ancestors play in the family's life and culture. Similarly, the feeling of loss through adoption, death or parental divorce is affected by the meaning of these events in given cultures. Jewett (1982) provides a useful guide for practitioners who are helping children cope with separation and loss.

Conclusion

Socio-genealogical knowledge is undoubtedly fundamental to our psychological integrity. It is essential to self-knowledge – who we are, where we come from, and where we belong in the order of things. It is important to adults and children, and so needs serious consideration in family work. Research supports the belief that, in order to progress developmentally, a child needs to be nourished on undamaging parental information. Children amalgamate their parents' personalities and backgrounds so that the cost to them of seeing their parent as 'bad' or 'undesirable' is too high. The clinical literature reveals that even abused and neglected or rejected children may demonstrate strong attachment to their parents or primary caregivers, although the attachment may be insecure, anxious or disorganised. Socio-genealogical connectedness goes some way to explain this apparent paradox. It indicates that even where there is a seeming absence of attachment behaviour or identification with the parent, this must not be seen as a sign of an absence of a child's need to feel a part of his or her birth parents.

With children and families' work becoming theoretically and culturally more eclectic and inclusive of diversity, the notion of socio-genealogical connectedness offers a useful framework for children's services policy and practice. Its acceptance in these areas is likely to increase and enhance the range of interventions available to children's services professionals in a multi-cultural society.

CHAPTER 7

The Influence of Parenting and Other Family Relationships

Hedy Cleaver

If you get love, then you're a family. But if you get nothing what's the point of having a mother and a father? Or a father or a mother?

(A boy of South Asian origin living with his mother,
quoted in Brannen et al. *2000)*

The family

Practically every one of us grew up in some form of family and our picture of what constitutes an acceptable family reflects our upbringing. However, our experience of family life will vary greatly, dependent both on our own particular circumstances and the community and society to which we belong.

For example, Young and Willmott (1957) found that in East London working class society, most families comprised three generations. A young woman in this society would have expected, once married, to live near her parents and turn to her own mother for both practical and emotional support. Mother and daughter frequently co-operated in bringing up the children.

In contrast, a young woman born into middle class British society during the 1950s and 1960s experienced greater educational opportunities and increased mobility. As a result she frequently moved away from her family and the community she was brought up in, and close intergenerational bonds were more difficult to sustain. Although young women from the British middle classes would have held similar expectations of marriage to those of her sisters in working class communities, child rearing, however, was solely her responsibility. At this time all women, irrespective of their class, were expected to want to become wives and mothers: 'Caring for others is assumed to be something all women do; it is the essence of being female' (Lewis 2002, p.33).

Because many professionals in the United Kingdom come from middle class homes or, through exposure to higher education, adopt the Western middle class concept of the family, the traditional two-parent family became the acceptable family structure during much of the twentieth century. This model of the family, with mother being the primary carer of children and father the economic provider, became widely accepted, suggesting that a 'properly-constituted' family requires two parents (Chester 1977). The two-parent family was assumed to be the 'best' environment to bring up healthy, well-adjusted children: 'Certainly it is this unit which now represents the sentimental ideal: the cornflakes-advertisement pattern of father, mother, boy and girl' (Oakley 1974, p.65).

The coming together of a number of factors after the 1970s destabilised this traditional concept of the family within British society. Changes in the law (Matrimonial Causes Act 1973), in the benefits system (from family allowance to child benefit meant the money went directly to mothers), and in the more recent removal of the married couple's allowance in favour of channelling support to families with children, all have had an impact. Other societal changes and developments have also affected the family, such as the greater acceptance of children born to unmarried mothers. While changes in educational and work opportunities for women, more reliable contraception, and a plethora of time-saving home innovations offer parents greater choice and control over their lives, an increasing number of children are living in poverty and there is great pressure for mothers to be economically active.

Recent research is beginning to challenge some of the assumptions about the specific roles of mothers and fathers explicit in this notion of the family. For example, the significance of the father's contribution to caring for his children has been highlighted in research (Daly 1993; Lewis and O'Brian 1987) and supported by policymakers with, for example, the introduction of paternity leave. Ryan (2000) notes that Article 6 of the European Communities Recommendations on Child Care states:

> As regards responsibilities arising from the care and upbringing of
> children, it is recommended that member States should promote
> and encourage, with due respect for freedom of the individual,
> increased participation by men, in order to achieve a more equal
> sharing of parental responsibilities between men and women and to
> enable women to have a more effective role in the labour market.
> (p.8)

Although there have been some shifts in relation to gender and parenting roles, the ideal of the mother as the main and natural carer remains powerful and much professional intervention with families continues to target women as 'mothers' (Lewis 2002; Ryan 2000).

Political pressure groups also played their part in changing society's views on the family. Gay rights movements and changes in the law enabled same sex couples to live together without condemnation and the Adoption and Children Act 2002 allows unmarried couples, including same sex couples, to adopt jointly.

Another key factor to have an impact on the concept of the family was the arrival in Britain of people from different cultures. The 1950s and 1960s saw Britain recruiting labour from the African–Caribbean population where the family had more in common with Young and Willmott's matriarchal model than that of the English middle class. In African–Caribbean society men often had a visiting rather than residential role in the lives of their children, leaving women (often from at least two generations) to carry out the day to day work of child rearing. Taking work in Britain frequently resulted in families being divided, as adults left their children in the care of grandparents while they established themselves in Britain. Children were generally sent for when parents could afford to support them, and joined reconstituted families where some but not all were blood relatives. Family patterns were reasserted but without the existence of the extended family, frequently leaving mothers to bring up their children with little support.

As a result of these historical, legal and economic factors, the structure of the family in British society underwent fundamental changes during the twentieth century. Individual children in Britain today will grow up in very different family units – at one extreme a child may live with both his or her birth parents and siblings from the same union. At the other, a child may live with parents neither of whom are related to him or her by blood (for example a stepmother and her new partner) and other children who may be related in a variety of different ways. Along this continuum is a great variety of different types of family unit: one-parent, or step-parent families, both parents and grandparents, or other relatives, or less common constellations such as same sex parents caring for children.

Whether members of the family are biologically related or not is linked to the differences in the relationships between children and their carers, which in turn is associated with the child's adjustment. The research suggests children have more positive relationships with parents to whom they are biologically related than with step-parents, irrespective of the age of the child (Dunn 2002). Children themselves hold sophisticated notions of the family and are aware of the different types of family structures: 'There isn't a right way to have a family. Like people say, a mum, a dad, daughter and a baby. But there are very few people who have families like that' (Tara, a mixed race girl aged between 10 and 12 years, living with a lone mother, quoted in Brannen, Heptinstall and Bhopal 2000).

This brief excursion into the minefield of what constitutes the family in multi-cultural Britain in the twenty-first century was ventured to alert professionals to their personal perspective of what constitutes an 'acceptable' family structure, because this will influence their perceptions and judgements when assessing children's needs and circumstances. For example, it is a generally held maxim that two parents are better than one in bringing up children, and that the extended family is a valuable support for parents. However, research has questioned these assumptions and shows that living in close proximity to wider kin may act as a support to children and their parents, but this assumes the existence of harmonious relationships. Moreover, close family links may, in exceptional cases, serve to perpetuate inter-generational abuse (Cleaver and Freeman 1996). Similarly, mothers and fathers may either support one another in parenting their children, or undermine each other's competence through hostility, criticism and aggressive competition (Jones 2001).

There are also cultural stereotypes that may affect professional perceptions. For example, it cannot be assumed that most African-Caribbean families in Britain benefit from the support of relatives, or that elders within the Jewish and Asian communities are best placed to resolve family problems, and social services intervention should be kept to a minimum. Applying such assumptions to individual families would be stereotyping and dangerous. Professionals responsible for assessing children's development must explore the strengths and weaknesses of that particular family structure, of the community in which they live, and explore how these have an impact on each individual child's health and emotional and behavioural development.

Parenting a child

> The aim of human parents is to rear their young to be autonomous individuals who will be capable of participating fully in the culture in which they live. (Jones 2001, p.256)

For children, the configuration of their family is irrelevant, as long as the main ingredients of love, availability, patience and continuity are present. Parker and colleagues (1991) identified seven dimensions that are salient for the health and development of all children. These have been incorporated into the Assessment Framework (Department of Health, Department for Education and Employment and Home Office 2000b, p.19), the Integrated Children's System (Department of Health 2002) and the Common Assessment Framework (Department for Education and Skills 2005c). The developmental dimensions are health, education, emotional and behavioural development, identity, family and social relationships, social presentation, and self-care skills.

To meet the child's developmental needs, parenting must: provide the child with basic care; ensure the safety of the child; provide emotional warmth; provide appropriate stimulation; offer guidance and provide boundaries; and provide the child with stability (see Box 7.1 for a detailed description of these parenting dimensions).

Box 7.1: Dimensions of parenting capacity

Basic care
Providing for the child's physical needs, and appropriate medical and dental care.

Includes provision of food, drink, warmth, shelter, clean and appropriate clothing and adequate personal hygiene.

Ensuring safety

Ensuring the child is adequately protected from harm or danger.

Includes protection from significant harm or danger, and from contact with unsafe adults/other children and from self-harm. Recognition of hazards and danger both in the home and elsewhere.

Emotional warmth

Ensuring the child's emotional needs are met and giving the child a sense of being specially valued and a positive sense of own racial and cultural identity.

Includes ensuring the child's requirements for secure, stable and affectionate relationships with significant adults, with appropriate sensitivity and responsiveness to the child's needs. Appropriate physical contact, comfort and cuddling sufficient to demonstrate warm regard, praise and encouragement.

Stimulation

Promoting child's learning and intellectual development through encouragement and cognitive stimulation and promoting social opportunities.

Includes facilitating the child's cognitive development and potential through interaction, communication, talking and responding to the child's language and questions, encouraging and joining the child's play, and promoting educational opportunities. Enabling the child to experience success and ensuring school attendance or equivalent opportunity. Facilitating child to meet challenges of life.

Guidance and boundaries

Enabling the child to regulate their own emotions and behaviour.

The key parental tasks are demonstrating and modelling appropriate behaviour and control of emotions and interactions with others, and guidance which involves setting boundaries, so that the child is able to develop an internal model of moral values and conscience, and social behaviour appropriate for the society within which they will grow up. The aim is to enable the child to grow into an autonomous adult, holding their own values, and able to demonstrate appropriate behaviour with others rather than having to be dependent on rules outside themselves. This includes not over protecting children from exploratory and learning experiences.

Includes social problem solving, anger management, consideration for others, and effective discipline and shaping behaviour.

Stability

Providing a sufficiently stable family environment to enable a child to develop and maintain a secure attachment to the primary caregiver(s) in order to ensure optimal development.

Includes ensuring secure attachments are not disrupted, providing consistency of emotional warmth over time and responding in a similar manner to the same behaviour. Parental responses change and develop according to child's developmental progress. In addition, ensuring children keep in contact with important family members and significant others.

(Department of Health *et al.* 2000b, p.21)

If the standard of parenting is particularly poor in any one of these areas, it may well have a detrimental effect on the child. Parenting, however, is not carried out in isolation. As discussed in Chapter 4, the relationship itself is a two-way process that functions in a circular fashion; the emotions and behaviour of one player (i.e. the parent) affecting the emotions and behaviour of the other (i.e. the child) and the consequent feedback resulting in each modifying their behaviour. Adjusting to a new baby tests the powers and capacities of any parent, but when the infant is born addicted to the drugs taken by the mother during pregnancy, or with special needs such as Down's syndrome or muscular dystrophy, the birth may present an additional challenge for parents. Many babies born to heroin or methadone users show any number of the following withdrawal symptoms: irritating and high pitched crying, rapid breathing and heart rate, disturbed sleep pattern, sweating and fever, vomiting and diarrhoea and feeding difficulties (see Hogan 1998). Similarly, babies with special needs may make far greater demands of parents, and may not respond to their parents' overtures in the expected manner: 'Mahmoud has multiple impairments resulting from meningitis at age nine weeks. He is thought to have very limited vision and hearing, and his physical frailty and extreme vulnerability dictate higher standards of consistency and continuity than for a baby without such needs' (Marchant and Jones 2001, p.68).

These early interactions between parents and their newborn baby will become an important element of their developing relationship. The foundation of this relationship will be stronger when parents have the capacity to respond to their child's emotional and behavioural needs, and find the reaction of the infant rewarding, as was discussed in Chapter 4.

Factors affecting parenting capacity

There is a considerable body of research that suggests issues such as mental health, learning disability, substance misuse, domestic violence, and/or a history of childhood abuse have an impact on the capacity of parents, or those with responsibility for parenting the child, to respond appropriately to children's developmental needs (see, for example, Aldridge and Becker 2003; Cleaver *et al.* 1999; Falkov 2002; Klee, Jackson and Lewis 2002; Moffitt and Caspi 1998; Rutter 1989; Saradjian 1997; Velleman and Orford 1999).

Such parental issues may influence parenting because parents' or carers' emotional and behavioural responses may change and the family's social and economic circumstances deteriorate: 'Substance misuse affects parenting capacity directly through its effects on mental state and judgement ability or, indirectly, through the parents' lifestyle or the adverse social environment in which such parents live' (Swadi 1994, p.237).

To anticipate the impact on parents' emotions and behaviours is not straightforward. For example, the impact of mental illness will depend on the parent's personality, the type of mental illness, its severity and the treatment given. Treatment has been shown to ease symptoms but may not totally prevent them.

> (The medication) keeps things under control and (the voices) stop enough for me to get it under control, they're not so intense. (But sometimes) I need to distract the voices and the only way I can do that is to hurt myself, you see they constantly want me to do nothing but kill myself so like if I hurt myself badly enough it convinces them, they stop a bit and then I get in control so it's a balancing act. (Mother with poor mental health, quoted in Aldridge and Becker 2003, p.42)

The impact of drugs or alcohol also varies in relation to the parent's current mental state, experience and/or tolerance of the drug, expectations, personality, and the quantity and combination of the drugs taken (Cleaver *et al.* 1999). Similarly, the impact of childhood abuse is difficult to predict and may be ameliorated through the experience of success that increases self-esteem and self-efficacy, and through the development of a good stable relationship with a non-abusive partner (Rutter 1989).

To compound the difficulties for professionals responsible for assessing parenting capacity, these issues frequently coexist (Cleaver *et al.* 1999; Cleaver and Nicholson 2003; Klee *et al.* 2002; Rutter 1989). Such co-morbidity has been found to escalate the negative impact on parenting and presents a much greater risk of children suffering significant harm (Cleaver *et al.* 1999; Hogan 1998).

The research findings suggest these issues adversely affect the parent(s)' capacity to respond appropriately to their children for the following reasons:

- Parents have difficulty organising their lives.

- Parents neglect their own and their children's physical needs.

- Parents have difficulty controlling their emotions.

- Parents are insensitive, unresponsive, angry and critical of their children. (Cleaver *et al.* 1999)

Parents have difficulty organising their lives

The behavioural and emotional consequences of issues such as mental illness, substance misuse, learning disability, domestic violence and childhood abuse affect the ability of parents to organise day to day living. A disorganised lifestyle will have a differential impact on children depending on their age, development and personality. Babies, young children and disabled children are particularly vulnerable if parental disorganisation leaves them unsupervised or in the care of inappropriate adults:

> 'You want to go out, you don't want to be sat in the house so you'd leave them with anybody. I never left them on their own, I really didn't, but I left them with people who weren't suitable really.' (Substance misusing mother, quoted in Klee *et al.* 2002, p.153)

Additional problems may arise when appointments for health checks are missed or when school attendance is not a priority. To assume older children escape unscathed from a disorganised lifestyle would be unwise. Some children and young people react by absenting themselves emotionally or physically from their family, while others may become angry and resentful. Many older children living in families that include a troubled parent assume the role of carer, which may interfere with school attendance and homework and curtail time with friends: 'Anthony said that he is left to look after his baby brother. He hasn't been to school all week' (child whose parent had an alcohol problem, quoted in ChildLine 1997, p.24). Some parents are aware of the burden that caring places on their children and are able to define the parameters even in difficult times: 'Well she has to do homework, she has to do the dishes, if I'm not feeling too good, you know what I mean it's just, the only thing I won't let her touch is an iron so the ironing is just piling and piling and piling up' (lone parent with mental health difficulties talking about her 11-year-old daughter, in Aldridge and Becker 2003, p.57).

Research by Aldridge and Becker (2003) found that half of the 40 young carers they interviewed described positive aspects of being a young carer, such as the closeness of their relationship with their parent, increased maturity, and a better understanding and empathy for vulnerable people. Caring for a troubled parent is not wholly negative or necessarily detrimental to the child's well-being. Nonetheless, although many young carers did not wish to relinquish this role, they wanted support that enabled them to continue caring without too great a sacrifice. The support they wanted included information, practical help, substitute care to let them have time off, financial support and equipment such as a mobile phone to help them keep in touch (Baldwin and Hirst 2002).

Parents neglect their own and their children's physical needs

When a parent suffers mental illness, or when alcohol or drugs become the prime focus of their attention, children's physical needs may be neglected: 'If you've got a habit – when you get up in a morning before you can even think about the children you've got to think about getting yourself better' (mother quoted in Klee et al. 2002, p.155). Neglect is not restricted to young children. When parental problems divert monies that would ordinarily be used for household essentials and clothes, children may find it difficult to keep up an acceptable appearance and friendships may be jeopardised: 'They spend all the money on drink. There's no soap in the house and all my clothes are too small. I lost my girlfriend because she said I smell. Others call me names and make fun of me. It hurts' (Paul, 14, quoted in ChildLine 1997, p.37).

Most mothers who are subjected to domestic violence continue to meet the physical needs of their children, although some reported periods of despair when they did not care what happened to either themselves or their children. 'I didn't bother do the housework, and I didn't bother to wash myself...I didn't give a shit about who said what about how the children looked...' (NCH Action for Children 1994, p.47). Research suggests, however, that the majority of parents employ strategies to minimise the impact of their personal problems on their children: 'I can get pretty bad-tempered when I'm coming down, that's why I try an' have a smoke (cannabis) or get someone to take the kids out' (substance misusing mother, quoted in Klee *et al.* 2002, p.154).

Parents have difficulty controlling their emotions

When parents display violent mood swings and ineffective and inconsistent behaviour, children may become very frightened. For example, drugs such as crack cocaine or alcohol and certain types of mental illness can result in unpredictable behaviour. Parents may quickly change from being caring, loving and entertaining to being violent, argumentative and withdrawn. In these circumstances children often believe that the rapid mood swings of their parents or the domestic violence is the result of their own behaviour. They blame themselves and try to ensure all their actions minimise the likelihood of further negative parental reactions.

Parents are insensitive, unresponsive, angry and critical of their children

In Chapter 4, we explored how the attachment process between children and their parents depends on parental sensitivity, responsiveness and support. Insecure attachments have implications for the child's intellectual, emotional, social and psychological functioning.

When a parent is suffering from mental illness, has a problem with alcohol or drugs or is the victim of domestic violence, the effects may render them physically unable to respond to the needs of their children. Alternatively, the effects of their own problems may leave parents emotionally flat with little or no desire or energy to interact with their children. Acute depression is associated with mothers being cold and unresponsive, and personality disorders have been found to be related to a 'callous unconcern for others, a low threshold for frustration, a discharge of aggression and an inability to feel remorse' (Stroud 1997, p.158): 'And when you've got children dependent on you it's very difficult to answer their needs because you're so wrapped up in your own. I don't want to be, I want to put them first, but I haven't been able to do that' (lone parent with mental health problems, quoted in Aldridge and Becker 2003, p.57).

Substance misuse can also result in a parent being emotionally unavailable to their children. Research has shown that substance misusing mothers are less responsive to their babies, less willing to engage in meaningful play and more likely to respond in a manner that curtails further engagement (see Kroll and Taylor 2003 for a review of the literature).

High levels of criticism and rejection are also associated with insecure attachments in children. Research suggests that opiate using mothers frequently rely on harsh verbal responses when communicating with their children, thus increasing risk of significant harm (Hogan 1998): 'I shouted at me son...you know what I mean. I shouted at him when I was coming down and I felt dead guilty. I went into the other room and started crying...it's not his fault I haven't got any speed' (substance misusing lone mother, quoted in Klee *et al.* 2002, p.154).

The difficulties of attachment may be confounded when excessive drinking or drug use during pregnancy have resulted in babies being born with damage to the central nervous system, born prematurely, or with behaviours such as poor feeding, tremors, irritability and occasional seizures. Substance misusing women fear the damage they may be causing to their unborn child and research suggests that the majority try to reduce their drug use during pregnancy: 'I've stopped everything but speed... really I need to have speed if I'm going out' (polydrug using mother, quoted in Klee *et al.* 2002, p.80). Unfortunately, there is no straightforward association between substance use during pregnancy and the baby's health when born: 'The unpredictability of the effects of drugs used by the mother during pregnancy is well known and there was no straightforward association between reported illicit drug use or methadone dose and the baby's health in these data' (Klee *et al.* 2002, p.133).

The other parent figure as an agent of support

There is considerable evidence that many if not most children of parents with problem alcohol and drug use, or poor mental health, eventually 'out-grow' their troubled childhood (Quinton and Rutter 1985; Velleman 1993). A key factor in the emotional and behavioural well-being of these children is the presence of a caring adult who is not experiencing difficulties. In two-parent families when one parent is unaffected, the negative consequences for the children of the mental illness, learning disability, or substance misuse of the other are reduced because one parent is able to respond appropriately to their developmental needs. For example, when postnatal depression prevents a mother feeling any empathy for her newborn baby, a father's warm emotional response can compensate, and strong bonds of affection and attachment can be successfully established (see Chapter 4 for a more detailed discussion of attachment).

Siblings as agents of support

Only children face the impact of their parents' difficulties alone and may be particularly vulnerable. An only child living with a mentally ill parent is more likely to be drawn into the parent's delusional world, a factor associated with long term emotional and behavioural difficulties (Cleaver *et al.* 1999). Research reinforces this notion of greater vulnerability. Only children report an unhappy and lonely childhood where the burden of responsibility for parenting difficulties is borne alone (Laybourn 1994). Most children hold themselves wholly or partially responsible for their parents' substance misuse, mental ill health or violence (Cleaver *et al.* 1999). However, the single status of a child may work in his or her favour; individual children are easier for relatives to look after than sibling groups.

When the family consists of more than one child, the presence of other children will affect how each child reacts to and copes with parents' difficulties. There is a widely accepted belief that brothers and sisters have fun together, support each other in times of stress and, by being with each other, learn to share and co-operate. Siblings can provide a number of forms of support for one another. They may be important attachment figures, act as role models, be sources of emotional support, offer a confidential ear, provide companionship, or offer care in a practical sense (Brannen *et al.* 2000; Dunn 1993): 'Helen (10) described how she had to look after her younger brothers and sisters because "Mummy's often in bed all morning"' (quoted in ChildLine 1997, p.24).

When children live with mentally ill or substance misusing parents, or where there is evidence of domestic abuse, siblings may act as a support and temper the impact of these issues and help them to develop coping strategies: 'Sometimes, when my parents were raging at each other in the kitchen, Lecia and I would talk about finding a shack on the beach to live in.

We'd sit cross-legged under the blue cotton quilt with a flashlight, doing parodies of their fights' (Karr 1995, p.38).

Although some children find support and comfort in sharing distressing experiences with a sibling, not all relationships are so rewarding. The commonly held idyllic notion of sibling childhood is a myth and siblings may or may not get on with each other, depending on their basic temperament and individual experiences. For example, siblings may express strong hostility towards each other: 'She's pretty disgusting and we don't talk to each other much. I don't really know much about her' (6-year-old boy talking about his sister, quoted in Dunn 1993). In some families a particular child may be scapegoated for all the family's difficulties and for these children siblings may be an additional source of active distress. 'My father did not let me sit on the sofa with my brother, I had to sit on the floor. When he got angry he held my head in the toilet' (7-year-old boy talking to a Women's Aid refuge worker, Greenwich Asian Women's Project 1996).

The quality of sibling relationships varies substantially. Some siblings have warm, affectionate and supportive relationships, while others are characterised by hostility, aggression and conflict (see, for example, Dunn *et al.* 1995; Pike and Atzaba-Poria 2003). How siblings get on is related to their temperaments; those with very different temperaments have been found to have more conflictual relationships (Dunn 1993).

What distinguishes sibling relationships from those between parents and children is that they include both complementary and reciprocal features (Dunn 1993). Because one child is older and more developmentally advanced, this sibling is frequently expected to take on some responsibility for the younger child, reflecting the power balance and nurturing behaviour epitomised by the parent–child relationship. Nonetheless, most siblings also interact more equally in their day to day game playing.

When the family includes a disabled child the relationship between siblings is affected; the give and take that characterises most sibling relationships is less evident. How children react to a disabled sibling is also dependent on the temperament of the siblings involved. Some children take on aspects of the caring role while others cope in different ways. The recollection of one man's experience of growing up with a severely disabled younger sister shows how children use different ways of managing chronic stressful situations: 'It hurt to look at Bridget's situation face on, and I shied away from it. Consequently, although she was a familiar presence, I never really got to know her very well as an individual human proposition' (Spufford 2002, p.15).

Sibling relationships are linked to whether or not they are biologically related. Step-sibling relationships are characterised by greater distance in that they are both less negative and less positive than relationships between 'full' biological siblings or half siblings. This means that the quality of the relationship between siblings that share one or more parent is more closely associated with the child's well-being and adjustment than relationships between step-siblings (Dunn 2002). The intensity of sibling relationships declines as children grow older. There is evidence to suggest that both the warmth and closeness of earlier relationships and the conflict and aggression decreases markedly in adolescence (Buhrmester and Furman 1990).

The impact of the wider family and the community

An additional factor that influences parental emotions and behaviour towards their children, and the experiences of children themselves, will be the attitudes and behaviour of their wider family, and the community. The proximity of relatives may be an important support for children when parents are experiencing difficulties in meeting their emotional and developmental needs. For example, relatives may be able to look after children when parental mental illness or substance misuse requires residential treatment, help parents with the day to day care of their children, or offer children a safe haven and ongoing emotional support. Research suggests that the level of help needed by many families who are experiencing difficulties in their parenting capacity approximates to 'that offered by a well-functioning extended family system' (quoted in Booth and Booth 1994, p.20). For example, the developmental needs of children of learning disabled parents may be adequately met when parents are well supported by their own families (Booth and Booth 1994).

Unfortunately parental substance misuse, poor mental health and domestic violence often disrupt and destroy the 'well-functioning extended family system'. Parents and children avoid contact with relatives outside the immediate household because they are ashamed of their circumstances and wish to keep the family's difficulties secret. Children frequently believe that talking about their family is disloyal and will result in professional intervention and family break-up. In some families the separation is imposed through the need of one partner to control and dominate the situation.

> I was kept in one room for six years. Six years of my life was in one room and kitchen. He kept me there. He wouldn't let me go out except sometimes with him... And if anything he didn't like about the cooking and the shopping, he'd start doing the beating. Just like I was his slave... (Asian woman who had three children, quoted in Malos and Hague 1997, p.403)

The quality of children's relationships with their grandparents or other relatives is also a factor that will influence the quality of support that they receive. However, the direction of effect is difficult to identify. For example, grandparents may find their relationships with grandchildren who are well adjusted and happy more rewarding and subsequently become closer to them than to grandchildren who are more disturbed (Dunn 2002). Consequently the children who have the most need of support may, through their disturbed and disturbing behaviour, find themselves rejected by those who could have offered help.

The attitude of the community and professional agencies also has an impact on families which are experiencing difficulties. For example, a community's negative perceptions of disabled children have a detrimental effect on the social experiences of children and their families (Baker and Donelly 2001): 'It's hard for people to cope with something that's less than perfect. And society is always teaching us to strive for the best and to be perfect. Most people just can't cope with someone who's less than that' (mother of a disabled child explaining discriminatory attitudes, quoted in Baker and Donelly 2001, p.73).

What works to support parenting capacity and children's development?

It is generally acknowledged that community-based services which focus on primary prevention are more acceptable to families than targeted services aimed at ameliorating long-standing family difficulties. Many community-based services seek to augment families' informal support networks and are frequently run by volunteers and/or families themselves (Home-Start is a good example). A key element of such community-based services that distinguishes them from more targeted professional services is their voluntary and open door approach to families based on the principle of working in partnership.

For statutory agencies adopting a partnership approach with families can be difficult because parents who seek their services, or are referred to them, rarely start from a position of strength. Whatever the good intentions of the professionals, the fact that parents are asking for help with their child or their parenting, or alternatively are having professionals' attention thrust upon them, places parents at a disadvantage. Families in this position frequently experience a range of competing negative emotions, including fear, shame, guilt and powerlessness. In these cases professional actions, even when they are compensatory gestures, such as offering to hold a tearful toddler, are interpreted as judgemental (Cleaver and Freeman 1995).

Nonetheless, regardless of whether the service is a community-based provision which is universally available or a service provided by a professional agency to families who meet certain specified criteria, research has identified particular features that are associated with better outcomes for children and families.

Professionals who are non-judgemental in their dealings with families

Families that are experiencing issues such as domestic violence, parental mental illness, parental substance misuse, or where a parent has a learning disability, value professionals who do not apply commonly held stereotypes. Whatever the door of entry to services, whether it be via children and families social services or adult services, families need a sympathetic worker who clearly communicates what is likely to happen, why, and the anticipated time-scale for events. To ensure parents and children whose first language is not English fully understand what is being said to them, an interpreter should be used. When parents perceive professionals as critical and judgemental towards them, or when parents are frightened of the process, they may become wary of seeking the support and help of professionals, and will comply with professional requests rather than fully co-operate.

Involving families in the decision-making process

A partnership approach between families and professional children's services is not always possible. True partnership depends on both parties (a) having equal power and (b) holding a similar perspective of key events.

Nonetheless, a degree of partnership is possible and is associated indirectly with better outcomes for children. Families are more satisfied with professional interventions when they have been involved in the assessment and decision-making process that led to the provision of services (Cleaver 2000; Cleaver and Walker, with Meadows 2004). Moreover, in order to bring about the necessary attitudinal and behavioural changes in families, individual members must feel they have fully participated with professionals in any assessments and decisions that affect them. Services need to be organised in a way that acknowledges and builds on the strengths within the family, reinforces the competencies of both children and their parents, and results in their having a part in solving their own problems and feeling in control of events. Finally, once an assessment of the child's needs and circumstances and, where appropriate, an assessment of the parent's difficulties has been completed, a clear plan should be drawn up in partnership with the family and the relevant professionals. This plan should identify specific issues that are to be addressed, the actions or services to be provided, who is responsible for providing them, and the expected outcomes.

For families, however, to participate fully in any decision making depends on the following factors:

- Children and their parents are empowered and supported in contributing their views and opinions.

- Sufficient time and resources are made available to ensure disabled or wary children and adults are able to contribute.

- Children and their parents perceive that professionals listen to their views and experiences, and take them seriously.

- Children and their parents believe that their contribution has been taken into account when decisions are made.

- The services that are provided are seen by children and their parents as appropriate and timely.

Increasing the awareness that social services offer support to families

Families that include a parent with, for example, poor mental health, learning disability, substance misuse, or perpetrating domestic violence, fear that discussing these issues with children and family social workers will result in legal intervention and the removal of their children. This fear also prevents many parents who are receiving professional help for themselves from talking about difficulties they are experiencing in parenting their children. Parents appreciate professionals who acknowledge the real bond that exists between themselves and their children and involve them in any decision to make a referral to another agency.

Clear policies and procedures on confidentiality and information sharing

When more than one agency is involved with the family, parents are distressed by having to start from the beginning in explaining the needs and circumstances of their family to a range of different professionals. Clear policies and procedures are required on confidentiality and information sharing, particularly in relation to cases where there is evidence of the domestic violence, substance misuse or mental illness.

An holistic approach to family difficulties

Although considerable research shows that issues, such as parental mental illness or parental substance misuse, have a negative impact on children's emotional and behavioural development, it is an over simplification to presume that addressing the parental issues will result in a reduction of harm to the child (Velleman 1992). Conversely, programmes which only address children's problems such as anti-social behaviour without incorporating parenting interventions are likely to be less effective (Gardner 1998; Webster-Stratton 1999). An holistic approach that addresses both the children's developmental needs and the factors affecting parenting capacity will be more successful.

Joint interventions

Services that work with both the children and parents are necessary. At present services are too often either adult or child focused. The challenge is the establishment of services that work specifically with *parents* who are experiencing, for example, substance misuse, which are able to work with the family in an holistic way and are particularly valued by parents.

CHAPTER 8

The Impact of Community and Environmental Factors

Monica Dowling, Anna Gupta and Jane Aldgate

As previous chapters have shown, caregiving and the child's family environment are major sources of influence on the developing child. These are, however, not the only sources of influence. The ecological developmental approach taken in this book provides a framework for understanding the mutual influence between children's development, the circumstances of their families, and the environment and neighbourhood in which the families live out their daily lives. This experience of everyday human ecology will also include children's experience of school and friendships (Bronfenbrenner 1979; Gilligan 1998; Jack 2000). The environment and neighbourhood in which children grow up will undoubtedly have both a direct and indirect influence on the developing child. Utting, Rose and Pugh (2002), for example, suggest that policymakers have increasingly recognised that: 'children's wellbeing amounts to more than the successful completion of developmental tasks at different ages and stages. Children's wellbeing, or their wellness, is determined by the level of family and community wellbeing' (p.12).

This chapter has several themes:

- The impact of families' permitting circumstances, employment and work on children's development.

- The influence of social exclusion on children's development.

- The potential of using community services to promote the well-being of children and families.

- The impact of school, peers and community on children's development.

It draws on the work of Jack and Gill (2003), who have written convincingly on what they describe as 'the missing side of the triangle', referring to the third side of the triangle in Framework for the Assessment of Children in Need and Their Families (see Department of Health, Department for Education and Employment and Home Office 2000b). This side of the triangle emphasises the importance of the context and environment in which children grow up. At the end of the chapter, we include a chart from Jack and Gill's book, which looks at strengths and pressures for children and families from communities in which they live. The chapter also draws on the work of Gilligan (1998) on the role of the school in building resilience.

The influence of income on children's development

Income may have both a direct and an indirect effect on children's development. For example, poverty may directly affect children's health: they may be poorly nourished and live in cold, damp houses and may be bullied at school. It may also affect them indirectly through the behaviour of their carers towards them. Parents and other caregivers cannot accomplish the parenting tasks unless they live in 'permitting circumstances' (Rutter 1974). Acknowledging the relationship between individuals and their environments is a fundamental part of the ecological perspective that underpins the philosophy of this book. Citing the Canadian commentators, Prilleltensky and Nelson (2002), the interaction of poverty, individual health and community is summarised by Utting et al.: 'Parents who enjoy physical and psychological health, and who have access to adequate financial resources, will be in a good position to provide a wellness-enhancing environment. Parental wellness, in turn, is based on the opportunities afforded them by the community in which they reside' (2002, p.12).

Financial deprivation is probably the most common stressful factor for families experiencing various forms of inequality in the UK with its consequent impact on the well-being and development of children in that family. The following quote provides a powerful reminder of the pervasive effects of chronic poverty:

> Poverty means staying at home, often bored, not seeing friends, not going to the cinema, not going out for a drink and not being able to take the children out for a trip or a treat or a holiday. It means coping with the stresses of managing on very little money, often for months, or even years. It means having to withstand the onslaught of society's pressures to consume. It impinges on relationships with others and with yourself. Above all poverty takes away the tools to create the building blocks of the future – your 'life chances'. It steals away the opportunity to have a life unmarked by sickness, a decent education, a secure home and a long retirement. It stops people being able to plan ahead. It stops people being able to take control of their lives. (Oppenheim and Harker 1996, p.5)

As many studies have shown, it is likely that many children 'in need', whose development is likely to be impaired without the provision of services, are characterised by very low income and impoverished material circumstances (see, for example, Department of Health 2001). Jack and Gill (2003) point out that poverty poses special problems for families that include a child with a disability or chronic illness, where the costs of caring for a severely disabled child may be three times greater than for a non-disabled child. Ethnic minority children may be particularly at risk of material disadvantage, where the take up of benefits tends to be lower than for other families (see Jack and Gill 2003). The impact of poverty on the developing child has an influence in two ways. First, the grind of poverty may diminish parents' energy and capacity to care for their children in a way that will give them the best opportunities for optimal development. Second, children may be relatively deprived vis-à-vis others in the community, which may lead to stigmatisation and bullying because they are different. Such experiences of discrimination and exclusion may in turn diminish children's developing sense of confidence. As Jack and Gill suggest: 'Living in an income-deprived family also has implications for children's social integration, the richness of their social world and their self esteem' (2003, p.60).

The impact of employment on children's development

There are two main issues:

1. The impact of *parents'* employment on children's development.
2. The impact of *children's* employment on their development.

The influence of working parents on children's development

The impact of having sufficient income to support children's development is important but the influence of work on parenting capacity is also a factor, which has to be considered. As Jack and Gill suggest, work can have positive or negative meaning for individuals.

> Work can influence parents' values and their views about what individual qualities are needed to succeed in the society in which they live. It also presents them with a range of different opportunities and constraints that affect their parenting capacity, including their physical and emotional availability, as well as the skills, knowledge and personal relationships that arise out of their employment. (2003, p.71)

For the developing child, the importance of parents' work is that the nature of employment can influence parental styles, as well as the time and energy parents have to spend with their children. Work can also provide opportunities for adults to be socially integrated into their communities. Conversely, redundancies and unemployment in a local workplace can affect not only the permitting circumstances in which parents are raising their children but also the morale and sensitivity of parental responses to their children. A stressed parent is less likely to be able to respond sensitively to the developing child. Jack and Gill also suggest that the workplace can be a source of social support through friendships and that social networks can also be an important route to finding employment.

Children's developmental needs can have an impact on parents' employment. Jack and Jack (2000) report that parents of disabled children experience restrictions on both their employment opportunities and earning potential (a point also made in Lawton's 1998 study). They found, for example, that few mothers with a disabled child worked outside the home. Where parents' work requires child care, the impact on the developing child will depend to a large extent on the quality and continuity of that care (see also Chapter 4).

In summary therefore, the impact of parents' working will affect the child positively or negatively, or more likely in a combination of both, according to the meaning that work has for the parents and the demands it makes on their energies and morale. The complex interplay of these factors will, accordingly, influence children's development. It cannot be assumed that working parents are always good for children. Neither can it be assumed that to be unemployed is always likely to have a negative impact on children's development. Much will depend on individual circumstances and attitudes.

Children, work and development

While parents' work will affect the developing child in complex ways, it is important to consider the impact of children's work on their development. The majority of children and young people have had experience of paid work before reaching the school-leaving age of 16 (Hobbs and Mackechnie 1997). Young people work in a wide variety of covert and overt paid work settings and for variable hours, so the question of whether work is beneficial or harmful to children is problematic. There are some differences in patterns of work according to gender. Girls are much more likely to work in the traditional 'female occupations' such as babysitting, being a waitress and shop work. Boys are more likely to do paper rounds and have formal paid jobs at higher hourly rates (Middleton, Shropshire and Croden 1998).

Bearing in mind the incomplete overall picture of which children work, when and how, what can be said about the benefits of working for children and young people? What are the protective factors which makes working an enjoyable experience? Conversely, what are the stressful factors that will have a negative effect on children's development?

The advantages for children and young people are that they gain increased financial independence from their parents, which in poorer families is a covert contribution to the family income. Work can foster self-esteem and social development, and enhances self-efficacy. It gives them a sense of independence and relieves boredom. It also develops their ability to work with others outside school and home, educates them on their responsibilities in a work setting, such as timekeeping and sharing responsibilities, and facilitates the transition from school to full time work. Protective factors include keeping working hours less than 20 hours a week, where research shows a positive or neutral effect on their school work and gives children the opportunity to balance their home, school, work and leisure activities (Steinberg, Fegley and Dorenbusch 1993).

The negative effects of work on children and young people's development are concerned with:

- injuries and accidents

- long hours and low pay – affecting the child's health and abilities at school.

The evidence indicates that it is poorer children who work the longest hours, are most in danger of being exploited and whose education is most likely to suffer (Pettitt 1998). Official Health and Safety statistics suggest that the number of severe injuries to employees under 16 is very small, but the under reporting of accidents of young workers is borne out by the findings of surveys that questioned young people themselves (Joliffe *et al.* 1995; Mackechnie, Lindsay and Hobbs 1994; Pond and Searle 1991). About one third of working young people in these surveys reported having had an accident while working. Boys had twice as many accidents as girls and one third of injuries needed medical attention (Pond and Searle 1991). One third of newspaper delivery boys and girls had suffered an injury including dog bites, falls from bicycles and trapping fingers in letter boxes. Protective factors suggested by young people themselves include having a complaints procedure young people could use if they were not happy with their situation at work; having a wage slip from their employers giving details of their hours and wage rate; and a range of user friendly leaflets explaining employment rights for children and young people (Campbell *et al.* 1998).

The negative effects of social exclusion on children and families

In addition to the negative and excluding effects of poverty, many children and families have to cope with the effects of other forms of social exclusion within their communities because they are perceived as being different. Every child's development will be influenced by the culture of family and kinship networks. This culture will be influenced by, amongst other things, the family's ethnicity, religious beliefs, class and political values. A black child growing up in a predominantly white society may receive negative messages about being black, and need a positive internal model of black identity to counteract negative stereotypes (Dutt and Phillips 2000). Many traveller, refugee and asylum-seeking children and families are likely to experience multiple stressors, including traumatic past experiences, poverty and poor housing, which are exacerbated by a hostile response from their local community and wider society. Such multiple stressors are likely to have a cumulative effect on children's development (Rutter 1995). A child may be able to cope with one or two, but as the stressors increase, so does the likelihood that the child's development will be impaired. For a child growing up in circumstances of poverty and social exclusion, the chances of experiencing multiple separate types of stressors are high.

In spite of the potentially negative effects on children's development of multiple stressors, many children living in poverty and experiencing other forms of social exclusion do achieve positive outcomes. Children growing up in a nurturing family with racially aware carers, positive role models and supportive, kinship and community networks are likely to develop a positive sense of themselves, which helps build resilience against racism and other forms of discrimination. Studies of resilient children suggest that certain characteristics or circumstances will help to protect children from the effects of adverse environments. Some factors will be intrinsic to the children, such as their health and temperament; some will come as a result of family functioning, for example, the fostering of good attachments by sensitive caregiving. Other protective factors relate to the context of children's lives outside of the family, such as positive experiences at school. Just as vulnerability is relative and depends on complex interactions, resilience is governed by a similar dynamic interaction among protective factors within the individual, their family environment and wider social context (Werner 1990)

The potential of community to enhance the well-being of children and families

The presence of appropriate community resources can be a positive buffer against the impact of social exclusion. Jack and Gill (2003) suggest that 'community resources' can be conceptualised in two ways:

> First it can refer to all the systems of help, support, advice, guidance, and general activities in the local area to which families have access. Secondly, it can refer to the 'social capital' within the community and include all of the informal contacts and networks of which the child and family are part. (p.9)

Jack and Gill (2003) also stress the importance of considering how children and their families define 'community' and their perception of the support they receive. The term community may have different meaning for individuals, even within one family. Children and parents may see resources in different ways, which will influence their individual definitions of community. While adolescents may complain about the absence of local recreational resources, parents may see the community offering a number of resources to support them in their parenting. There may be a local group to support grandparents who are looking after children, for example. Resources may be available to mothers but not to fathers, which might influence how fathers engage with their children. 'The level and nature of resources for different family members may have a significant impact on how they perform their role as parents' (Jack and Gill 2003, p.10).

Community is not necessarily confined to geographical locality. For example, many families from cultures and religions that differ from the majority in their geographical area may receive considerable emotional and practical support from kinship networks, places of faith worship and community groups in another part of their city. Conversely, locality can facilitate positive interaction within families. Some large extended families, who live in an area where housing policies support kinship groups, may define community in terms of both their kinship connections and proximity of family within the same locality. Nevertheless, in looking at the influences of community on the developing child, both locality and networks must be taken into account. Resources may be available for children and parents to use but are not supportive to the developing child if parents and children live in isolation from others. Aldgate and Bradley (1999), for example, found that, although families sometimes lived near extended family, it could not be assumed that they automatically turned to their kin for social support. Much depended on the relationship that existed between them.

One of the well-documented consequences of isolation from social support is the effect this can have on parenting capacity. Social supports have a preventive role and can produce buffering effects on families and children. Jack and Gill (2003) summarise research that associates mothers' social support with more sensitive caregiving to infants. They suggest, for example, that children's security of attachment can also be influenced by positive maternal patterns of social support (Crittenden 1985).

The association between positive communities and the developing child

Community resources for children and young people, such as constructive clubs, can contribute to children's development. Holman (1981 and 2000) suggests several factors contribute to positive places for children to spend time and energy that will promote their physical, social and emotional development. These include safe, local meeting places, which are open to all and are easily accessed. Holman's groups offered activities, trips and some-times holidays for those who attended. An important aspect of the groups was an adult who could give individual support to young people as well as run group activities. Adults who looked back on the clubs in Holman's fol-low-up study said that the groups helped them at a critical stage in their development. They also helped to counteract any negative experiences at home or at school.

Jack (2000) suggests that the influences of positive community resources can be equally effective for both children and parents. Facilities that provide social support, including emotional support, instrumental help, and information and advice, are associated with positive influences on parenting capacity and children's development (Jack 2000).

There is an ongoing debate about the merits of the community resource of day care for small children. As suggested in Chapter 4, many children experience multiple carers from an early age but recent work on the impact of day care on children's attachments suggests that it cannot be assumed that day care is intrinsically good or bad for children. Reviewing key studies, Bee (2000, p.413) concludes that 'the quality of alternative care is the critical factor'. Good quality care is generally linked with positive or neutral outcomes, whilst poor quality day care can be detrimental to children. Key factors are stimulation, safety and nurturing, and continuing responsive relationships with a small number of adults (see also Chapter 4).

Studies on family support to families of children in need (see, for exam-ple, Tunstill and Aldgate 2000) are less contentious in showing how parents value help with the challenges of parenting, provided these are focused and offered in a way that does not undermine their self-esteem. Health and social services both have positive roles to play here. Other less formal community sources of support aimed at enhancing parenting behaviour include Sure Start support groups, family centres, and home visiting programmes, as well as groups to support various aspects of parenting. Some of these may be aimed at both mothers and fathers (see Jack and Gill 2003; also Department for Education and Skills 2004b).

Positive experiences of community that children and families experience may be described as social capital. This includes both informal and formal interactions, which are important in fostering a collective sense of trust and mutual respect, and thereby creating environments conducive to promoting children's development. However, social capital can also be seriously undermined by inequalities, and divisions within communities such as poverty, homelessness, unemployment and racism, which act as barriers to the development of open and reciprocal relationships (Jack and Jordan 1999).

Jack and Gill (2003) suggest the factors in communities that promote positive outcomes in children are those in which:

- children feel their community is a good place to live (this might include those with anti-poverty resources, as well good quality and accessible leisure activities, organised clubs and out-of-school activities)

- children feel safe and valued in their community (this emphasises geographical communities where children perceive their immediate area to be safe, rather than threatening, and communities in which children can have positive contact with significant adults from different generations and where it is safe to play with peers)

- children can develop a positive identity, self-esteem and security, via activities, groups and services, which convey a positive sense of identity and belonging, and provide access to opportunities to develop their talents and interests.

Jack and Gill (2003) have developed a model for use by practitioners for analysing the impact of community on parents and children (see Table 8.1). They identify six categories of information which may be perceived either positively or negatively by different family members, i.e. as strengths or pressures:

1. Practical resources within the community.

2. Natural networks in the community.

3. Child and family safety in the community.

4. Community norms around children and child care.

5. The individual family and child in the community.

6. The cumulative impact of all of the above.

Positive experiences lead to low 'environmental stress', where children and their families feel their community is a good place to be living and bringing up children. Such experiences lead to the 'development of positive identity, self-esteem and security'.

Table 8.1: The missing side of the triangle: a model for analysing the impact of community in parents and children

Strengths		Pressures	
Parents	*Children*	*Parents*	*Children*
1 Practical resources in the community			
Employment (links to income and social integration)	Anti-poverty resources (e.g. breakfast clubs, subsidised holidays)	High local levels of unemployment	Leisure facilities, outings and holidays not affordable or accessible
Good local Shops (e.g. good quality/value food)	Good quality, accessible play resources	Inadequate local shops (including rural accessibility)	Lack of safe, local play areas/facilities
Transport available (access to employment and leisure facilities) Anti-poverty resources (e.g. credit unions, welfare rights advice)	Specific resources for black, other minority ethnic or dual-heritage children, and children with disabilities	Transport expensive, infrequent, unreliable	Few organised clubs and out-of-school activities
Affordable local childcare (access to employment for parents)	Social network development (e.g. clubs, playgroups)	No access to financial advice or services	No specific resources for black, other minority ethnic or dual-heritage children, or children with disabilities
Social network development (e.g. drop-ins, community centres)	Local schools provide inclusive and supportive environment	Expensive credit facilities	Local schools provide poor educational and social environments (e.g. low achievement, bullying)
		Childcare resources inadequate (opening hours, location, cost)	
2 Natural Networks in the community			
Reciprocal 'helping' relationships in community	Established and supportive social networks	Culture of people 'keeping themselves to themselves'	Lack of positive contact with range of people in community
Long-term residence of families	Good contact with immediate neighbours	High rates of mobility into and out of neighbourhood	Children's networks disrupted by high mobility of residents
Non-threatening relations with immediate neighbours	Positive contact with significant adults from different generations in community	Lack of links between wider family networks and community networks	Lack of links between school and community networks
Balanced community – mixed age structure	Integration between school and community networks		
3 Child and family networks in community			
Community members perceived as safe (people safety)	Children perceive their immediate area to be safe, rather than threatening (people safety, crime/drugs safety, physical safety)	Parents see community as unsafe (people safety, crime/drugs safety, physical safety)	Children perceive local environment as threatening (people, crime/drugs, physical danger)
Community activities are seen as safe (crime/drugs safety)		Harassment from neighbours (including racial)	Harassment from local adults and children (including racial harassment)
Community area is perceived as physically safe (e.g. roads, buildings)			

Continued on next page

Table 8.1 cont.

	Strengths		Pressures	
	Parents	Children	Parents	Children
4 Community norms around children and childcare				
	Established positive community norms	Children experience stable and established community norms	Lack of established positive community norms	Children do not experience stable and established community norms
		Positive sense of identity conveyed to all children		Negative sense of identity conveyed to certain children (e.g. teenagers, poor children, black, other minority ethnic and dual-heritage children, children with disabilities)
5 The individual family and child in the community				
	Personal resources and knowledge to access available facilities	Developing confidence in using available facilities	Lack of personal resources or knowledge to access available facilities	Lack of personal resources to access available facilities and networks
	Personal resources to develop and maintain supportive networks	Developing confidence in local networks with other children	Personal demands too high to develop reciprocal supportive relationships	Alienates other children/other children bully or stigmatise them
	Perceptions that local facilities are accessible for their family	Perception that facilities are accessible to them (e.g. disabled child and black or dual-heritage child sees facilities as accessible)	Alienates potential sources of support	Family networks either very limited or difficult
			Networks produce demands rather than support	Child has had frequent moves (including homeless)
			Perception that facilities are not accessible for their family (e.g. black families)	Perceptions that facilities are not accessible to her/him
			Experience of frequent house moves including homeless	
6 Cumulative impact of all of the above				
	Low level of individual 'environmental stress'	Children feel their community is a good place to be living	High level of individual 'environmental stress' (e.g. poor quality housing, unemployment, lack of childcare)	Children feel threatened, frightened, and unvalued in their community
	Feel supported in the community in their parental role of bringing up children	Children feel safe and valued in their community	Parents feel unsupported, threatened, or frightened in their community (mental health issues, isolation)	Anxiety, depression, anti-social behaviour, school failure/exclusion
	Community is perceived as a 'good place to bring up children'	Development of positive identity, self-esteem, and security	Parents ambitions are to leave the community	

Source: Jack and Gill 2003

The influence of school on children's development

Children spend much of their childhood in school. Most children in ᴜ. attend school for at least 10 years of their lives. A child's experience of this educational institution is relevant to many aspects of their development. In terms of development, in our view, school settings should be able to offer children and young people:

- opportunities for cognitive development

- a growing understanding of the world around them

- formation of friendships

- development of mental, social and physical skills

- development of confidence and self-esteem

- experimentation with roles and responsibilities, utilising examples of role models among staff and older pupils

- a source of personal support and a gateway to the workplace.

A positive school experience is associated with the development of resilience, and is therefore a protective factor, which should be encouraged (Daniel *et al.* 1999). As Howe and colleagues explain: 'School life, with its rich environment of new relationships and tasks, presents children with occasions to identify, develop and establish fresh, more robust and socially valued aspects of the self' (1999, p.260).

Although education is one of the few universal services, the experience is very different for individual children. In child development terms it is not useful to have an homogeneous notion of school, because an individual child's experience will be influenced by a variety of factors. These include: the environment and opportunities before the child arrives in the classroom (Rutter 2001); the quality of their education (Barber 1996); their relationships with teachers; the support provided by their family; the relationships with their peers; their abilities; their race, class and gender.

A relationship with a significant adult outside a child's immediate family who offers consistent encouragement and support, and serves as a positive role model and advocate, is a factor associated with positive outcomes and the promotion of resilience (Department of Health 1996; Gilligan 2001). In the example that follows, action by Theresa's social worker in conjunction with the education authorities, her foster family and her parents resulted in her being able to make positive comments about her current experience of education. At 14 she had been extremely disruptive both at home and at school.

> In year 10 and 11 we are all put in the same class and there are two teachers for seven pupils – so we get a lot of attention – all the teachers are like social workers – you can talk to them – they don't have favourites we are all treated the same – which is good – not like a larger school where they have favourites – I was never a favourite of any teacher… Social Services sent me there, so that was one good thing they did for me, it took three months to get into that school. (Dowling 1996)

Gilligan (1998) suggests that school may, in the right circumstances, play several important roles in children's development. School can be seen as an *ally*, offering children important adult role models and sources of support outside the family. Such adults have been found to be a protective factor associated with resilient children (see also Jack and Gill 2003). They will also be important in relation to avoidance of gender stereotyping. Boys and girls need to feel that there are opportunities for them to develop their cognitive and social skills.

School can be seen as *guarantor* of children's well-being. Gilligan suggests that school: 'represents the most accessible and natural setting in which to gather evidence about a child's social functioning and attachment to home, peer group and community. In a sense, schools act as guarantors of the well-being of school aged youngsters at risk' (1998, p.15).

Research eliciting children's views on school suggests that children are generally happy at school, unless there are specific circumstances that are affecting their well-being (Barber 1994). These include:

- not having access to teachers – at lunchtime or after school – to ask about things they do not understand but know are important

- feeling that it is not legitimate to want to learn and discuss their learning with their peers

- not having access to the necessary books and equipment to do their work. (pp.1–2)

School can be a *capacity builder* for children, providing children with opportunities to build their self-esteem and competence. Gilligan believes schools help children in adversity and can divert children from deviant or risk-taking activities through constructive programmes. Teaching children to raise their capacity is also linked to the development of self-efficacy. Gilligan (1998) goes on to suggest that what is taught in the classroom is only part of the developmental experience of school. Helping children shape their attitudes and behaviours may be equally important for their development.

School can be a *secure base*: 'school is a place in which to develop confidence and social belonging, in which to rehearse adult roles and identities and from which to explore oneself and the world... Routines and rituals may convey consoling security to a troubled child' (Gilligan 1998, p.16).

School is an *integrator*, being a universal institution 'providing non stigmatizing access to all school children and through them to their parents' (Gilligan 1998, p.16). Parental involvement in their child's education, such as attendance at parent–teacher meetings and supervision of homework, can make children more motivated, competent and achieve better outcomes. For some parents this is harder to achieve than for others, e.g. if a parent has a learning disability or does not speak English. For particularly vulnerable groups, such as refugee and traveller children and their families, strategies by the school to encourage parental involvement and to help children settle are important. Some examples include befriending schemes and home liaison workers (Save the Children and the Refugee Council 2001).

School can be a *gateway to opportunities in adulthood*. Gilligan (1998) suggests that schools can have an enduring and positive effect on students' friendships and special skills. Positive experiences at school may have long term effects on acting as a buffer against adversity in childhood. For example, Quinton and Rutter (1988) found that a group of care graduates coped better than a control group in adulthood because of their good experiences at school. School may also 'be a source of life-long friendships and sporting and cultural interests' (Gilligan 1998, p.17).

The education of looked after children has been a continuing concern for many years but according to the Department for Education and Skills, there are signs that there has been an improvement in the educational attainment of young people looked after. Forty-three per cent of the 6700 young people leaving care in England in 2003–2004 had at least one GCSE or GNVQ on leaving care (National Statistics/Department for Education and Skills Bulletin (2005). Professional help from teachers, social workers, school counsellors, the youth service or community workers can make a difference for these children who are experiencing disadvantage and disruption in other aspects of their life. The use of visitors to schools to act as mentors is also being promoted in many children's services authorities (Jackson and Sachdev 2001).

Finally, school may be a *resource to parents and communities.* 'Involvement with their child's academic and extra curricular activities may help otherwise isolated parents to become part of adult neighbourhood networks through their association with their child's school' (Gilligan 1998, p.17). Such contacts may, in turn, give parents more confidence to respond positively to their children. Schools can also be a physical resource for communities, a place where meetings and gatherings can take place. They can give all children access to computers, thus combating an absence of opportunity in families who cannot afford to buy computers at home. Gilligan (1998) also suggests that schools may increasingly become the focus for the location of social services and cites several international examples of such initiatives in the US and Europe. This has been recognised in UK Government policy so that schools are being encouraged and supported to provide a range of extended services which are right for their school and community (Department for Education and Skills 2004b).

Research has consistently demonstrated the existence of significant and enduring difference in educational attainment for children of different social backgrounds, at all levels (Bradshaw 2001; Coard 1971; Douglas 1964; Halsey, Heath and Ridge 1980). In response to evidence to suggest that children living in low-income families start off at school at a disadvantage compared with other children (Bradshaw 2001), the Government's Sure Start programme, aimed at early cognitive development, parent education and health for the entire family, was initially targeted on deprived areas (Pierson 2002).

The role of schools in responding to negative experiences for children

If schools are to act as buffers and positive resources for children's development, it is important that they pay attention to combating harassment and bullying, and develop effective school policies for the provision of safe environments and the development of positive social values. The experience of bullying can have a long lasting adverse effect on children's development. There are many reasons for bullying, all of which are generally related to identification of individuals as 'different'. Poor children can be stigmatised by their lack of ability to wear designer clothing or have the latest popular toy. Children in kinship care have reported being stigmatised because of not living with their parents (see Hunt 2001). Children may also be bullied because of personality issues, physical appearance, disability, and race and cultural background. A ChildLine study (1996) found that Black and minority ethnic children in Britain experienced high levels of racial harassment, which affected many children's self-esteem and confidence.

Another negative experience for children, which can threaten their growing sense of self-esteem, is being excluded from school. Race is a key factor when considering school exclusions in Britain. African-Caribbean students, particularly boys, are four times more likely to be excluded from school than their white colleagues. Kundani (1998) found that African–Caribbean children who had been excluded had different characteristics from other excluded children, e.g. less deep-seated trauma, higher average ability and less chronic behavioural problems, which would suggest the operation of institutional racism in the form of negative stereotyping and labelling. Such attitudes can have a serious effect on the sense of identity of the developing child. Remedial services such as Pupil Referral Units can be effective for the child who has been excluded by giving him or her a temporary respite from school, while building up confidence and abilities. A children's advocate system within the school can also help in individual cases.

Despite the 1944 Education Act encouraging disabled children to be educated in mainstream schools, in practice local education authorities have generally developed separate rather than integrated provision. In the last five years, government policy has encouraged all education authorities to move towards a fully integrated education service. Those disabled children who go to schools specifically geared around their needs can benefit from, for example, learning British Sign Language or Braille and may develop a stronger sense of their own identity as a disabled person within a supportive environment. However, they can also feel frustrated that they are being kept apart from the wider range of pupils, with whom they would like to mix. They may be aware that their education may not be preparing them adequately for entry into the wider society and a work culture (Connors and Stalker 2003; Tomlinson 1982) and they may not have full access to the National Curriculum.

Children with special needs often find the conventional school system is too inflexible to fit with their particular special needs. For example, a hearing loop system for the child, ramps and lifts for wheelchair access, access to staff for support for incontinence, health or learning disability needs or even extra resources for larger print books and handouts can be problematic. They may have specialist health appointments and need help catching up with their schoolwork, or want to keep fit like other children but need support and encouragement to work out games and routines that they can enjoy despite their impairment. They may need an advocate within the school to help them deal with bullying and teasing (Dowling 1992).

Within this structure, disabled children may be impaired not by their disability but by the attitudes of the education authority, the school, its staff and other pupils to the idea of disabled children participating in the learning environment. Changing attitudes to disability is a long and slow process, and the task for health, welfare and education professionals cannot be underestimated (Dowling 2001). However, progress has been made as Kluth (2003) demonstrates, in her accounts of adapting classroom routines at both primary and secondary levels to include children with autism. This accords with the Government's strategy spelt out in *Removing Barriers to Achievement* (Department for Education and Skills 2004c). An integrated approach to disability means not only education authorities and health authorities having a positive joint approach, but also youth, probation and social services participating in improving the educational opportunities for disabled children. Such developments help to ensure that disabled children have every opportunity to reach their maximum potential.

Peer relationships

Friendships with peers are important for children, as they are for adults. Having generally positive peer relationships, and specifically a close friendship, is a protective factor associated with the promotion of resilience (Cleaver *et al.* 1999; Daniel and Wassell 2002). Children's friendships with each other can provide:

- opportunities to learn social skills of interacting with peers, e.g. competition and co-operation
- fun and companionship
- self-knowledge and knowledge about others

- emotional support in times of stress (Hartup 1992; Schaffer 1996).

A lack of friends can stunt children's development in a variety of ways, including poor school adjustment and attainment and emotional problems (Schaffer 1996). As suggested in Chapter 4, children and young people who have experienced secure relationships are more likely to relate to peers in positive and responsive ways whereas children with poor attachment experiences and emotional and behavioural difficulties are more likely to have difficulties making and sustaining friendships, even though they have the most need (Daniel and Wassell 2002; see also Chapter 4). The association between peer rejection at a younger age and anti-social behaviour has been explored by Rutter, Giller and Hagell (1998).

Young children's access to friendship networks is largely dependent on their families, where they live and their school. School widens the opportunities to develop relationships based on personal choice. During adolescence, complex peer relationships independent of the family environment assume greater importance. Thompson (1995) suggests that friendships in adolescence are:

- more extensive

- more exclusive (involving intimacy and loyalty)

- more multi-dimensional (mix of friendships and sexually intimate relationships)

- important for reducing stress, mediating stress and preventing stress.

Types of friendships are also important when considering their impact on developmental outcomes for children. Conformity to peer group values and behaviours increase in adolescence. Anti-social behaviours such as offending or substance abuse are likely to have been influenced by the child's earlier experiences, and are compounded, for some children, by peer group relationships. Adolescents are likely to develop relationships with peers similar to themselves, so negative peer pressure is more likely to affect young people already showing anti-social behaviour (Bee 2000; Daniel *et al.* 1999). Daniel and Wassell (2002) cite a study conducted in the US, which found that the more 'assets' that teenagers have, including positive values, the less likely they are to become involved in 'high-risk' behaviours. These 'assets' are similar to resilience factors. Interventions need to be aimed at promoting positive social values, and other factors promoting resilience at the group and individual level are required for these young people.

Family income, class, race, gender, disability and sexuality may have an impact on the development of peer and other relationships in a variety of complex ways. Poverty, for example, can limit children's ability to participate in peer group activities, such as school trips and going out with friends to the cinema and clubs. An inability to afford the latest electronic game or designer label can have an impact on children's self-esteem and sense of belonging within a peer group. Many ethnic minority children in Britain will experience difficulties and conflict managing peer relationships within a dominant culture different from their own (Dwivedi 2002). Sexual orientation is often explored during adolescence. As homosexuality is stigmatised and considered deviant by many in British society, rejection can occur in peer as well as familial relationships, when young people 'come out' as gay or lesbian (Remafedi 1987).

Implications for practice

In this chapter we have considered the influence of income, work, social inclusion, community, school and peer relationships on children's development. Throughout we have highlighted how poverty and other forms of social exclusion can impair children's development, and suggested positive ways of addressing adverse environmental factors. All professionals working with children must strive to provide services which promote children's and families' strengths and protective factors within their environment. Positive interventions are required on different levels, including government policies, organisational structures, access to supportive community resources and interpersonal relationships, which respect and value individual children. In understanding child development and understanding the range of factors in society that can promote or damage a child's development, we can work towards achieving better outcomes for all children.

Part 2

Children Developing: Early Childhood to Adolescence

CHAPTER 9

Developmental Progression

Wendy Rose, Jane Aldgate and David Jones

In the previous eight chapters we have outlined some of the main themes, constructs and influences on the developing child. This part of the book provides three detailed chapters that look at children's development at different stages of childhood.

The concept of childhood progressing through a series of stages is not a contemporary device or construction. The division or categorisation of human life into different periods, which incorporate childhood as well as adulthood, are to be found in writings as far back as the seventh century CE. Orme, in his work on medieval children, cites schemes that were well known with six or seven ages or epochs, all mentioning childhood: 'They occur in the influential Latin dictionary, *Liber Entymologiarum*, by Isidore of Seville (d. 636); in the chief encyclopaedia read in England during the later middle ages, *De Proprietatibus Rerum*; and, most famously, in Jacques' speech on the ages of man in Shakespeare's *As You Like It*' (2001, p.6).

Orme makes the interesting point that the words for the stages of childhood in Latin were *infantia, puerita* and *adolescentia* but that only infancy and adolescence remain in use in English. The word denoting the period from 7 to 14 never came into common usage (except, perhaps, it might be suggested in the more derogatory sense of puerile). It was usually expressed as 'childhood' (Orme 2001, p.7). It could be argued that it reflects the neglect of this period of change and development in children, early childhood and adolescence having received much more attention in the research literature (notable exceptions being, for example, Pringle *et al.*

1966; Williams and Stith 1974; and more recently, Brannen *et al.* 2000; Cleaver 1991; Cleaver 2000; Quinton *et al.* 1998).

The idea of children progressing from one distinctive period of change to another is obviously useful both to parents and to professionals working with children and families. Boyden and her colleagues (1998, p.31) have identified three major reasons for this:

> Defining development in terms of progressive stages fits the empirical observation that children everywhere grow bigger and stronger with age and master new skills and new insights daily. It also seems to make feasible the measurement of developmental progress in individual children through the application of behavioural and developmental tests. And very importantly, it apparently provides a benchmark of well-being upon which child care services and education programmes at all levels, pre-school through to higher education, can be built.

It can help new parents to know what to expect, to understand something of what their child is experiencing and to stimulate and foster areas of competence where required. For professionals, the concept of developmental stages provides a framework for assessing what is happening to a child and for discovering what may be influencing a child either negatively or positively as the basis for any intervention. There are, however, a number of issues raised by the adoption of a developmental framework, underpinned by the idea of child development as a universal process.

First, there is the debate raised by Woodhead, Boyden and others (Boyden *et al.* 1998; Woodhead 1990) about whether such a framework can encompass the very different childhoods experienced by children across cultures: 'Different societies have their own ideas about children's capacities and vulnerabilities, the ways in which they learn and develop and what is good for them and what is bad' (Boyden *et al.* 1998, p.32). Their particular interest is in the way in which basic concepts such as 'child work' and 'child exploitation' are interpreted so differently. Thus the extent to which any delineation of general patterns of development is socially and culturally as well as biologically determined requires careful consideration.

Second, the tension has always existed as to how far descriptions of developmental stages are interpreted as normative or prescriptive, and how far they can accommodate the strong individual differences and variability between one child and another even within the same family. This tension is acknowledged, from the moment of birth, by Murray and Andrews in their magical book *The Social Baby* (2000, p.6):

General descriptions of the development of babies are given in this book, but their purpose is to help parents appreciate the baby's early capabilities, rather than to set out what 'ought' to happen at any given time. It is important for parents to realise that babies will vary a great deal in how these capabilities are shown and develop.

Third, there is not only a question of the range of difference between one child and another at each period of development, but also the question of how far each stage is truly distinctive and separate from an earlier stage of development. Winnicott reminds us that each stage is building on the previous stage, characterised by increasing complexity in the process. However 'any stage in development is reached and lost and reached and lost over and over again' (1988, p.37). He concludes:

> It is a highly artificial procedure, this dissection out of stages of development. In fact, the human child is all the time at all stages, even although one stage can be said to dominate. The primitive tasks are never completed, and throughout childhood their incompleteness presents a challenge to the parent and the educator, though originally they belong to the realm of infant care. (p.34)

Thus the notion of children progressing through different, observable stages is an old idea and has been found to be useful. However, it is an artificial construction. It has to be remembered that the experience of childhood is strongly socially and culturally influenced as well as biologically determined and expectations of children's competencies will vary from one society to another. There is likely to be considerable variability between individual children at any given stage of development, for both genetically inherited and social and environmental reasons. Finally, the developmental stages themselves as constructed are not discrete but build one on the other and the developmental tasks are never entirely completed. There are usually no sudden leaps in development: adolescence happens over a period of years, for example. These caveats do not undermine the value of a framework of developmental progression, which describes general patterns, but suggest caution and care is taken in the application of any such models to the assessment of individual children.

Describing and understanding how these changes take place is useful so that practitioners can have a broad idea of the process of development, even though there will be many variations. Often development in certain areas will occur in bursts. Young children move from crawling to walking very fast. Looking at different epochs is also helpful in identifying the parenting or caregiving response needed at different stages. For example, being a parent to a small child will require very different skills from dealing with the enquiring mind of a middle years child who has discovered spirituality and abstract thinking, or responding to the turbulent emotions of an adolescent.

The central unifying idea, which transcends culture and differently constructed childhoods, is that all children progress in their development. In order to progress, it is generally agreed that children need to accomplish certain developmental tasks and achieve specific developmental competencies in a logical order. In Chapter 1, we suggested that the idea of a logical order and an orderly progression is universal in child development. It is generally accepted that first steps of progression need to be taken before progressing to the next step. If children have missed the first steps, it is not impossible for them to start again or change but it does call for a more sensitive and intensive response from caregivers. In Chapter 4, for example, it was suggested that children who are disorganised in their attachments will need to learn to trust caregivers and change their internal working models of the world before they can take steps towards becoming securely attached.

Writers such as Masten and Coatsworth (1998) and Morrison and Anders (1999) talk about children achieving 'mastery' in specific areas. As Marchant (Marchant and Jones 2000) has pointed out, such progression applies just as much to disabled children but there will be much more variation in timing and, in some areas, progression will be very slow. Some children will compensate for lack of progression in one area by developing other areas to a heightened level. Meggitt and Sunderland (2000) use the expression that children with special needs 'often seem to dance the developmental ladder', moving through developmental stages 'in unusual and very uneven ways' (p.v).

The main areas of developmental progression can usefully be represented in a developmental grid (see Table 9.1). There are many writers in the field of developmental progression whose works are a useful point of reference. These include the following:

1. Sheridan (1997) *From Birth to Five*——Mary Sheridan's research from the 1950s has been found to provide a useful framework by many professionals working with children. Sheridan's chart illustrating the developmental progress of infants and young children in the key areas of posture and large movements, vision and fine movements, hearing and speech, and social behaviour

and play is reproduced in *Assessing Children in Need and their Families: Practice Guidance* (Department of Health 2000, pp.23–28).

2. Meggitt and Sunderland (2000) *Child Development: An Illustrated Guide (Birth to 8 Years)*——Meggitt and Sunderland build on Mary Sheridan's work and extend it by incorporating additional research. It is based on children growing up in Western Europe and covers four areas of development:

    o physical, including sensory

    o cognitive and language

    o emotional and social

    o moral and spiritual.

3. Morrison and Anders (1999) *Interviewing Children and Adolescents* Morrison and Anders identify the developmental milestones of childhood and early adolescence in a number of key areas:

    o gross motor movements

    o fine motor movements

    o affect/mood

    o language/speech

    o relationships

    o intellectual/symbolic capacity.

    They list 'those behaviors and accomplishments that a parent or a teacher might ordinarily perceive in the course of ordinary interactions with a child, or that simple testing procedures would reveal' (p.52). They note the variability between the ages at which children accomplish specific tasks and warn that milestones should be seen as guidelines not standards, as discussed by Aldgate in Chapter 1.

4. Fahlberg (1982) *Child Development*——Fahlberg's aim with this workbook was to assist social work professionals and others involved in placements of children in out-of-home care, by highlighting special developmental issues of which professionals and parents would need to be aware. She pursues these themes in relation to children for whom the plan is foster care in *A Child's Journey through Placement* (1994).

Here we provide our own example of a grid showing developmental progression (Table 9.1), adapted from Masten and Coatsworth (1998) and Morrison and Anders (1999).

Table 9.1: Developmental progression

Age period	Principal aspects of change and growth
Infancy to pre-school	Attachment to caregivers.
	Gross and fine motor skills.
	Communication and early language.
	Increasingly complex expressions of emotion.
	Differentiation of self from others.
	Self control and compliance.
Middle childhood	Developing friendships with peers.
	Increasing complex physical capabilities and coordination.
	Capable of long periods of concentration.
	Moods becoming more stable, beginning of capacity for empathy and worry.
	Developing sense of values (right versus wrong, what is fair, etc.).
	Beginning to regulate behaviour appropriately in different settings.
	Able to communicate ideas and expression of wishes.
	Literacy and numeracy skills become established.
Adolescence	Forming a cohesive sense of self-identity.
	Increasing ability to reason about hypothetical events.
	Forming close friendships within and across gender.
	Academic achievement (learning skills required for further education and work).
	Frequently questioning the belief system with which brought up.
	Period of experimentation.

Source: adapted from Masten and Coatsworth 1998 and Morrison and Anders 1999.

This grid provides what we might wish to call an overview of progression. It highlights areas which represent developmental aspects of change and growth. The grid is not prescriptive but can be used to trigger questions about children's development. If children are not progressing in one area, such questions need to be asked. We should ask why is this so for this child? Is there progression but at a slower pace? For example, is there an area of life in which there is less progress than in other areas? A good example is the development of speech. If a child has problems with language development, is this out of step with other development or is language one of many other areas of a child's development that do not seem to be progressing?

We also present a second table (Table 9.2) which provides greater detail of expected changes as the child grows and develops, in order to assist the practitioner making an assessment of an individual child.

There may be many reasons why change and growth in one area is not happening. Identifying that there is a question to be raised allows the professionals to engage in different developmental assessments to make sense of what is happening. In the words of the Children Act 1989, practitioners need to ask, is this a child in need whose development will be impaired or is likely to be impaired without the provision of services (Children Act 1989 s17(10))? The emphasis should be on finding out what can be done to enhance development where there is an issue. Such intervention will always need to be seen in a positive light – with the aim of helping a child reach his or her optimal level of development. Working on an ecological developmental model means that it may also be necessary to help caregivers or the community play their part in giving this child the best possible opportunity for development. Do facilities need to be adapted to promote the welfare of a child with a particular disability? What is available to help caregivers develop their skills? What part are schools playing in responding to children with specific developmental needs? It is not a question of identifying difference and leaving it there but of asking what can be done to give this child the best developmental opportunity for him or her? Such an approach embraces a social justice model: one which recognises the value of family, and community being involved in standing up for each and every one of their children. This child-centred approach is one which combines the right of every child not to be disadvantaged, with a positive and flexible attitude within services. Such an approach is optimistic and sees professionals being willing to adapt to children rather than children being fitted into unsuitable services that will not help them change and grow.

Table 9.2: Developmental progression: indications of expected changes and growth

	1 month	3 months
Physical change, posture and large movements	Lies back with head to one side; arm and leg on same side outstretched, or both arms flexed; knees apart, soles of feet turned inwards.	Now prefers to lie on back with head in mid-line.
	Large jerky movements of limbs, arms more active than legs.	Limbs more pliable, movements smoother and more continuous.
	At rest, hands closed and thumb turned in.	Waves arms symmetrically. Hands now loosely open.
	Fingers and toes fan out during extensor movements of limbs.	Brings hands together from side into mid-line over chest or chin.
	When cheek touched, turns to same side; ear gently rubbed, turns head away.	Kicks vigorously, legs alternating or occasionally together.
	When lifted or pulled to sit head falls loosely backwards.	Held sitting, holds back straight, except in lumbar region, with head erect and steady for several seconds before bobbing forwards. Placed downwards on face lifts head and upper chest well up in mid-line, using forearms as support, and often scratching at table surface; legs straight, buttocks flat.
	Held sitting, head falls forward, with back in one complete curve.	Held standing with feet on hard surface, sags at knees.
	Placed downwards on face, head immediately turns to side; arms and legs flexed under body, buttocks humped up.	
	Held standing on hard surface, presses down feet, straightens body and often makes reflex 'stepping' movements.	
Vision and fine movements	Turns head and eyes towards light.	Visually very alert, particularly interested in nearby human faces.
	Stares expressionlessly at brightness of window or blank wall.	Moves head deliberately to look around him.
	Follows pencil flash-lamp briefly with eyes at 1 foot.	Follows adult's movements near cot.
	Shuts eyes tightly when pencil light shone directly into them at 1–2 inches.	Follows dangling toy at 6–10 inches above face through half circle from side to side, and usually also vertically from chest to brow.
	Notices silent dangling toy shaken in line of vision at 6–8 inches and follows its slow movement with eyes from side towards mid-line on level with face through approximately quarter circle, before head falls back to side.	Watches movements of own hands before face and beginning to clasp and unclasp hands together in finger play.
	Gazes at mother's nearby face when she feeds or talks to him with increasingly alert facial expression.	Recognises feeding bottle and makes eager welcoming movements as it approaches his face.
		Regards still objects within 6–10 inches for more than a second or two, but seldom fixates continuously.
		Eyes converge as dangling toy is moved towards face.
		Defensive blink shown.

Hearing and speech	Startled by sudden loud noises, stiffens, quivers, blinks, screws eyes up, extends limbs, fans out fingers and toes, and may cry.	Sudden loud noises still distress, provoking blinking, screwing up of eyes, crying and turning away.
	Movements momentarily 'frozen', when small bell rung gently 3–5 inches from ear for 3–5 seconds, with five second pauses; may 'corner' eyes towards sound.	Definite quietening or smiling to sound of mother's voice before she touches him, but not when screaming.
	Stops whimpering to sound of nearby soothing human voice, but not when screaming or feeding.	Vocalises freely when spoken to or pleased.
	Cries lustily when hungry or uncomfortable.	Cries when uncomfortable or annoyed.
	Utters little guttural noises when content.	Quietens to tinkle of spoon in cup or to bell rung gently out of sight for 3–5 seconds at 6–12 inches from ear.
	(*Note.* Deaf babies also cry and vocalise in this reflex way, but if very deaf do not usually show startle reflex to sudden noises. Blind babies may also move eyes towards a sound-making toy. Vision should always be checked separately.)	May turn eyes and head towards sound; brows may wrinkle and eyes dilate.
		Often licks lips in response to sounds of preparation for feeding.
		Shows excitement at sound of approaching footsteps, running bath water, voices, etc,
		(*Note.* Deaf baby, instead, may be obviously startled by mother's sudden appearance beside cot.)
Social behaviour, relationships and play	Sucks well.	Fixes eyes unblinkingly on mother's face when feeding.
	Sleeps much of the time when not being fed or handled.	Beginning to react to familiar situations – showing by smiles, coos, and excited movements that he recognises preparation for feeds, baths, etc.
	Expression still vague, but becoming more alert, progressing to social smiling about 5–6 weeks.	Responds with obvious pleasure to friendly handling, especially when accompanied by playful tickling and vocal sounds.
	Hands normally closed, but if opened, grasps examiner's finger when palm is touched.	Holds rattle for few moments when placed in hand, but seldom capable of regarding it at same time.
	Stops crying when picked up and spoken to.	Mother supports at shoulders when dressing and bathing.
	Mother supports head when carrying, dressing and bathing.	
Understanding and intellectual capacity	Watches parent when talked to.	Increasing interest in people and objects
	Opens and closes mouth when parent speaks.	

Continued on next page

Table 9.2 cont.

	6 months	9 months
Physical change, posture and large movements	Lying on back, raises head from pillow.	Sits alone for 10–15 minutes on floor.
	Lifts legs into vertical and grasps foot.	Can turn body to look sideways while stretching out to grasp dangling toy or to pick up toy from floor.
	Sits with support in cot or pram and turns head from side to look around him.	Arms and legs very active in cot, pram and bath.
	Moves arms in brisk and purposeful fashion and holds them up to be lifted.	Progresses on floor by rolling or squirming.
	When hands grasped braces shoulders and pulls himself up.	Attempts to crawl on all fours.
	Kicks strongly, legs alternating.	Pulls self to stand with support.
	Can roll over, front to back.	Can stand holding on to support for a few moments, but cannot lower himself.
	Held sitting, head is firmly erect, and back straight.	Held standing, steps purposefully on alternate feet.
	May sit alone momentarily.	
	Placed downwards on face lifts head and chest well up, supporting himself on extended arms.	
	Held standing with feet touching hard surface bears weight on feet and bounces up and down actively.	
Vision and fine movements	Visually insatiable: moves head and eyes eagerly in every direction.	Very observant.
	Eyes move in unison: squint now abnormal.	Stretches out, one hand leading, to grasp small objects immediately on catching sight of them.
	Follows adult's movements across room.	Manipulates objects with lively interest, passing from hand to hand, turning over, etc.
	Immediately fixates interesting small objects within 6–12 inches (e.g., toy, bell, wooden cube, spoon, sweet) and stretches out both hands to grasp them.	Pokes at small sweet with index finger. Grasps sweets, string, etc, between finger and thumb in scissor fashion.
	Uses whole hand in palmar grasp.	Can release toy by pressing against firm surface, but cannot yet put down precisely.
	When toys fall from hand over edge of cot forgets them.	Searches in correct place for toys dropped within reach of hands.
	(Watches rolling balls of ½ to ¼ inch diameter at 10 feet).	Looks after toys falling over edge of pram or table.
		Watches activities of adults, children and animals within 10–12 feet with eager interest for several seconds at a time.
		(Watches rolling balls 2/8 inch diameter at 10 feet.)

Hearing and speech	Turns immediately to mother's voice across room.	Vocalises deliberately as means of interpersonal communication.
	Vocalises tunefully and often, using single and double syllables, e.g. ka, muh, goo, der, adah, er-lah.	Shouts to attract attention, listens, and then shouts again.
	Laughs, chuckles and squeals aloud in play.	Babbles tunefully, repeating syllables in long strings (mam-man, bab-bab, dad-dad, etc.)
	Screams with annoyance.	Understands 'No-No' and 'Bye-Bye'.
	Shows evidence of response to different emotional tones of mother's voice.	Tries to imitate adults' playful vocal sounds, e.g. smacking lips, cough, brr, etc. (Immediate localising response to baby hearing tests at three feet from ear and above and below ear level.)
	Responds to baby hearing test at 1½ feet from each ear by correct visual localisation, but may show slightly brisker response on one side.	
	(Tests employed – voice, rattle, cup and spoons, paper, bell, two seconds with two seconds pause.)	
Social behaviour, relationships and play	Hands competent to reach for and grasp small toys.	Holds, bites and chews biscuits.
	Most often uses a two-handed, scooping-in approach, but occasionally a single hand.	Puts hands round bottle or cup when feeding.
	Takes everything to mouth.	Tries to grasp spoon when being fed.
	Beginning to find feet interesting and even useful in grasping.	Throws body back and stiffens in annoyance or resistance.
	Puts hands to bottle and pats it when feeding.	Clearly distinguishes strangers from familiars, and requires reassurance before accepting their advances.
	Shakes rattle deliberately to make it sound, often regarding it closely at same time.	Clings to known adult and hides face.
	Still friendly with strangers but occasionally shows some shyness or even slight anxiety, especially if mother is out of sight. Displeased if toys removed.	Still takes everything to mouth.
	Will laugh, show excitement.	Seizes bell in one hand, imitates ringing action, waving or banging it on table, and pokes clapper or 'drinks' from bowl.
		Plays peek-a-boo.
		Holds out toy held in hand to adult, but cannot yet give.
		Finds partially hidden toy.
		May find toy hidden under cup.
		Mother supports at lower spine when dressing.
		Beginning to show stranger anxiety.

Continued on next page

Table 9.2 cont.

	6 months	9 months
Understanding and intellectual capacity	Smiles at self in mirror.	Pats image of self in mirror.
	Tries to recover dropped toy.	Responds to own name.
	Imitates – blowing bubbles, tongue protrusion.	Recognises tone of voice.
	Peek-a-boo.	Responds to 'no'.
	Starts to show likes and dislikes of foods.	Reaches persistently for toys out of reach.
		Shows excitement and pleasure.
		Increasing concentration.

	12 months	15 months
Physical change, posture and large movements	Sits well and for indefinite time.	Walks unevenly with feet wide apart, arms slightly flexed and held above head or at shoulder level to balance.
	Can rise to sitting position from lying down.	Starts alone, but frequently stopped by falling or bumping into furniture.
	Crawls rapidly, usually on all fours.	Lets himself down from standing to sitting by collapsing backwards with bump, or occasionally by falling forward on hands and then back to sitting.
	Pulls to standing and lets himself down again holding on to furniture.	Can get to feet alone.
	Walks round furniture stepping sideways.	Crawls upstairs.
	Walks with one or both hands held.	Kneels unaided or with slight support on floor and in pram, cot and bath.
	May stand alone for a few moments.	May be able to stoop to pick up toys from floor.
	May walk alone.	

Vision and fine movements	Picks up small objects, e.g. blocks, string, sweets and crumbs, with precise pincer grasp of thumb and index finger.	Picks up string, small sweets and crumbs neatly between thumb and finger.
	Throws toys deliberately and watches them fall to ground.	Builds tower of two cubes after demonstration.
	Looks in correct place for toys which roll out of sight.	Grasps crayon and imitates scribble after demonstration.
	Points with index finger at objects he wants to handle or which interest him.	Looks with interest at pictures in book and pats page.
	Watches small toy pulled along floor across room 10 feet away.	Follows with eyes path of cube or small toy swept vigorously from table.
	Out of doors watches movements of people, animals, motor cars, etc., with prolonged intent regard.	Watches small toy pulled across floor up to 12 feet.
	Recognises familiars approaching from 20 feet or more away.	Points imperiously to objects he wishes to be given.
	Uses both hands freely, but may show preference for one.	Stands at window and watches events outside intently for several minutes.
	Clicks two bricks together in imitation.	(Watches and retrieves rolling balls of $2\frac{1}{8}$ inches at ten feet.)
	(Watches rolling balls $2\frac{1}{8}$ inches at ten feet.)	
Hearing and speech	Knows and immediately turns to own name.	Jabbers loudly and freely, using wide range of inflections and phonetic units.
	Babbles loudly, tunefully and incessantly.	Speaks 2–6 recognisable words and understands many more.
	Shows by suitable movements and behaviour that he understands several words in usual context (e.g. own and family names, walk, dinner, pussy, cup, spoon, ball, car).	Vocalises wishes and needs at table.
	Comprehends simple commands associated with gesture (give it to daddy, come to mummy, say bye-bye, clap hands, etc.).	Points to familiar persons, animals, toys, etc., when requested.
	Imitates adult's playful vocalisations with gleeful enthusiasm.	Understands and obeys simple commands (e.g. Shut the door, give me the ball, get your shoes).
	May hand examine common objects on request, e.g. spoon, cup, ball, shoe.	(Baby test 4½–6 feet.)
	(Immediate response to baby tests at 3–4½ feet but rapidly habituates.)	

Continued on next page

Table 9.2 cont.

	12 months	15 months
Social behaviour, relationships and play	Drinks from cup with little assistance. Chews. Holds spoon but usually cannot use it alone. Helps with dressing by holding out arm for sleeve and foot for shoe. Takes objects to mouth less often. Puts wooden cubes in and out of cup or box. Rattles spoon in cup in imitation. Seizes bell by handle and rings briskly in imitation, etc. Listens with obvious pleasure to percussion sounds. Repeats activities to reproduce effects. Gives toys to adult on request and sometimes spontaneously. Finds hidden toy quickly. Likes to be constantly within sight and hearing of adult. Demonstrates affection to familiars. Waves 'bye-bye' and claps hands in imitation or spontaneously. Child sits, or sometimes stands without support, while mother dresses. Will express several emotions, such as affection, anger, anxiety, sadness. May show separation anxiety.	Holds cup when adult gives and takes back. Holds spoon, brings it to mouth and licks it, but cannot prevent its turning over. Chews well. Helps more constructively with dressing. Indicates when he has wet pants. Pushes large wheeled toy with handle on level ground. Seldom takes toy to mouth. Repeatedly casts objects to floor in play or rejection, usually without watching fall. Physically restless and intensely curious. Handles everything within reach. Emotionally labile. Closely dependent upon adult's reassuring presence. Needs constant supervision to protect child from dangers of extended exploration and exploitation of environment.
Understanding and intellectual capacity	Increasing language understanding. Prefers certain toys.	Looks at pictures with interest. Points to familiar objects, on request. Can find an object screened from view. Imitates behaviours of parents. Likes to play with adult possessions.

	18 months	2 years
Physical change, posture and large movements	Walks well with feet only slightly apart, starts and stops safely.	Runs safely on whole foot, stopping and starting with ease and avoiding obstacles.
	Runs stiffly upright, eyes fixed on ground 1–2 yards ahead, but cannot continue to run round obstacles.	Squats to rest or to play with object on ground and rises to feet without using hands.
	Pushes and pulls large toys, boxes, etc, round floor.	Walks backwards pulling large toy.
	Can carry large doll or teddy-bear while walking and sometimes two.	Pulls wheeled toy by cord.
	Backs into small chair or slides in sideways.	Climbs on furniture to look out of window or open doors, etc, and can get down again.
	Climbs forward into adult's chair then turns round and sits.	Walks upstairs and down holding on to rail and wall; two feet to a step.
	Walks upstairs with helping hand.	Throws small ball without falling.
	Creeps backwards down stairs.	Walks into large ball when trying to kick it.
	Occasionally bumps down a few steps on buttocks facing forwards.	Sits astride large wheeled toy and propels forward with feet on ground.
	Picks up toy from floor without falling.	
Vision and fine movements	Picks up small sweets, beads, pins, threads, etc, immediately on sight, with delicate pincer grasp.	Picks up pins and thread, etc, neatly and quickly.
	Spontaneous scribble when given crayon and paper, using preferred hand.	Removes paper wrapping from small sweet.
	Builds tower of three cubes after demonstration.	Builds lower of six cubes (or six+).
	Enjoys simple picture book, often recognising and putting finger on coloured items on page.	Spontaneous circular scribble and dots when given paper and pencil.
	Turns pages two or three at a time.	Imitates vertical line (and sometimes V).
	Fixes eyes on a small dangling toy up to ten feet.	Enjoys picture books, recognising fine details in favourite pictures.
	May tolerate this test with each eye separately.)	Turns pages singly.
	Points to distant interesting objects out of doors.	Recognises familiar adults in photograph after once shown.
	(Watches and retrieves rolling balls of 2½ inches at ten feet.)	Hand preference becoming evident.
	(Possibly recognises special miniature toys at ten feet.)	(Immediately catches sight of, and names special miniature toys at ten feet distance. Will now usually tolerate this test with each eye separately.)
		(Watches and retrieves rolling balls of 2⅛ inches at ten feet.)

Continued on next page

Table 9.2 cont.

	18 months	2 years
Hearing and speech	Continues to jabber tunefully to himself at play.	Uses 50 or more recognisable words and understands many more.
	Uses 6–20 recognisable words and understands many more.	Puts two or more words together to form simple sentences.
	Echoes prominent or last word addressed to him.	Refers to himself by name.
	Demands desired objects by pointing accompanied by loud, urgent vocalisation or single words.	Talks to himself continually as he plays.
	Enjoys nursery rhymes and tries to join in. Attempts to sing.	Echo(s) are almost constant, with one or more stressed words repeated.
	Shows his own or doll's hair, shoe, nose.	Constantly asking names of objects.
	(Possibly special five toy test. Possibly four animals picture test.)	Joins in nursery rhymes and songs.
		Shows correctly and repeats words for hair, hand, feet, nose, eyes, mouth, and shoe on request.
		(Six toy test, four animals picture test.)
Social behaviour, relationships and play	Lifts and holds cup between both hands.	Lifts and drinks from cup and replaces on table.
	Drinks without spilling.	Spoon-feeds without spilling.
	Hands cup back to adult. Chews well.	Asks for food and drink. Chews competently.
	Holds spoon and gets food to mouth.	Puts on hat and shoes.
	Takes off shoes, socks, and hat.	Verbalises toilet needs in reasonable time.
	Indicates toilet needs by restlessness and vocalisation.	Dry during day.
	Bowel control usually attained.	Turns door handles. Often runs outside to explore.
	Explores environment energetically.	Follows mother round house and copies domestic activities in simultaneous play.
	No longer takes toys to mouth.	
	Remembers where objects belong.	Engages in simple make-believe activities.
	Casts objects to floor in play or anger less often.	Constantly demanding mother's attention.
	Briefly imitates simple activities, e.g. reading book, kissing doll, brushing floor.	Clings lightly in affection, fatigue or fear.
		Tantrums when frustrated but attention readily distracted.
	Plays contentedly alone, but likes to be near adult.	Defends own possessions with determination.
	Emotionally still very dependent upon familiar adult, especially mother.	As yet no idea of sharing.
	Alternates between clinging and resistance.	Plays near other children but not with them.
	Onset of negativism.	Resentful of attention shown to other children.

	2½ years	3 years
Understanding and intellectual capacity	Likes to explore cupboards. Recognises miniature objects. Points to own or doll's nose, eyes, hair, on request. Imitates parents' domestic activities.	Pulls people to show them objects. Onset of fantasy play (e.g. with dolls). Can remember one or two pieces of information, e.g. numbers or words.
Physical change, posture and large movements	Walks upstairs alone but downstairs holding rail, two feet to a step. Runs well straight forward and climbs easy nursery apparatus. Pushes and pulls large toys skilfully, but has difficulty in steering them round obstacles. Jumps with two feet together. Can stand on tiptoe if shown. Kicks large ball. Sits on tricycle and steers with hands, but still usually propels with feet on ground.	Walks alone upstairs with alternating feet and downstairs with two feet to step. Usually jumps from bottom step. Climbs nursery apparatus with agility. Can turn round obstacles and corners while running and also while pushing and pulling large toys. Rides tricycle and can turn wide corners on it. Can walk on tiptoe. Stands momentarily on one foot when shown. Sits with feet crossed at ankles.
Vision and fine movements	Picks up pins, threads, etc., with each eye covered separately. Builds tower of seven (or seven+) cubes and lines blocks to form 'train'. Recognises minute details in picture books. Imitates horizontal line and circle (also usually T and V). Paints strokes, dots and circular shapes on easel. Recognises himself in photographs when once shown. Recognises miniature toys and retrieves balls of 2⅛ inches at ten feet, each eye separately. (May also match special single letter-cards V, O, T, H at ten feet.)	Picks up pins, threads, etc., with each eye covered separately. Builds tower of nine cubes, also (age 3½) bridge of three from model. Can close fist and wiggle thumb in imitation. R and L. Copies circle (also V, H, T). Imitates cross. Draws man with head and usually indication of features or another part. Matches two or three primary colours (usually red and yellow correct, but may confuse blue and green). Paints 'pictures' with large brush on easel. Cuts with scissors. (Recognises special miniature toys at ten feet.) Performs single-letter vision test at ten feet. Five letters.)

Continued on next page

Table 9.2 cont.

	2½ years	3 years
Hearing and speech	Uses 200 or more recognisable words but speech shows numerous infantilisms.	Large intelligible vocabulary but speech still shows many infantile phonetic substitutions. Gives full name and sex, and (sometimes) age.
	Knows full name.	Uses plurals and pronouns.
	Talks intelligibly to himself at play concerning events happening here and now.	Still talks to himself in long monologues mostly concerned with the immediate present, including make-believe activities.
	Echolalia persists.	Carries on simple conversations, and verbalises past experiences.
	Continually asking questions beginning 'What?', 'Where?'.	Asks many questions beginning 'What?', 'Where?', 'Who?'.
	Uses pronouns, I, me and you.	Listens eagerly to stories and demands favourites over and over again.
	Stuttering in eagerness common.	Knows several nursery rhymes.
	Says a few nursery rhymes.	(Seven toy test, four animals picture test. first or second cube test, six 'high frequency' word pictures.)
	Enjoys simple familiar stories read from picture book.	
	(Six toy test, four animal picture test, first cube test. Full doll vocabulary.)	
Social behaviour, relationships and play	Eats skilfully with spoon and may use fork.	Eats with fork and spoon.
	Pulls down pants or knickers at toilet, but seldom able to replace.	Washes hands, but needs supervision in drying.
	Dry through night if lifted.	Can pull pants and knickers down and up, but needs help with buttons.
	Very active, restless and rebellious.	Dry through night.
	Throws violent tantrums and when thwarted or unable to express urgent need and less easily distracted.	General behaviour more amenable.
	Emotionally still very dependent upon adults.	Affectionate and confiding.
	Prolonged domestic make-believe play (putting dolls to bed, washing clothes, driving motor cars, etc.) but with frequent reference to friendly adult.	Likes to help with adult's activities in house and garden.
	Watches other children at play interestedly and occasionally joins in for a few minutes, but little notion of sharing playthings or adult's attention.	Makes effort to keep his surroundings tidy.
	Expresses pride in own accomplishments.	Vividly realised make-believe play including invented people and objects.
		Enjoys floor play with bricks, boxes, toy trains and cars, alone or with siblings.
		Joins in play with other children in and outdoors.
		Understands sharing playthings, sweets, etc.
		Shows affection for younger siblings.
		Shows some appreciation of past and present.
		Decline of negativism. Enjoys showing off.

	4 years	5 years
Understanding and intellectual capacity	Copies vertical and horizontal strokes with pencil. Relates to objects, e.g. spoon in the cup. Helps to put things away. Matches colours. Enjoys familiar stories from picture books.	Understands 'big' and 'small', 'under' and 'on'. Recognises object by use. Knows some nursery rhymes. Vivid make-believe. Dresses and undresses doll. Comprehends the meaning of two or three parts of an item. Can state own gender. Can state own full name. Uses objects to represent people in play.
Physical change, posture and large movements	Turns sharp corners running, pushing and pulling. Walks alone up and downstairs, one foot per step. Climbs ladders and trees. Can run on tiptoe. Expert rider of tricycle. Hops on one foot. Stands on one foot 3–5 seconds. Arranges or picks up objects from floor by bending from waist with knees extended.	Runs lightly on toes. Active and skilful in climbing, sliding, swinging, digging and various 'stunts'. Skips on alternative feet. Dances to music. Can stand on one foot 8–10 seconds. Can hop 2–3 yards forwards on each foot separately. Grips strongly with either hand.
Vision and fine movements	Picks up pins, thread, crumbs, etc., with each eye covered separately. Builds tower of ten or more cubes and several 'bridges' of three on request. Builds three steps with six cubes after demonstration. Imitates spreading of hand and bringing thumb into opposition with each finger in turn, R and L. Copies cross (also V, H, T and O). Draws man with head, legs, features, trunk and (often) arms. Draws very simple house. Matches and names four primary colours correctly. (Single-letter vision test at ten feet, seven letters: also near chart to bottom.)	Picks up minute objects when each eye is covered separately. Builds three steps with six cubes from model. Copies square and triangle (also letters; V, T, H, O, X, L, A, C, U, Y). Writes a few letters spontaneously. Draws recognisable man with head, trunk, legs, arms and features. Draws simple house with door, windows, roof and chimney. Counts fingers on one hand with index finger of other. Names four primary colours and matches 10 or 12 colours. (Full nine-letter vision chart at 20 feet and near test to bottom.)

Continued on next page

Table 9.2 cont.

	4 years	5 years
Hearing and speech	Speech completely intelligible.	Speech fluent and grammatical.
	Shows only a few infantile substitutions usually k/t/th/f/s and r/l/w/y groups).	Articulation correct except for residual confusions of s/f/th and r/l/w/y groups.
	Gives connected account of recent events and experiences.	Loves stories and acts them out in detail later.
	Gives name, sex, home address and (usually) age.	Gives full name, age and home address.
	Eternally asking questions 'Why?', 'When?', 'How?' and meanings of words.	Gives age and (usually) birthday.
	Listens to and tells long stories sometimes confusing fact and fantasy.	Defines concrete nouns by use.
	(Seven toy test, first picture vocabulary test, second cube test. Six 'high frequency' word pictures.)	Asks meaning of abstract words.
		(12 'high frequency' picture vocabulary or word lists, third cube test, six sentences.)
Social behaviour, relationships and play	Eats skilfully with spoon and fork.	Uses knife and fork.
	Washes and dries hands. Brushes teeth.	Washes and dries face and hands, but needs help and supervision for rest.
	Can undress and dress except for back buttons, laces and ties.	Undresses and dresses alone.
	General behaviour markedly self-willed.	General behaviour more sensible, controlled and responsibly independent.
	Inclined to verbal impertinence when wishes crossed but can be affectionate and compliant.	Domestic and dramatic play continued from day to day.
	Strongly dramatic play and dressing-up favoured.	Plans and builds constructively.
	Constructive out-of-doors building with any large material to hand.	Floor games very complicated.
	Needs other children to play with and is alternately co-operative and aggressive with them as with adults.	Chooses own friends.
	Understands taking turns.	Co-operative with companions and understands need for rules and fair play.
	Shows concern for younger siblings and sympathy for playmates in distress.	Appreciates meaning of clock time in relation to daily programme.
	Appreciates past, present and future.	Tender and protective towards younger children and pets. Comforts playmates in distress.
	May attempt to control emotions (e.g. crying).	
Understanding and intellectual capacity	Can make and honour an agreement.	Beginning sense of values, right versus wrong, fairness.
		Can evaluate own capabilities with some accuracy.
		Counts to ten.

	7–8 years	9–10 years
Physical change, posture and large movements	Can bounce a ball on floor several times. Can ride a bicycle. Can hop, jump, run, skip, and throw.	Increasing strength. Participation in individual and team sports.
Vision and fine movements	Can tie a bow, or shoelaces. Can print letters. Can copy a diamond shape. Capability for cursive writing develops.	Writing well established Mastery of drawing and fine movement tasks
Hearing and speech	Can tell left from right, controls own grammar. Verbally expresses fantasies, and needs, and wishes. Start of puns, riddles and word games.	Expresses ideas with complex relationships between elements. Increasingly subtle use of language to express thought, feelings, categories of things and comparisons between them.
Social behaviour, relationships and play	Develops peer and best friend relationships. Beginning capacity for empathy and concern about others. Moods more stable. Gender identity now well established.	Best friends become increasingly important. Mood now normally regulated and stable.
Understanding and intellectual capacity	Begins to develop an ability to regulate own behaviour (ability to wait, check aggression). Increasing curiosity. Emerging morality, and concerns about opinions of others. Recognises that the whole comprises its parts. Now 'talks to him/herself' – inner speech as part of growing understanding.	Memory capacity well established. Several strategies for memorising events and facts. Increase in logical thinking. Capacity for inference develops.

Continued on next page

Table 9.2 cont.

	11–12 years	15 years
Physical change, posture and large movements	Onset of puberty Puberty lasts for 4–5 years on average.	Attainment of adult height Rapid physical growth coinciding with sexual maturation.
Vision and fine movements		
Hearing and speech	Reading capacity now increasingly important for new information.	Reading more important than listening for new, complex information.
Social behaviour, relationships and play	May develop animal phobias. Increasing importance of peer friendships, based on shared values and understanding. Well established empathic concern for others.	Demand for conformity to group. Ambivalence towards parents. Increasing development of self identity and esteem (including sexual and ethnic). Social identity outside the family. Increasing emotional and social emancipation in later adolescence. Further development of empathy and awareness of others. Transient homosexual feelings and activities. Powerful heterosexual 'crushes', usually about unobtainable figures.
Understanding and intellectual capacity	Can reason about hypothetical events. Awareness of other's different perspectives. Conscience becomes increasingly refined.	Can hold in short term memory seven or eight independent units (e.g. numbers or words). Abstract thinking. Concept of probabilities.

In the three chapters that follow, the developmental tasks and competencies have been divided into three epochs:

- children in their early years

- children in their middle years

- adolescence and transitions to adulthood.

Each chapter stands in its own right but together they demonstrate the changing emphases of the developing child.

CHAPTER 10

Early Childhood: Zero to Four Years

Brigid Daniel

Introduction

The term 'infancy' is used for the first two years of life, a time characterised by total dependency upon a more mature caregiver. During the next two years, known in many societies as 'pre-school' years, children are still highly dependent but they develop more autonomy. This autonomy is partly associated with increased independent mobility, but also an increased understanding of the separateness, but inter-dependence of people. From the very beginning children are active participants in their development; they are constantly working out how the world of objects and people works, usually through the medium of play. This active participation can be enhanced or blunted by the quality of encouragement offered by people in the child's world.

Physical development

The speed and number of changes that can be seen in the early years is underpinned by massive brain development. There is extensive growth in neural connections, more in fact than will finally be required. The connections that are most used become fixed and the others die back, so some predictability and patterns of experience are important (Berger 2001; Gebhardt 2004; Glaser and Balbernie 2001). Although good nutrition is important for brain development, severe emotional neglect means an absence of the stimulation that allows patterns of connections to become fixed. This is why it is so important to take neglect of the very young child seriously. By the time the child is 5 years old, the brain is at 90 per cent of its adult weight.

The two key early physical developmental tasks are learning to use the hands and fingers and learning to get about. Babies start to have control over their trunk first of all and then gradually this control moves out to their extremities, so that by 9 months they can use the forefinger and thumb to pick up small objects. They also gradually gain control from head to foot and by 12 months can crawl well and begin walking. From the age of 2 growth slows and during the next couple of years children refine their walking and running ability, their manipulative ability and stability. During these years children also need proportionately fewer calories and even small amounts of sweet foods can negatively affect their appetite. This decrease in appetite can be a trigger for problems if parents worry and start to force children to eat.

It is tempting for social workers and other children's services professionals to pay less attention to physical development than to socio-emotional development, but physical development occurs within a social context (Thelen and Smith 1994). With encouragement from others, the baby's natural tendency to try new things is enhanced, and children enjoy the pleasure that others take in their physical achievements. For some parents, the child's active attempts to develop his or her physical skills are seen as 'naughty' or a nuisance. Practitioners should be concerned, for example, if they encounter a young child who spends significant amounts of time restrained in a buggy. It is natural for a young child to grab at pretty objects and this will include treasured ornaments. Some parents may need help to understand their child's cognitive limitations and be encouraged, for example, to put precious objects away. Finally, the tired, hungry, anxious, abused or frightened baby is far less likely to want to try crawling and reaching.

Cognitive development (including language and communication)

Piaget (1952) depicted cognitive development as a product of two processes: assimilation and accommodation, and as progressing through stages. The first stage, which he called *sensorimotor*, is characterised by an absence of mental representation of events and the assimilation of objects into reflex responses, for example, by sucking them. Gradually infants begin to accommodate reflexes to different objects, for example, by sucking toys in a different way from sucking a teat. In the second year behaviour becomes more goal directed as they move into *pre-operational* thought where some internal representations begin, although with some limitations as illustrated by Piaget's classic *conservation* experiments. For example, when liquid is poured from a short fat glass into a tall thin one, pre-school children are beguiled by the salient feature of height and miss the other features such as width and think there is more liquid in the taller glass. Children cannot fully conserve liquid, number, mass or length until about 6 or 7 years.

Piaget also described young children's thought as *egocentric*, or self-centred. This does not mean that young children do not show empathy, but it does explain *magical thinking* where young children mistakenly attribute events as related to their own actions or thoughts, and are prone to blame themselves for external events such as the loss of a parent. More naturalistic experiments show that children can achieve some cognitive tasks earlier than Piaget surmised, and that they are less egocentric than he described. However, his descriptions of the qualitative changes in thinking can help with understanding some of the cognitive limitations of young children.

Vygotsky (1962) emphasised the role that a trusted other plays in cognitive development. An adult (or older child) uses *guided participation* to encourage the child to try something just beyond their capabilities. They will use all sorts of naturally occurring situations to encourage cognitive development, and routine activities are turned into games whereby children can learn about objects; activities are pitched at the optimal level to encourage the child. If the people around the child are preoccupied with their own circumstances, are not interested in the child or have no energy, then the child is left to work much more out alone. The neglected child's cognitive abilities will gradually develop, but he or she will not experience the fun of learning in a social context and the learning experiences will not be so rich.

Young children can remember important events, and memories include sensory associations. Many 'memories' result from reminders and descriptions of childhood events by others (Rovee-Collier 1999). The importance of positive stories from childhood is emphasised by Owusu-Bempah in Chapter 6 on socio-genealogical connectedness, particularly for those children growing up away from their families. If a child has suffered a lot of disruption of care, they can miss out on this reinforcement of positive memories. At the same time it cannot be assumed that traumatic events will be forgotten. Children as young as 2 or 3 years can recall past events accurately and children of 3 years have testified competently in court (Graffam Walker 1999).

The foundations for conversation are laid in the first few months when babies take great pleasure in games that involve reciprocal turn-taking and, by 5 months, they take an active part in nursery rhymes and other word games. In the sixth month babbling starts, and there is evidence that deaf babies reared in signing households play with gestures in a version of babbling (Petito and Marentette 1991). Understanding of vocabulary and grammar develops in advance of expressive abilities. As they approach their first year, children comprehend simple words and soon after start to produce recognisable words. At 18 months there is a spurt in vocabulary and, by 2 years, multi-word sentences are produced. By 5 years, many children are proficient speakers. Children actively try to work out grammar and in fact may appear to regress as they start to over-apply regular rules to irregular verbs, for example, by saying 'runned' instead of 'ran'.

Practitioners need to be aware that children may use words that they do not fully understand. As Graffam Walker (1999) indicates, young children use and interpret language very literally and tend to understand concrete rather than abstract terms. They have difficulties with categorisation and may not be clear about relative terms such as 'before', 'above' and so on. Young children also know that a question requires an answer and supply one even if it is not correct; usually they will respond 'yes' when they do not know the answer. Practitioners need to check carefully that children really have understood them.

One of the key developmental tasks in the early years is the ability to understand that others think and feel and that other people's thoughts and feelings may be different from your own. This is known as *theory of mind*. By 3 years, children have the beginnings of theory of mind and by 4 years, know that others can have false beliefs. This can be tested in a number of ways. For example, a child is shown a box that normally holds sweets but in which pencils have been put in instead. When asked what they think is inside young children will say 'sweets', and when they look inside are surprised. If asked what they thought was inside before they looked, younger children will say 'pencils', and if asked what another child will think is inside, will say 'pencils'. After about 4 years, children are more likely to say that another child will think that there are sweets inside: in other words, they know that other people can be fooled by appearances.

Psychosocial development

During the early years children develop a sense of who they are, what other people feel and learn to direct their attention and recognise and control their own emotions and behaviour.

There is considerable evidence to suggest that infants are born with particular temperamental tendencies that are evident within the first months. Thomas and Chess (1977) suggest that about 40 per cent of babies can be described as *easy*; they seem to be generally happy, take easily to routines and adapt well to change. Ten per cent of babies are described as *difficult*; they cry a lot, are hard to settle, do not adapt well and are hard to distract when they are upset. Fifteen per cent of babies are *slow to warm up*; they tend to be rather passive, and somewhat negative in response, but will respond with time. The concept of *goodness of fit* captures the extent to which the adult and child temperaments mesh and most people adapt their parenting very effectively to fit the child. But people have different tolerance levels for normal infant behaviour and therefore such temperamental distinctions have to be treated with care. Children's sense of self is affected by the way other people describe and relate to them. Descriptions of the child cannot always be taken at face value, for example, an unwanted child or a child whose parent is struggling with other issues may be more likely to be described as 'difficult'. Observation of the child in different circumstances and with different people can help with an assessment of temperament.

Pre-school children observe and notice gender and race differences. By 2 years, most can label self and others by gender, and notice differences in skin colour. By 4 and 5 years, they know about gender stability. They can also pick out a picture or doll whose ethnicity matches their own and classify themselves and others by race, but they may have limited understanding of more subtle distinctions of customs and religion (Schaffer 1996). From as early as 3 years, children tend to choose same-sex playmates and already have absorbed many of society's expectations of 'typical' gender role behaviour. Resilience in children is associated in girls with encouragement towards autonomy and in boys by encouragement of expression of emotions (Werner and Smith 1992). Perhaps this acts as a balance to the characteristics that are quickly picked up and reinforced as being associated with particular genders.

By 5 or 6 months infants can distinguish some emotional expressions and between 9 to 12 months begin to recognise different emotions in others. By 2 years, they can use a number of words to describe emotions such as 'happy' and 'scared' and soon after this they can begin to comment on others' thoughts and feelings. Dunn (1991) observed second-born children in their second and third years as they interacted with siblings and saw signs of simple teasing early in the second year, demonstrating an understanding of what might affect other people. In their pretend play in the third year, the children played out the feelings that another might feel in different situations. By 5 years, they could describe the kind of situations that lead to a range of emotions in themselves or in others. The importance of shared fun and humour should not be underestimated as it clearly helps with this important developmental task. Professionals, therefore, need to be alert to the emotional climate that the child shares in. It is especially helpful for young children to have the opportunity to play with other children.

Tiny babies are not able to control responses to strong stimuli; if they feel pain they cannot help but cry out, if they are tired they will fall asleep, if frightened they show automatic startle responses. Infants can, to some extent, control and direct their attention to objects of interest, but by 15–18 months they show more selective attention and also show 'joint attention' where they look at what the mother looks at (Butterworth 1995). At 2½, children are less distractible and improve their ability to pay attention to the important features of a task and become more systematic in attempting tasks (Flavell 1985). By the second year, self-control also emerges as children learn socially accepted behaviour. They become more autonomous and can become very upset if a task is beyond their ability. They may show some *instrumental* aggression to get what they want, but this should decline and by the age of 4 they should be reasonably good at controlling their aggression. If aggression or challenging behaviour does not decline, then it needs to be taken seriously as pre-school conduct disorder is highly predictive of later problems of aggression (Rutter and Rutter 1993).

Emotional development

Emotional well-being and long-term resilience is underpinned by the experience of being loved and feeling lovable. Infants have an inherent need to attach and much early social behaviour is an assertion of that need

(Bowlby 1969), as was discussed in Chapter 4. Initially (0–2 months) infants show rather indiscriminate responses in that they respond to all people and, although they can recognise the primary carer within days, they do not show active preferences (Vasta, Marshall and Miller 1999). They then develop more discriminate social responses (2–7 months) and are more interested in the main caregiver and begin to look to them for guidance on how to respond to novel situations (*social referencing*). More focused attachment springs from this discrimination (9–24 months). It is during this stage that children may first develop a fear of strangers and then demonstrate anxiety when separated from the primary attachment figure, although children who have had extensive contact with other people may show less wariness of strangers.

The quality of the interaction with significant others provides the context in which the child develops a sense of him or herself as lovable and others as dependable, and provides a template of relationships or *internal working model* (Howe *et al.* 1999). The majority of children develop secure attachments, facilitated by adult caregiving that is sensitive and warm. However, as previously discussed in Chapter 4, some children develop attachment styles that have been described as insecure (Ainsworth *et al.* 1978). *Avoidant* insecure attachment is associated with somewhat cold and rejecting parenting and is characterised by children showing little distress at separation and avoiding contact with the carer. *Resistant* or *ambivalent* insecure attachment is associated with parenting that is warm but not particularly sensitive to the child's individual needs. It is characterised by children showing great distress at separation but not gaining great comfort from reunion with the parent. Some children's behaviour is more contradictory and includes avoidance and resistance and is known as *disorganised, disoriented* attachment (Downes 1992). There tends to be a relationship between the styles of attachment to different significant people, but it is important for professionals to know that this is not always the case. Fox *et al.* showed, for example, that 31 per cent of children could be securely attached to one parent and insecurely attached to the other (Fox, Kimmerly and Schafer 1991).

The adult acts as a safe haven to retreat to, particularly when the child is distressed, anxious or frightened. However, the attachment figure also serves the very important function of a secure base from which the child can explore the world of other people and objects. Some children who are insecurely attached lack the sense of trust in the attachment figure to feel safe exploring the world.

When children are abruptly separated from an attachment figure, they feel loss and recovery is facilitated by the grieving process (Fahlberg 1994). A child who is securely attached is likely to react to separation with the following sequence:

- initial protest and attempts to recover the lost person

- despair and watchfulness, preoccupation and depression

- emotional detachment and loss of interest in carers (Bowlby 1969).

Children between 6 months and 4 years are the most vulnerable to the worst effects of separation because they have developed selective attachments and are laying the foundations of autonomy (Rutter 1981). They may react to separation by regression to less autonomous behaviour. During these early years children lack the cognitive skills to comprehend the events leading to separation and this, coupled with the propensity for magical thinking, means that young children are highly likely to blame themselves for the loss. A child who has had a previous experience of a secure attachment is more likely to be able to develop new attachments. Practitioners can minimise the impact of losses upon young children by ensuring that:

- there is adequate preparation for anticipated separation

- warm consistent substitute care is available

- as many routines as possible are retained

- wherever possible ongoing contact with the attachment figure is enabled

- any signs of self-blame are quickly picked up and defused.

Moral and spiritual development

Moral development covers a range of different features of interpersonal life, including acting kindly towards others, showing empathy for another's situation, being able to inhibit actions that you know to be wrong and developing an internal conscience. Young children's cognitive skills are not sufficiently sophisticated for them to understand complex social moral principles such as justice, truth and honesty. Nor can they understand the need for mutual social pacts about laws and social cohesion. Young children's understanding of right and wrong tends to be in terms of punishment and reward: something is wrong if it leads to a punishment. Kohlberg described this as *preconventional* morality (Kohlberg 1969). It is clear to see the potential for a link with magical thinking in that if a child experiences something is bad, they are likely to see it as a punishment and assume that they did something wrong. In these early years it is parents and others who provide the external regulation of behaviours and act as the primary 'conscience'. Gradually children internalise these messages and can increasingly regulate their own behaviour.

Very young children can show empathy for, and kindness towards, others and such pro-social behaviour is a key building block for satisfying interpersonal relationships. Kind behaviour towards others is associated with longer term resilience to adversity (Werner and Smith 1992). From before they are 2 years old, babies can become upset if someone else is upset or unhappy and they then begin to make active efforts to provide comfort. As they develop a theory of mind, they realise that each person might take comfort in different things. A child who is treated with kindness and respect and observes the people they care about treating others with kindness and respect is more likely to develop kindness and morality (Zahn-Waxler *et al.* 1992). A child is also more able to recognise the perspective of others and converse about inner states if the family encourages the discussion of feelings and motives (Dunn 1991; Webster-Stratton 1992).

Developmental texts do not routinely examine spiritual development in any detail (Beek 2000). Crompton (1998) suggests that the whole care of the child must incorporate attention to spiritual development, and not only for children of minority ethnic origin. Consideration of spiritual development is frequently confined to the realm of organised religion development, but in a broader sense it is concerned with the young child's notion of things greater than they are and things unexplained, as Seden noted in Chapter 2. Very young children can ask questions about the nature of the world and existence, as Bettelheim observed. He suggested that myths and fairy tales help children to deal with some of these questions and the fears associated with such questions about existence (Bettelheim 1982).

Conclusion

Practitioners have to balance two considerations when working with young children. The first is that it should never be assumed that abuse, neglect or trauma in infancy have a lesser impact than in later years. Every effort must be taken to protect the very young child from circumstances that are likely to stunt their physical, cognitive and emotional development because such trauma in early years can be associated with significant problems in the longer term. By the same token, though, it should not be assumed that early trauma is disastrous and will necessarily blight the rest of the child's life. Practitioners who offer appropriate intervention can make a long-term difference because adversity in early life can be compensated for and the worst effects can be ameliorated if the appropriate support is offered.

CHAPTER 11

Middle Childhood: Five to Eleven Years

Gillian Schofield

The period from five to eleven years old is often seen as a relatively quiet period developmentally, as suggested by Freud's term 'latency', in contrast to the more dramatic changes of the early years or of adolescence. However, the developmental tasks, challenges and opportunities involved in the development of the self in this period, in the context of a wide range of social relationships, lay down the basis on which adolescence and the transition to adulthood will be more or less successfully navigated. From a practitioner perspective, the transition to school at age five is very often a point at which some children whose behaviour and relationship difficulties may have been managed, tolerated or overlooked in the home setting are revealed to have significant developmental problems when faced with the expectations of school. Middle childhood is also particularly significant for children's services workers, since it is a period when many major developmental concerns, such as conduct disorders, attention deficit hyperactivity disorder and learning disabilities, are likely to be picked up and will require an accurate and appropriate response. The sources of such difficulties need to be understood in the context not only of what we know about children's previous development in early childhood, but also what we should expect in the normal developmental processes of middle childhood. This requires an understanding not only of the separate areas of development but of how these interact. It also requires an awareness of how the child's characteristics interact with the community and family environments in which they are growing up.

Physical development

Although the rate of physical growth slows during this period, the pattern of that growth will continue to be affected by the interaction of genetic and environmental factors. Genes influence body shape and size, but the quality of nutrition will also have an impact on physical development, with this period seeing the onset of obesity in increasing numbers of children, for example. Boys tend to be stronger than girls, girls tend to be more agile than boys, but diet will have an impact on both, affecting the extent to which boys *and* girls have the energy to benefit from the increased complexity and agility of gross motor skills that occurs in this period. This is an age when physical play and activity remain important sources of self-expression and shared fun, but there is a wide range of levels of activity, from children who may be hyperactive to those who are listless and lack energy – with healthy children likely to display energetic but focused and purposeful physical activity.

Towards the end of this age period some girls will be reaching puberty. It is important to remember that the timing of puberty can affect self-esteem, with the additional possibility that early maturing children will mix with older adolescents who may engage them in more risk taking activities. The interaction here of physical development, a sense of self and peer group relationships, important particularly in thinking about the impact of sensory and physical disabilities in this age group, suggests the need to be very aware of the role of physical development as a source of potential strengths and difficulties.

Cognitive development (including language and communication)

The changes in a child's thinking in middle childhood are major influences in all areas of development: psychosocial, emotional and moral. This is an age period when children become better able to think logically, to be able to work things out for themselves – what Piaget called the *concrete operational* period (6–11) (Piaget and Inhelder 1969). As Vygotsky (1978) suggests, however, although children can learn through their own exploration, there is a gap, which he called the *zone of proximal development*, between the developmental level achievable by independent problem solving and the level of potential development achievable in a social context i.e. with the support and direct teaching of adults and other more competent children. This model promotes the targeted use of learning guidance for all children, but is especially relevant for those children who have disabilities or other special needs and who arrive in school without the skills or the capacity to make purposeful use of the materials available independently.

Children in middle childhood make big strides in terms of understanding the rules of the physical world, such as conservation of mass (discussed in Chapter 10 in relation to early childhood), but they also start to understand, apply and indeed insist on the application of rules in other contexts, particularly in their playing of rule-based games. Thinking is the way in which children make sense of themselves and their environments and learn the rules relevant to their lives. They need effective ways of processing all the new information that is coming to them. Children in middle childhood not only have increasingly powerful memories, they also develop increasingly complex strategies for retrieving information from their memories and for problem solving generally. They develop metacognition, the ability to reflect on their own mental life. They know, for example, that they need to concentrate in order to remember a difficult fact or to complete a task. They also begin to reflect on thoughts and feelings in a more subtle and complex way. The development of *theory of mind* in the pre-school years equips middle childhood children with the capacity to think about their own minds and the differences in the minds of others, in order to deal more successfully with the complexity of the social world they now face.

For children growing up in adverse family environments, and for maltreated children in particular, the capacity to think has often been damaged or distorted. They may not have had the kind of predictable emotional environment or the kind of safe access to the mind of a protective caregiver that provides a cognitive scaffolding and enables children to mentalise, to think about their own minds and the minds of others and to come up with options and strategies (Fonagy *et al.* 1991). Research on children in foster care suggests that these difficulties can emerge not only in relation to academic learning and the social world but also in relation to apparently simple things, such as the ability to tell the time (Schofield *et al.* 2000). Just at the age when these troubled children are looking most urgently for rules to make sense of the world in order to feel safe in it, they find that their worlds often do not make much sense.

For looked after and adopted children, there are, in addition, complicated kinds of information that need to be processed. Brodzinsky (1990) suggested that it is at the age of 7 or 8 that adopted children often start to question who they are and where they come from. Adoptive parents and their support workers need to understand that the sudden asking of such questions does not indicate a problem in the adoption, but is simply a normal consequence of a cognitive developmental need to make logical sense of information – including, and perhaps most significantly, information about the self. Practitioners should be aware that children of this age have an increasing developmental need to understand themselves and their circumstances. Middle childhood children in foster care and adoption, who have complex histories to make sense of, will often have the least capacity to process the information, particularly if their thinking has been distorted by their early caregiving experiences. Involving children in decision making and life story work is all the more important, but the challenges for the child and the worker should not be underestimated (Schofield 1998b, 2005).

The use of *language and communication* in this age period is inevitably an important way for the child to learn, to manage information, to make sense of the social world and to build relationships. Children are increasingly competent communicators, adding to their vocabulary by on average 20 words a day between the ages of 5 and 11 (Berk 2003). But middle childhood children can also understand and use more subtleties of language, knowing that some words such as 'cool' have multiple meanings and that feeling words, such as 'like' and 'dislike'/'love' and 'hate', have different meanings and impact differently on other people. Here too, however, we know that children who have not experienced the appropriate cognitive and linguistic stimulation or clarity in early childhood often lack the foundations on which they can build in middle childhood. This affects children's learning in an academic context, but also affects the capacity to communicate their needs and feelings in subtle and accurate ways, leaving them prey to social withdrawal or to frustration and aggression.

As in early childhood, language provides the *scaffolding* that assists children to see the world as predictable and to learn its rules. This process not only promotes children's learning and development, it reduces anxiety and promotes self-efficacy. Parents and children's services professionals therefore need to talk children through the changes that are happening to them and what is now expected of them. The language used to help the child needs to be appropriate, in terms of cognitive stage and emotional age, as well as in terms of other factors such as culture and ethnicity. Disabled children have the same developmental need to understand their environments, but may lack receptive or expressive language and communication skills. However, even children with very severe learning disabilities who have no speech can benefit from nonverbal scaffolding and can be enabled, for example, to anticipate contact with birth parents or to express a preference for the colour of their new bedroom (Beek and Schofield 2004a, 2004b).

Psychosocial development

In middle childhood, children enter school and find a world of new physical environments and new relationships with other people, adults and children from outside the family. In order to 'fit in' and benefit from the opportunities now available, they have a number of developmental tasks as they adapt to the rules of these new worlds (Collins 1984):

- developing a relatively stable and comprehensive understanding of the self
- refining one's understanding of how the social world works
- developing standards and expectations of one's own behaviour
- developing strategies for controlling or managing one's behaviour.

Developing a relatively stable and comprehensive understanding of the self
From birth onwards children are developing a sense of self – who they are and how they are valued by important people around them. The challenge of middle childhood is to build on those foundations and to find ways of accommodating the messages they already have about who they are, their self-concept and their self-esteem, in the wider social world. This process is strongly linked with their new cognitive capacities. The search for logic and for rules means that issues such as racial, cultural and gender identities have to be clarified, justified and defended to others. Most children are likely to have some clear sense of who they are even at the age of five, but there are still many lessons to be learned, for example about how a boy or girl of a

certain age is expected to behave in this particular playground. They are at the height of their need to find rules that define themselves and others. Stereotyping rules are often applied insistently once learned and it is not surprising that the most rigid attitudes towards gender, towards those who speak a different language or towards those of a different ethnicity are expressed by 7–8 year olds (Doyle and Aboud 1995). However, this then declines in late middle childhood into adolescence as thinking becomes more abstract and more flexible.

The key message for practitioners in this area of psychosocial development is that it presents particular challenges for children who find themselves unable to define themselves in ways recognised and accepted by other children, which may include children from minority cultures, children looked after or adopted, children from stigmatised groups such as traveller children or asylum-seeking children. These children need help to place themselves in their own minds in terms of identity so that they can manage their diverse social worlds and the in-group/out-group nature of middle childhood peer groups. Self-concept and self-esteem go hand in hand here, since it is knowing who you are *and* valuing it that will enable the primary school child not just to cope with but to enjoy social relationships. But the more vulnerable child in the more challenging environment (for example, a racist or bullying group culture) will also need more practical and active social supports.

Refining one's understanding of how the social world works

Learning from and thriving in the social world requires lessons to be learned about how the world works in terms of social roles, how to behave and how to manage the self in relationships. This is what Dunn (1993) refers to as 'social intelligence'. Children at this age should have already learned about the basic differences between what doctors and postmen do, for example, and that queuing is expected at bus stops or to pay for shopping. But they now need to learn more subtle social skills, such as how to gain entrance to a game of skipping or football, how to judge who would make a trustworthy friend and so on. Their social expertise is often promoted by the diversity of situations and relationships to which they are exposed in activities and clubs, a source of growth and resilience that is often targeted in residential care, foster care and adoption (Beek and Schofield 2004b; Gilligan 2000; Schofield *et al.* 2000) but also needs to be a focus in family support.

Some children by the age of 5 will already have begun to learn these lessons in the home and at the playgroup or nursery, but it is very striking that for many children who come from more deprived, chaotic families even the most basic understanding of how the social world works is missing. Often these are children who have not attended playgroups and nurseries. On entering school, the etiquette of the classroom, the school assembly or the dinner queue is a mystery to them and this can be a source of anxiety for the child which drives their disruptive behaviour.

Developing standards and expectations of one's own behaviour

An important consequence of sensitive parenting in early childhood, which has facilitated the development of a stable self-concept and a knowledge of the social world, is that these secure children are enabled to enter middle childhood with a wide-ranging set of standards and expectations of their own behaviour. This might include the tone of voice that is appropriate for a child when speaking to different adults. It would include knowing that fighting to get another child's toy is not acceptable. Such core social and moral principles need to be extensively developed and become much more sophisticated by the time the child reaches adolescence. However, where children have not been given role models or clear messages about how to behave, then developing these standards from scratch in the school and community settings is often hard to achieve. This is an area of development which family centres and other support services or the foster carers and adopters of looked after children need to target specifically.

Developing strategies for controlling or managing one's behaviour

At the heart of the successful negotiation of this period developmentally is the notion that children become largely self-regulating. Children who have received positive messages about the value of the self, who have had clear messages in early childhood about what is expected, who have internalised standards *and* who have had their autonomy and self-efficacy promoted can monitor and manage their own behaviour. This can be seen in children as young as 3, but certainly by 5 the process should be well established and continues to evolve during the primary years as children move towards being able to walk to school on their own, sit still in assembly, work patiently through school tests and so on. This process is assisted by the cognitive shifts that allow for more sophisticated information processing and more sophisticated strategies for thinking through options. Children use their strategies to learn how to manage their behaviour in new situations and stay within the rules. They may also enjoy and learn from playing with the rules. As Dunn has suggested in her research on early childhood (1988, 1993), children learn the pleasure of breaking rules and testing the boundaries, joking and treating the rules humorously. This certainly continues in middle childhood. But it can become apparent that although for most children this testing out simply confirms their core knowledge of the rules and their ability to manage their behaviour in the light of those rules, some children find it impossible to regulate their behaviour. Many children causing concern to practitioners appear to lack strategies to manage their behaviour so that boundaries are repeatedly and excessively crossed. While one child may give another child a gentle push in the playground, that other child may completely lose control and retaliate causing serious physical hurt to the child who has upset them. This is exceptional behaviour but not untypical of middle childhood children who lack strategies for managing their behaviour, often the case for those who have experienced poor or maltreating parenting.

Although there is in theory plenty of time as they move through the primary years for children from troubled backgrounds to learn these important lessons about the self and the social world and to learn how to regulate their behaviour, in practice disastrous starts at primary school can shock anxious and confused children into extreme withdrawal or into highly aggressive behaviour. It may seem excessive to find children excluded from school at the age of five or six, and yet when teachers and other children have been taken to hospital as a result of attacks by a particular child with a history of abuse or neglect, the gap between the normal expectations of children entering school and what some children can manage is stark. Systems of rewards and sanctions designed to change behaviour at school appeal to reason and a capacity for self-regulation, whereas children with poor parenting experiences, and particularly children who have been maltreated, often find it impossible to plan and manage their behaviour in terms of its consequences. These problems almost certainly existed in the pre-school years, but are thrown into sharp relief by the school context and the developmental demands and expectations of middle childhood.

Emotional development

Just as increasing self-regulation of behaviour is an important part of psychosocial development in middle childhood, so self-regulation of emotions is an important milestone in emotional development. It is useful to think of these two areas as closely related, since the failure to regulate behaviour, the extreme aggressive attack in the playground for example, is likely to derive not only from a difficulty in understanding and meeting behavioural expectations, but from two related factors in emotional development – first, the child may be overwhelmed by anxiety and emotions such as jealousy or anger and, second, the child may lack the emotional understanding and perspective taking skills needed to empathise with the child who is being hurt.

As with behavioural self-regulation, the process of regulating their own emotions will for most children have started young – towards the end of the first year. In attachment theory terms (Bowlby 1969; Howe et al. 1999; Schofield and Beek forthcoming), explored in Chapter 4, as the infant or toddler starts to use the caregiver as a secure base and can physically move towards exploration and back again, it becomes possible to avoid being overwhelmed by sadness or anger by seeking comfort. In middle childhood this process of regulating emotion is more likely to be occurring at the level of mental representations. The secure child at home or at school may need to seek comfort actively from an attachment figure or a teacher if distressed, but is more likely to manage their emotions in most situations by drawing on an internal working model that represents themselves as loved and effective and others as available and protective. This enables them to be appropriately assertive when stressed – they may demand their ball back – but they would not feel so much under threat as to attack if refused. Not only do they have a repertoire of behavioural strategies (for example, ask the teacher, find another ball), their self-esteem and range of cognitive strategies for explaining the situation and dealing with it in a positive way allows them to regulate their emotions.

As these origins of emotional self-regulation suggest, however, insecurely attached children will have a range of difficulties in regulating their emotions (George 1996). In middle childhood avoidant children, for example, continue to defend against affect and inhibit the expression of emotion, even though they remain intensely anxious and suppress emotion in order to achieve safe proximity. However, the behavioural avoidance of early childhood is replaced by psychological inhibition in this age group

(Howe *et al.* 1999) and it is possible to see compulsive compliance developing among some children, for example. Positive self-regard for these children is conditional on the suppression of anger and hurt and the display of self-reliance and achievement. However, for some avoidant children the tendency to be dismissive of their own and others' emotions, combined with experiences of rejection, can lead to their becoming bullies.

Emotional self-regulation is particularly difficult for ambivalent/ resistant children who are disinhibited and attempt to achieve proximity by excessive emotional demands for attention, switching from displays of need to displays of anger. This is often reflected in switches from coy to coercive behaviour and back to coy behaviour, to protect the self from the rejection arising from the coercive behaviour. Difficult to manage at home, the child will export this behavioural strategy into relationships with teachers and friends. The pattern makes for stormy friendships, with special friends becoming worst enemies in an instant and with groups of friends left in turmoil. Extravagant claims may be made about friendships by a troubled child in foster care, for example, but often the child is actually isolated, disappointed and angry (Beek and Schofield 2004b). Severely neglected children in this group may be more passive and helpless, with displays of emotion that simply communicate distress. Such children are often unable to regulate their shows of distress, lacking both self-esteem and self-efficacy.

As Crittenden (1995) emphasises, disorganised children in infancy are helpless and chaotic, but in the later pre-school years and into middle childhood they are forced to construct a survival strategy. They are likely to become increasingly controlling and manipulative in order to stay in charge, but there also may be outbursts of distress and rage, since they have poor emotional scaffolding and poor affect regulation. Disorganised attachment in infancy is found to be associated with hostility and aggression in early and middle childhood (Lyons-Ruth 1996). However, disorganised children may show a range of behaviours, including compulsive self-reliance, compulsive caregiving or punitive behaviour. The goal for them is to be or to feel safe by controlling the distance between themselves and others. This often includes the development of a false self. Thus disorganised children of five or six meeting their new adoptive or long-term foster parents may present as quiet, well behaved and smiley, but the lack of genuine emotional expression and engagement can rapidly undermine the placement.

Moral and spiritual development

Firmly linked to the concept of regulation and arising from much that has been described in terms of understanding the social world is the nature of moral development in middle childhood. Kohlberg's model of the development of moral reasoning builds on Piaget's theory of cognitive development and has parallel shifts in thinking at different ages (Kohlberg 1976). Although some aspects of moral development, such as empathy for others, are present among pre-schoolers, at age five to six, Kohlberg suggests that the child is likely to adhere to moral rules in order to avoid punishment and simply conform to the superior power of adults. By the age of seven or eight, the child starts to make decisions based on self-interest, aware that each person has their own interests and that these will be different from his or her own. The major shift in this period, according to this model, is around age eight to nine, when there begins to be a clearer sense that making the 'right' decision and obeying moral laws is a matter of living up to what is expected of you by people important to you. There is the wish to be 'a good person' in one's own eyes and the eyes of others. Although it seems likely that there is a progression of this kind, the social emotions of shame and guilt, the decision to act in certain ways in order to conform to standards set by others, will for many children be developing in the pre-school years if they have been enabled to be sensitive to the feelings of others in the context of secure relationships.

Moral *behaviour* and the making of moral and pro-social choices will rely not only on the development of moral reasoning, but also on social cognition, the capacity to 'read' other people and to be able to understand their perspective. In this sense, moral choices are likely to depend on cognitive, psychosocial and emotional development, since these bridge the gap between the child *knowing* the right thing to do in a particular situation in a particular culture at a particular point in time and the likelihood of his or her *doing* it.

The spiritual development of children (Crompton 1992) is connected with moral development, but has many other layers that connect with religion and culture. As with other aspects of their world, children of this age can adopt and draw on models that go beyond the merely physical or social. They are looking for a direction and moral rules to guide them. Children who have been brought up with access to constructive ways of interpreting the world through faith, that make sense and give them comfort and reassurance, need to have this resource valued and promoted in their lives.

Conclusion

As this account demonstrates, development across these various domains can be understood as interlocking, with growth in one area facilitating growth in others. This integrated and interactive approach to understanding the mind and behaviour of the child in middle childhood helps us to understand how upward spirals, based on firm cognitive and emotional scaffolding, self-esteem and self-efficacy, self-regulation of behaviour and emotion, contrast with downward spirals, arising from adverse early and current experiences in the home, the school and the community, which leave them ill-equipped to take these next developmental steps. The interaction of home, school and community as environments offers opportunities for growth, fun, learning and intimacy, but also represents major challenges for children who lack the basic developmental building blocks. There are clearly arguments here for targeting the early years as an area for intervention. But for children who have arrived in school or started to move out into their communities and almost immediately find failure and rejection, professional regrets about the tardiness of the intervention are not helpful. Very active interventions in middle childhood, that acknowledge the need to target cognitive, psychosocial, emotional and moral development simultaneously, are required.

CHAPTER 12

Adolescence and Beyond: Twelve Years Onwards

Susan Bailey

> I would there were no age between ten and three and twenty, or that youth would sleep out the rest, for there is nothing in the between but getting wenches with child, wronging the ancientry, stealing, fighting. (*The Winter's Tale,* Act III Scene III, William Shakespeare, c.1611)

More than any other time in the life-course, adolescence is the stage of possibility and of promises and worries (Oyserman and Martois 1990). Adolescence is a transitional stage of development between childhood and adulthood. The developmental tasks of adolescence centre on autonomy and connection with others, rebellion and the development of independence, development of identity and distinction from and continuity with others. The physical changes of puberty are generally seen as the starting point of adolescence whilst the end is less clearly delineated. Adolescence ends with attainment of 'full maturity'. A range of social and cultural influences, including the legal age of majority, may influence the definition of maturity. As writers such as Owusu-Bempah and Howitt (2000b) have pointed out, definitions of maturity may differ in other cultures from Western views of 'independence' and embrace a view of maturity that emphasises integration into designated groups.

The aim of this chapter is to explore some of the developmental processes during the period of adolescence and the practical implications for working with young people. It looks particularly at mental health issues and the factors which may influence adolescent mental health problems. Finally, it explores the vulnerabilities that transition to adulthood may bring. Throughout the chapter, the author has drawn on the accumulated works of John Coleman, on the theme of adolescent development.

As the following statistics show, the adolescent population in the UK constitutes half the child population and there are around 7.5 million young people in the transitional stage between childhood and adulthood.

Table 12.1: Young people in the United Kingdom

Adolescent population	7.5 million
Age 10–14	3.9 million
Age 15–19	3.6 million

Source: Social Trends 32, 2003 edition, Office for National Statistics.

Mortality among adolescents, in contrast to almost all other age groups, did not fall during the second half of the twentieth century, the main causes being accidents and self-harm (Coleman and Schofield 2003). Health needs are greater in this age band than in children in middle childhood (5 to 12 years) or of young adults, and arises mainly out of chronic illness and mental health problems.

The main concerns of young people, in relation to health, focus on issues of immediacy that have an impact on their relations with peers and include problems with skin, weight, appearance, emotions and sexual health including contraception (Gleeson, Robinson and Neal 2002).

The growing evidence for the fundamental inter-relationship between physical, mental and social health is strong. Problems in adolescence in any of these areas indicate the likelihood of long-term adverse health and social consequences. Patterns of health behaviours established in adolescence are significant and may be maintained through adult life. These behaviours may include:

- smoking
- substance misuse
- eating disorders
- physical activity (or inactivity)

- obesity

- sexual risk taking.

Their prevalence and consequences are likely be exaggerated by the impact of poverty.

Development process in adolescence

There are many significant writers who have influenced our understanding of adolescence in the West. For example, in his developmental classification, Sigmund Freud suggested that normal development from the age of 11 constitutes the genital stage, a final stage of psychosexual development beginning with puberty and the biological capacity for orgasm but importantly involving the capacity for true intimacy. Erikson (1968) conceptualised age 11 through to the end of adolescence as 'identity vs. role diffusion', where there is:

- a struggle to develop ego identity (a sense of inner sameness and continuity)

- a pre-occupation with appearance, hero worship and ideology

- risk of role confusion (doubts about sexual and vocational identity)

- psychological moratorium (a stage between morality learnt by the child and the ethics to be developed as an adult).

For some, the adolescent's route to sexual maturity may be complicated (for example, by the experience of direct sexual abuse as a younger child). This leaves multiple points of possible and untoward departure, although strands of development eventually combine to produce the sexual adult. In girls, normal puberty begins with breast development (between the ages of 8 and 13) and extends over about four years with menarche occurring on average at 13 years, although there can be considerable variation. In boys, the first change is in testicular size, although this can be preceded by the growth of pubic hair. Pubertal changes begin between 10 and 15 years of age and last for 5 years before sexual maturity is reached. First ejaculation occurs on average at 13 years. Psychosexual maturation involves the development of gender identity, gender role and sexual behaviour.

In addition to the basic function of reproduction, sexual behaviour may fulfil the following functions:

- assertion of masculinity or femininity

- bolstering or maintenance of self-esteem

- exertion of power or dominance

- bonding dyadic relationships and fostering intimacy

- source of pleasure

- reduction of tension

- expression of hostility

- risk taking as a source of excitement

- material gain.

The period of adolescence is likely to be one of experimentation when one or more of these functions may be tested out.

Cognitive development

Cognitive development is a main feature of developmental process at this stage, attracting the attention of developmentalists (see, for example, Morrison and Anders 1999; Rutter and Hay 1994; and Mussen *et al.* 1990). The classic theorist on child development, Jean Piaget (1932) suggested, within his theoretical framework, that 11 years through to the end of adolescence constitutes the formal (abstract) age characterised by:

- hypothetical deductive reasoning, not only on the basis of objects but also on the basis of hypotheses and propositions

- being capable of thinking about one's thoughts

- an ability to grasp the concept of probabilities

- an ability to think in abstract forms.

Emotional and social development

In general, in our society, the adolescent exists in a world with which parents are unfamiliar and in which they share less. Home is a base. The school experience accelerates and intensifies the degree of separation from the family. The real world is school and the most important relationships are those with people of similar ages and interests.

The development of empathy and concern for others has occurred by late childhood. In early adolescence (11 to 14 years) puberty starts with an increase in the sex drive, this being most often vented through masturbation. Boys are easily aroused by stimuli and erections are frequent. Sexual impulse is more closely related to other feelings, which view sex and love as related. The early adolescent is still attached to the family and it is suggested that there is some resurgence of oedipal feelings with even sexual fantasies towards the opposite sex parent. In general, these thoughts and feelings are repressed, and young people's sexuality is directed outwards, in the form of crushes, hero worship and idealisation of film and pop stars (Calam 2001).

In middle adolescence (14 to 17 years) the following commonly occur:

- social behaviour and experimentation with a variety of sexual roles

- masturbation occurring equally in both sexes

- heterosexual crushes, usually with someone unobtainable.

Homosexual activity may also occur at this time although it is usually but not always transient.

The peer group, with its membership constantly shifting, and its roles never formally defined, is a vital agency for social growth and change (as discussed in Chapter 8). For the first time, the adolescent is likely to form relationships that lack the familiarity and security of those with parents and siblings. For most adolescents, the peer group consists of a core of a small number of sustained and emotionally significant friendships, from which emanate numbers of less defined contacts with others who come and go. Peer groups have the capacity for great social pressure, exercised in the context of basic acceptance and support. Social pressure does much to shape both the adolescent's character and values, with a very heavy demand for conformity to the group ideal.

Personality characteristics are seen to develop as an interaction with the environment, with an intricate balance and interplay with innate determinants and unconscious processes. In the passage to late adolescence (17 to 20 years), adolescents slowly start to blend many different values from all kind of sources into their own existing values.

Moral development

Moral understanding subsumes cognitive and emotional factors that have an impact on young people's awareness of the consequences of their behaviour for self or others.

Morality is used to describe a set of personal principles conforming to social standards of behaviour, rectitude, emotions, guilt and shame, and pro-social activities, such as helpfulness, generosity and enthusiasm. Guilt involves the appreciation of negative outcomes resulting from acts of omission. Shame is associated with negative feelings about the self, and perception of self as bad or unworthy. Cognitive appreciation of wrong involves an awareness of rules, both personal and social and the consequences of breaking such rules.

In early adolescence, thinking processes that become more abstract, multidimensional and self-aware mean adolescents can generate more alternatives when making decisions. They can check out both their own thought processes and those of others for inconsistencies. They start to look back with regret and forward with apprehension. Key to the development of moral understanding in childhood and on into early adolescence are the role of family, family rules, notions of blame and the emotional quality of family relationships. Family disruption can result in impaired attachments and capacity to appreciate one's own and others' feeling states. In turn, impaired attachments can lead to impaired empathy and decreased understanding of wrongfulness of actions.

Utilising Kohlberg's (1970, 1984) theoretical framework of moral development, as discussed in the previous chapter, by adolescence young people have usually reached the stage of *conventional morality*:

> *Kohlberg's Stage 3* is characterised by the desire to attain and maintain harmony in relationships, to be good and to seek the approval of others.

> *Kohlberg's Stage 4* brings with it the concept of morality opening out to include societal norms rather than solely the confines of family and close associates. The young person will then be orientated towards obeying laws and performing duties, the notion of just rewards becomes salient.

The adolescent then progresses to *postconventional morality*:

> *In Kohlberg's Stage 5*, the individual believes that laws are a social contract that should be recognised in the interest of democracy.

There may be conflict between moral justice and the law but there must be a democratic way of challenging the law. At the beginning of this stage, moral behaviour tends to be thought of in terms of general rights and standards agreed upon by society as a whole, but at later moments there is an increasing orientation towards internal decisions of conscience.

Kohlberg's Stage 6 introduces the universal ethical principle. At this stage there is an attempt to formulate and be guided by abstract ethical principles.

When relating moral development to adolescents, it is important to remember:

- cultural biases are of great importance – what is morally reprehensible in one society may be acceptable in others for example, polygamy, child labour

- moral reasoning, but not necessarily a person's morality, is affected by intellectual ability

- theory of mind is important

- social experience can shape moral development

- socio-political contexts influence both the evolution of theoretical frameworks and the adolescent at his or her point in present history.

Thinking and reasoning

The shift in the early teenage years towards more abstract thought needs to be taken into account by any adult who comes into contact with this age group. A growing capacity for logical and scientific reasoning will affect the young person's skills in communication, decision-making and negotiation. This has implications for education in the way that formal teaching can encourage critical thinking. Young people can appear to those who live and work with them as extremely self-centred. Awareness of the fact that egocentrism is a normal element of the cognitive development of adolescence can assist adults to put this behaviour into perspective.

Self-concept develops rapidly during the adolescent period and is linked to concomitant physical, cognitive and emotional growth. For those working with young people, it is important to recognise the impact that the development of the self-concept has on interpersonal relationships.

Self-esteem has a powerful influence on adjustment across a wide range of domains in a young person's life, as was discussed in Chapter 5. Educational achievements, social relationships, mental health, ability to deal with stress are all affected by self-esteem. In practice, interventions with adolescents have to be shaped so that they are appropriate to the individual's own developmental pathway.

Erikson (1968) placed emphasis on the concept of identity crisis in adolescence. However, although identity development is central during this developmental stage, it does not necessarily have to take the form of a crisis. Rather, an individual is likely to pass through various stages with considerable fluctuation from one stage to another, only reaching a resolution of the identity during later years of adolescence. It must be remembered that the desired identity will be shaped by cultural expectations (Quinton 1994).

The importance of ethnic identity

The importance of ethnic identity (Phinney and Rosenthal 1992) cannot be over-emphasised. Those working with young people need to recognise the importance of this dimension of adolescent development. There will be wide individual differences, and culture, context and social background will all have their effect on the salience or otherwise of this feature of identity.

Where children and their families have migrated from one culture to another, for the children there may be tensions because of clashes of expectations between the two cultures. As Quinton suggests:

> Cross cultural migrants are especially subject to these problems, as well as to stresses associated with dislocation of family and friendship ties, and to poor housing and occupational restriction due to prejudice. For the second generation, further stresses arise through conflicts between parental cultural beliefs and the children's desire to acculturate and become more like the young people in the new culture. (1994, p.168)

Phinney and Devich-Navarro (1997) describe these patterns as assimilation and fusion with the mainstream culture, where individuals manage to fuse the two cultures so they become one. The two cultures are perceived as overlapping, with the individual occupying the middle ground.

Alternatively, there may be those who identify solely with one culture and reject the other, or are forced to find a position outside both cultures. Such choices are particularly demanding for adolescents.

The influence of parenting and peers

Parenting styles (Rutter *et al.* 1998) that are shown to be 'consistently authoritative' have the most beneficial effect on adolescent development since this includes warmth, structure and support for autonomy. Rutter *et al.* (1998) and others stress the importance for adolescents of parental knowledge about what children are doing, including monitoring and supervision of activities outside and inside the home, but suggest the effects are more influential upon girls, whereas boys may be more influenced by peer pressure in spite of parental activity. Authoritarian, indifferent or indulgent parenting styles have effects which, whilst differing to some extent, all encourage less adaptive adolescent development. Fathers are equally as important as mothers. Equal effort and attention in a practical situation should be applied to the role of fathers and how to support fathers during the stage when children become teenagers.

Divorce will have an effect on teenagers (Butler *et al.* 2003) but divorce is part of a process. Adjustment to this event in the life of adolescents will be influenced by a range of experiences rather than by the divorce itself, not least the quality of communication throughout the process (as is noted in Chapter 16). Normally, the fewer life changes the young person has to manage, the better they will cope with parental separation.

The development of autonomy in young people may not occur entirely during the adolescent stage. There is a continuing connectedness with parents for both young men and young women and it forms a helpful transition to adulthood. Whilst there may be many issues about which parents and young people disagree, in general relationships appear to be more positive than negative and, in the majority of families, there is still no evidence of substantial inter-generational conflict. In practice, a major factor that will have an impact on the level of conflict is good communication between parents and young people. Conflict is highest where parents themselves have poor relationships, where the families have experienced stress or difficulty because of environmental factors, and where there has been long standing impairment of parental capacity.

Although a peer group becomes more influential during the adolescent years, this does not mean to say that parents no longer have any part to play.

Parents and peers need not necessarily be in opposition to each other, rather the two groups may be influential in different areas. Young people will listen to their friends when it comes to questions of fashion or social convention but will refer to their parents over school issues, careers and morality. Young people often choose friends who have views similar to those of their parents but they may deny these similarities. Because friendship and acceptance in the peer group are so important during adolescence, those who are isolated or rejected are highlighted and, in particular, disadvantaged. Loneliness can be difficult to deal with especially when everyone else appears to be part of a group.

The extension of compulsory schooling, and the development of further education with its economic consequences, generally contributes to a delay in reaching full independence (Coleman and Schofield 2003). This has an especially powerful effect on all young people. Leisure patterns follow developmental trajectories with a typical pattern involving a gradual evolution from home and school based activities to those located in the wider social setting. Leisure patterns are determined by both gender and social background. Difficult times, such as being unable to find employment or living within a troubled family, may lead young people to seek pleasure in the here and now, since there appears to be little hope in the future.

Despite media views, the fact that more young people are engaged in pro-social activities needs to be recognised. Family plays a key role in fostering involvement in voluntary and campaigning activities but schools and community agencies have a part to play in this by providing opportunities. Volunteering and campaigning has a benefit to all young people irrespective of their circumstances. This applies equally if not more so to young people who are disabled. The greater the opportunities for adolescents to be of service to others, the more beneficial in terms of their own personal and social development.

Sexual activity and health

From the evidence (Coleman and Hendry 1999) available today, there are more young people who engage in sexual activity and at an earlier age. This change is closely linked to the changes in the pattern of adult sexual behaviour and cannot be seen in isolation from other social trends. It has particular implications for educators and parents and underlines the importance of the timing of effective health and sex education. To be effective, sex education has to be conceptualised in an holistic manner, incorporated into a healthy living curriculum in schools or integrated with other health provision in the community.

The impact of HIV and AIDS on young people has been considerable. It has led to a widespread focus on safer sex, young people's knowledge about sexual matters, their attitude to contraceptive practice and the accessibility of condoms. There is growing knowledge about the recognition of the circumstances that affect young people who develop as gay, lesbian or bi-sexual during adolescence. These groups can face difficulties as the result of prejudice and negative stereotyping.

Teenage parenthood has received a high degree of attention particularly in the UK where rates of teenage pregnancy are higher than in other Western countries (Coleman and Schofield 2003). It is important that appropriate support to young people can be given to help them to become effective parents. Practitioners need to concentrate on strategies that facilitate parenting skills amongst young parents rather than emphasising their limitations.

Understanding what lies behind young people's risk-taking behaviour will be helpful in any health intervention. Whilst risk-taking is normally perceived by adults as a bad thing, for adolescents risk behaviour carries with it a number of rewards. In particular, risk-taking assists in securing recognition in the peer group or enables the young person to push against adult boundaries, and therefore contributes to identity development.

It is essential for adult professionals to recognise that adolescent concepts of health and health risk are not the same as those understood by older people. Young people may not worry about the future, may not avoid all risks, but this does not mean that they are not concerned about their health. Health interventions that will be most effective will be those where appropriate emphasis is given to the factors which influence young people rather than those which are set in the minds of adults.

Working with adolescents – practical implications

As well as recognising the influence of young people's attitudes towards their health, those working with young people need to be aware of mismatches between different aspects of development. Not all aspects of development proceed at an even pace and there are reasons to suppose that a mismatch between the various aspects of development is a particularly potent contributor to difficulties. This mismatch may be between aspects of intellectual functioning, or between physical and emotional development.

For example, specific reading delay, i.e. a delay greater than two years beyond that which would usually be expected for an individual child, seems to have a greater association with conduct disorder than general delays of equivalent magnitude (Gowers 2003).

Similarly, it is probable that a mismatch between physical and emotional development leads to comparable problems. Emotionally immature boys or girls who are physically mature and look older than their years may find themselves involved in demanding relationships with which they feel ill equipped to cope. Those working with young people need to be aware that outward appearances may belie the inner changes taking place.

Adolescents who are properly prepared for the arrival of puberty adjust better than those who have had little preparation. Parents, teachers and others who work with young people have to have a greater sensitivity to the needs and potential difficulties of early and late maturers (as both may be vulnerable). Support at the right time from a concerned adult may make a difference to the adjustment of the young person.

In any assessment of and in working with adolescents in difficulties, engagement has particular challenges (Gowers 2004). Problems are often brought to professionals in the form of someone who is complaining about the adolescent. Some adolescents lack confidence in their ability to put their ideas into words and may have experienced several poor relationships with authority figures at home, school and the police. Those working with adolescents require a mindset that does not compound former problems but one which recognises that the young people themselves have many strengths and potentialities, if only they are allowed to lead professionals into their perspectives on the world. It has been demonstrated that developing adolescents can be critical actors in shaping the environment in which they live, for example, by bringing abut improvements in libraries, leisure facilities and bus services in partnership with adults in local schools and councils (Cairns 2001). Such advances emanate from a mindset which values young people. As Cairns (2004, p.4) suggests: 'It seems reasonable to me that we provide a platform for young people to express their views of the world and their interpretation of events. There will be times when their views don't match ours and their interpretation differs from ours, but that's what you would expect.'

Anti-social behaviour

One of the main issues which challenges adults in relation to young people is anti-social behaviour. There are different types of anti-social behaviour with different developmental trajectories. It is important to make a distinction between behaviour which is life-course persistent and that which is adolescent limited. Factors underlying these behaviours will not be the same and, therefore, interventions will need to be tailored to the specific type of anti-social behaviour in question.

Much has been learnt about the possible interventions available for those involved in antisocial behaviour, including the development of social and cognitive skills, the enhancement of parenting capacity, the modification of disadvantaged environments and the support of positive peer groups. Studies of interventions show that opportunities for employment are possibly the more powerful of all options but, in addition, those interventions which are multimodal are more likely to be successful than those which concentrate on one modality at a time (Bailey 2002; Rutter *et al.* 1998).

Mental health

There is still stigmatisation associated with contact with mental health services. It is clear that a significant number of adolescents experience a range of difficulties in the arena of mental and emotional health, in particular problems around bullying, conflict at home or with close friends, feelings of depression or even suicide (Hawton *et al.* 1999). It is not unusual to find that health services and interventions for young people have been planned by adults with little reference to the needs of those most concerned. Where resources exist, those which have been planned jointly with young people have a much higher rate of success. Mental health is an area where all too often adult concerns obscure the real needs of young people.

Psychiatric disorders of adolescence

Psychiatric disorders in adolescence tend to fall into three developmental categories, namely, continuing childhood disorders, mental illnesses typical of adulthood, and disorders which, although not confined exclusively to adolescence, seem characterised by difficulties surmounting this stage of development. In the first category, a number of presentations, particularly developmental and conduct disorders, will continue from middle childhood into the teens. In the category of adult mental illnesses, schizophrenia and bipolar disorder are both extremely rare before the age of 12.

Disorders in the third category, which are typical of adolescence, can be seen as representing a difficulty in mastering the tasks of this developmental stage. The development of a personal identity is the main task of adolescence with the supplementary tasks of:

- proficiency in the adult sexual role

- the transition from being nurtured to being able to care for others

- learning to work and be self-supporting

- working towards independence, which may include leaving home.

As well as arising from task failure, adolescent disorder usually interferes with satisfactory completion of these tasks.

Chronic physical disorders illustrate some of the issues in the interplay between adolescent development and disorder. In diabetes mellitus, metabolic control is dependent on adherence to a dietary and pharmacological routine. This requires a discipline and sense of responsibility, which mirror those being addressed by the adolescent in the rest of his or her life and in relationships with adults. It may be expected to result in some ambivalence since compliance with any treatment regime is a constraint upon autonomy. Each family has to negotiate the appropriate level of protectiveness and supervision. Concern about one's health may be offset by resentment at having to comply overly much, particularly in comparison with peers. Experimentation with alcohol is just one aspect of normal adolescence which is more loaded with meaning in the diabetic, when drinking behind parents' backs involves 'cheating' and putting the adolescent's health at risk. Failure of adherence results not only in a greater challenge to authority than that posed by peers, but also may result in being faced with parents' own worries about the adolescent's illness. Frequently, teenagers with such a disorder are faced with a choice between being overly protected and relatively lacking in independence, or becoming 'super mature' and more responsible than their peers. This responsibility may include the burden of protecting parents from distress, by concealing fears and doubts (Bridging the Gaps, Health Care for Adolescents 2003).

Influences on mental health

Development

Given the transitional nature of adolescence, any assessment of mental health will involve a consideration of the presence or absence of illness or disorder, but also an evaluation of various components of development. Assessment of development encompasses personality, social and moral development, including such things as empathy and the ability to form relationships. It also includes physical and intellectual development, both of which have a considerable bearing on psychological development (Changing Minds 2002).

Physical factors

The relationship between physical development and disorder in adolescence is an important one. Psychological disorder can, on the one hand, influence physical development and, on the other, be influenced by it. Anorexia nervosa is an example of the former case; when it arises before linear growth and pubertal development are completed, it can result in stunting of growth and reversal or retardation of the process of puberty. Some of these physical effects are completely reversible, others only relatively so. Confidence and self-esteem, meanwhile, can be adversely affected by small stature or delayed pubertal development (particularly in boys) leading to anxiety or depression, sometimes influenced through bullying.

Resilience and vulnerability

The interplay between assessment of development and presence or absence of disorder is highlighted in the assessment of adjustment to a trauma, life event or change of social circumstance. The ability of an adolescent to cope, for example, with a placement in a residential home will include the presence of depression or anxiety, in addition to factors such as personality and social adjustment. Resilience and vulnerability are important concepts in understanding the variations in children's ability to cope in different circumstances, as discussed in Chapter 2.

Adolescents into young adulthood – a vulnerable transition

Part of the process of transition to adult status involves disengagement from parental influence, girls being much readier to leave home than boys. By the ages of 23–24, half the male population still lives with parents compared with one third of young women. Young people who are particularly vulnerable at this stage of their development in progressing towards independent living include those living in circumstances of:

- family conflict
- living in deprived areas
- having 'special needs'
- leaving school early with poor qualifications
- leaving care.

Adolescents as carers

As discussed in Chapter 7, as many as 175,000 young people in the UK are involved in the care of an adult with a physical or mental health problem. Chapter 7 explored how these adolescents worry about their parents. They may blame themselves for the illness, fear they will develop the same illness, can feel unsupported and experience sleeplessness and anxiety. Their role as carers may not be recognised by adults, including professionals, and may not be seen as an inappropriate role for them to carry. All professionals, including those working with adults with mental illness who are parents, need to encourage adolescents to describe their experiences, to seek their views when parents are admitted to hospital, and to help to encourage the partnerships between patients, professionals and carers who are also adolescents (Cooklin 2004).

Stress in adolescence

Stress is a common experience in adolescence. Breaking down the components of stress helps in assisting practitioners to evaluate a young person's circumstances and to assess the range of interventions that might help most (Coleman and Hendry 1999). This assessment will include:

- nature of the stressor
- internal resources of the adolescent
- available social supports
- the coping process itself.

Much attention has been paid to the distinction between problem-focused and emotion-focused coping. The former refers to actions which might be taken to modify the stress or its source, while the latter applies to an alteration of the feelings, which are engendered by the stressor. These responses can be referred to as active coping and internal coping. A third reaction to stress is withdrawal. Emotion-focused coping increases with age, although problem-focused coping remains at much the same level in different age groups.

There are gender differences in coping during adolescence. Boys are more likely to use active coping but girls are more likely to deny a problem or to withdraw from the stress. Girls, on the other hand, are more likely to use social support as a means of coping and to utilise emotion-focused coping strategies. Girls are also more affected by stress and perceive events as being more stressful than their male counterparts. The distinction between problem-focused coping and emotion-focused coping assists us in identifying a key developmental task. Problem-focused strategies are more adaptive in situations when the stressor can be modified. Emotion-focused strategies are more help when stressors cannot be altered. For this reason, a goal for those working with young people on the development of coping skills should be to facilitate the learning about whether stressors can be changed or not. This will enable young people to classify sources of stress, to think about types of coping and to develop skills around event appraisal, which can all contribute to emotionally healthy development during adolescence.

Conclusion

In Western society, in some respects, those of 9 or 10 years of age are experiencing the beginning of adolescence whilst young adults of 19, 20 and 21 remain economically dependent and thus take longer to leave adolescence behind. The stage is an extended one, in which a range of major emotional, physical and social transformations occur. Adolescence is not in itself a stage of trauma and disorder but a natural developmental process.

Writers about adolescence generally agree that the timing of stresses, the extent and number of changes experienced by the young person, and the synchronicity of changes, all contribute to whether the adolescent will cope well or not. The role of social support is critical as is the impact of environmental factors. We know that a young person growing up in multiple disadvantage, or living in a family with a parent whose capacity for caregiving may be limited, or who is exposed to the experience of violence, abuse or racial harassment, will not have the same opportunities for development as those living in a supportive, settled and economically stable environment. Hence, the importance of the concept of developmental contextualisation. Above all, it has to be acknowledged that the young person makes a personal contribution to managing the changes he or she experiences through the adolescent transition. Adolescents cope as well as they do by being active agents in their own development.

Part 3

Promoting Positive Developmental Outcomes for Children

CHAPTER 13

Direct Work with Children

Jane Aldgate and Janet Seden

The first two parts of this book have looked at the developing child from several perspectives. Part 1 laid out some of the most important frameworks and theories for understanding the developing child. Part 2 traced the pathways that development usually takes across a range of dimensions, influences and age-related considerations.

The third part of this book is concerned with translating the theory into practice. This chapter makes the case for working directly with children to help them make sense of events and relationships that may be affecting their emotional and social development. The chapter looks at the rationale for working directly with children to safeguard their development. In the next chapters, David Jones explores the skills required for communicating with children and young people about difficult subjects in adverse circumstances, and David Jones and his colleagues write about the critical processes involved in responding to children's developmental needs in situations where children's welfare is threatened by maltreatment. Finally, the book ends with a chapter by Wendy Rose on children's views on aspects of their lives which are relevant to their development.

The rationale for direct work with children

The rationale for working directly with children comes from three sources:

- A rights perspective, which recognises that all children are competent to have a voice on issues which directly affect their lives and that this position is only tempered by children's age, understanding and disability. Such differences do not diminish the child's right to involvement in decision making but will demand a repertoire of communication skills from adults who are working with them.

- A safeguarding and promoting welfare perspective, where it is recognised that children are a competent source of evidence about their own abuse or neglect. They are equally well able to take an active part in promoting their optimal development.

- A therapeutic perspective, grounded in developmental theory, which asserts that children need the opportunity to make sense of events which may pose a danger to their development, such as the loss of attachment figures, or harm done to their development by neglect or maltreatment.

These three approaches are not mutually exclusive and are brought together in a theoretical framework, such as the developmental ecological approach to children's development with which we started in Chapter 1. This approach not only recognises that children can play a major part in shaping their development but also acknowledges that they will be influenced by the relationships that surround them and the wider circumstances in which they grow up. Working directly with children has a part to play in helping children whose development is likely to be impaired or, more seriously, those at risk of significant harm to make sense of their experiences and ensure they do not suffer developmental damage.

A rights approach

The recognition that children have rights to be consulted through direct work because they are children is encapsulated in the UN Convention on the Rights of the Child. Article 12 stresses the importance of involving children in decision-making about their lives:

1. States Parties shall assure to the child who is capable of forming his or her own views the right to express those views freely in all matters affecting the child, the views of the child being given due weight in accordance with the age and maturity of the child.

2. For this purpose, the child shall in particular be provided the opportunity to be heard in any judicial and administrative proceedings affecting the child, either directly, or through a

> representative or an appropriate body, in a manner consistent with the procedural rules of national law. (UN Convention on the Rights of the Child 1989)

Thus the importance of direct engagement with children has been embedded in legislation relating to the welfare and upbringing of children in the UK. This includes the Children Act 1989, the Children (Scotland) Act 1995, and the Children (Northern Ireland) Order 1995. The Children Act 2004 has amended the Children Act 1989 and now social workers are required to ascertain the wishes and feelings of children and give them due consideration when deciding what services are to be provided (s17 of the Children Act 1989) and making decisions under section 47 of the Children Act 1989.

Evidence from studies accompanying the Children Act 1989 suggests that children really do want decision-making relating to their lives and development to be 'child-centred'. Furthermore, they are fully capable of responding to the challenge of participating in decision-making when given the opportunity. Reviewing 11 studies out of 24 that had elicited children's views for the Department of Health, Aldgate and Statham suggest:

> Given the right support, many children are capable of participating fully in decision making. To enable them to take part, they need skilled, direct work and adults who are reliable and will champion their needs. Children with severe impairments that inhibit their communication skills will need additional, specialist help. (Department of Health 2001, p.94)

> In the end what children need is straightforward: enough food, warmth, adults who love and nurture them, consistency, achievements and to be treated with dignity as properly befits child citizens. (Department of Health 2001, p.95)

Each piece of primary legislation cited above stresses the responsibility of adults to attend to children's developmental needs, as well as consulting them. This includes the making of decisions within timescales that will ensure children's development will not be further impaired. Research suggests that sometimes the practice does not live up to the reality (see, for example, Department of Health 2001) and that children can be waiting for crucial decisions from courts for far longer than is recommended to be in their best interests.

A safeguarding and promoting welfare approach

The second argument for working directly with children relates to their protection from significant harm. This approach places working directly with the child alongside other aspects of assessment of children's developmental needs, including careful assessment of children's social ecology, the quality of caregivers, and the impact of a child's physical and social environment upon his or her development. The extent to which a child's needs are met and his or her welfare safeguarded depends on good practice in all the basic areas of professional practice. When good practice is neglected the child can be placed in mortal danger, as for example, in the case of Victoria Climbié. The Victoria Climbié Inquiry (CM 5730 2003) shows how concerns about systems and procedures led to assessments happening *around* Victoria while opportunities for direct engagement with her as a 7-year-old person with developmental needs were lost. A theme from the report is that a focus on *seeing and hearing* children is essential. Recommendation 40 (p.376) says:

> Directors of social services must ensure that no case that has been opened in response to allegations of deliberate harm to a child is closed until the following steps have been taken.
>
> - The child has been spoken to alone
> - The child's carers have been seen and spoken to
> - The accommodation in which the child has to live has been visited
> - The views of all the professionals involved have been sought and considered
> - A plan for the promotion and safeguarding of the child's welfare has been agreed. (paragraph 5.187)

Direct work with Victoria and her carers was not undertaken properly. A specific example of an opportunity missed occurred when Victoria was in hospital, where the social worker decided neither to speak to nor see Victoria. There are reasons given for not having seen and/or spoken to her both on this occasion and at other times. One reason was lack of parental permission, another the need for an interpreter, and another the necessity of avoiding prejudice to any enquiries carried out by the field social work team which might have been used as evidence for proceedings. A picture emerges (p.238) of several people telling the Inquiry that they were cautious about speaking to Victoria in case they contaminated evidence. However, the report, while recognising that good practice guidelines for interviewing children should be observed, goes on to comment:

> the guidelines do not prevent a simple exchange of conversation with the child, the content of which should be properly recorded. Seeing, listening to and observing the child must be an essential element of an initial assessment for any worker, and indeed any member of staff routinely working with children, and this can be of great importance when dealing with child protection cases. (p.238)

This is not the first inquiry report to identify flawed operational practice taking place around a disempowered and isolated child. Like similar children before her, Victoria's situation was not fully understood by adult professionals. It could only have been improved by placing Victoria at the centre of their enquiries, by talking with her directly and listening sympathetically to her. If an interpreter was required, no action was taken to find one (see Department of Health, Department for Education and Employment and Home Office 2000b, para 3.41); in other words, as the Cleveland Inquiry suggested over a decade ago, seeing the child as a 'person' not an 'object of concern' (Butler-Sloss 1988). There is a clear message to practitioners that routine practice includes making observations of, talking to and listening to children as well as interviewing and observing parents, carers and other family members. This has been reinforced in government guidance about assessing children in need and their families (Department of Health *et al.* 2000b) and working together to safeguard children (Department of Health, Home Office and Department for Education and Employment 1999).

A therapeutic approach

The third argument for working directly with children relates to the therapeutic value of responding appropriately to children's emotional developmental needs at times of distress or anticipating transitions. It has been shown that children value the opportunity to talk to air their anxieties with someone they can trust (see, for example, Aldgate and Bradley 1999).

Some children's experiences may have been poor over a considerable period of time with a proportionate effect on their development. This applies particularly to children whose emotional development has been affected by maltreatment. Fahlberg, for example, suggests that some children may have gaps in their development and may appear to become 'stuck' at an earlier chronological age. She describes the way children can become 'stuck' in four areas:

- developmental delays in any or all of three major areas – physical, cognitive and psychological

- the child may have developed abnormal patterns of behaviour – maladaptive patterns

- unresolved separation issues may cause the child to become stuck

- misperceptions can hinder the usual progression of growth and change. (Fahlberg 1984, p.17)

Though Fahlberg was writing two decades ago, her work is still relevant for practitioners in many different disciplines. Those working with children with conduct disorders will recognise the development of patterns of social behaviour which cause children both to reject social exchanges with others and in turn be further rejected by adults and peers (see, for example, Rutter *et al.* 1998). There is a wealth of literature on the importance of helping children resolve their feelings of loss, especially loss of those to whom they were attached, however insecurely (see Chapter 4). Children who have suffered neglect and inconsistent caregiving may well see the world as a hostile place, where no one can be trusted except themselves, to the detriment of their emotional and social development (see Chapters 4 and 16).

The rationale for working with children in such circumstances is summarised by Simmonds:

1. Children need to be able to communicate what they feel about what they have experienced – even if this is painful...

2. That many children because of past experiences have blocked off the feeling part of them and hence do not have the means to know what they feel or the tools to express these feelings. Development of the senses – of the 'contact function' – looking, taking, touching, listening, moving, smelling and tasting has therefore become an important work with children and a significant part of the development of the sense of self.

3. There is concern to provide children with the means to express what they feel – that they can be happy/good/angry/sad and have

these feelings about important people in their past, present or future. (Simmonds 1992, pp.14–15)

Because of the emphasis on children's emotional development, this kind of direct work has been called 'an education in the emotions' (Simmonds 1992, p.15). The essence of such work with children is summarised by the eminent practitioner in the 1970s, Violet Oaklander:

It is up to me to provide the means by which we will open doors and windows to their inner worlds. I need to provide methods for children to express their feelings, to get what they are keeping guarded inside out into the open, so that together we can deal with this material. (1978, p.193)

Examples of direct work with children

There are many techniques available to practitioners who are undertaking direct work with children. The use of ecomaps, life story books and CDs, play with dolls and other toys, drawings and photography have become part of the standard tool kit of any worker engaged in direct work with children. There is a rich array of workbooks to help children understand their emotions in a tangible way. A story such as *The Huge Bag of Worries* (Ironside 1994), which tells the tale of a child with a bag of worries who manages to find empathic adults upon whom to offload the burden, is a good example of contemporary aids to practice.

Some techniques are almost classics in their own right. One example is the use of a jug of water, glasses and clingfilm to help explain to a child how feelings have been blocked in or out. The child learns that when a glass of water (representing the child's feelings) is covered with clingfilm (the child's 'suffering skin'), nothing, i.e. no feelings, can get in or out of the glass because of the barrier. Once the barrier is removed, feelings can flow to and from the child (see Aldgate and Simmonds 1992).

Another well-tried technique sometimes used with children who are moving from one family to another is the candle ritual. Candles are used to represent all the significant people in the child's life, and the new family. The child learns that old candles do not have to be extinguished to light new ones. In other words, it is possible to love and be loved by old and new carers (see Aldgate and Simmonds 1992). Such an approach resonates with Owusu-Bempah's work on socio-genealogical connectedness recounted in Chapter 6.

As well as using training resources to help think about strategies for communicating with younger and older children, both singly and in groups (such as *Turning Points*, NSPCC 1997; *Listening to Young Children Resource Pack*, Lancaster 2003; *All Join In* video/DVD, NSPCC and Triangle 2004; '*Say it Your Own Way*': *Including Children's Voices in Assessment: A Guide and Resource*, Hutton and Sugden 2006), some practitioners are very imaginative and work with children using a range of resources, such as books, cameras, games, videos, CDs and other materials. For example, a fostering and adoption worker undertaking an adoption assessment wrote:

> I needed to talk to two children aged 7 and 5 about adoption and thought that Harry Potter provided a wonderful opportunity. So I talked about how his parents were dead because of You-Know-Who, and his aunt and uncle were not kind to him and then how the Weasleys, kind of, adopted him, having him for school holidays etc. I think the parents were more impressed than the children! It also helped them to see how they could use stories that children already know to talk about big issues in life. (Jeffries 2002)

Other aids for assisting children to talk about themselves and their circumstances include questionnaires and scales.

The Strengths and Difficulties Questionnaire for young people aged 11–16 years and the Adolescent Wellbeing Scale (scale rating for depression in young people), published as part of the Family Pack of Questionnaires and Scales (Department of Health, Cox and Bentovim 2000), are useful for working with young people, and can be used with children as young as 8 years although the results are more reliable for children aged 11 and over. The Questionnaires and Scales enable the practitioner to engage with the young person about sensitive and difficult areas that young people are often reticent to talk about. An example of this is in the Adolescent Wellbeing Scale in which the young person is given prompts such as 'I feel very lonely' or 'I think life isn't worth living' and answers either most of the time, sometimes or never. Young people tend to answer these questions quite frankly, providing responses that would have been far harder to elicit in a standard interview.

The completed Questionnaires and Scales provide the basis for a discussion with the young person about their feelings, their perception of their current situation, strengths and difficulties. This discussion can lead on to consideration with the young person of their hopes and aspirations for the future. It is vital that the practitioner clarifies the young person's understanding of the question and the meaning of their answer during the subsequent discussion.

In My Shoes (Calam *et al.* 2000) is a computerised assisted interview for children. It can assist them to share information in ways that could not be achieved through traditional interview methods. A valuable guide for practitioners on planning and undertaking work in such situations is *Communicating with Vulnerable Children* (Jones 2003), which forms the basis of the next chapter and takes a developmental perspective to communicating with children.

Is direct work effective?

Although the rhetoric for working directly with children is persuasive, if for no other reason than its affirmation of children as individuals with a right to be heard, there has been little evaluation of the effectiveness of different types of direct work with children. Children in need have told researchers that they appreciate being consulted (see, for example, Department of Health 1995, 2001) and have complained when nobody listens to them (Thomas and Beckford 1999) but there has been little in-depth study of the impact of direct work on children's development.

One rare evaluation of direct work to prepare children for permanent placements suggested that direct work demands considerable skills and a high level of training if it is to be effective. A study by Rushton *et al.* (1997/8) of a group of children aged between five and nine years, moving from being looked after to permanent placements, found that the level of direct work to prepare children for placements had little association with outcome in terms of improvements in children's behaviour problems. However, the authors suggest many variables may have influenced the outcome, including the skills and confidence needed in workers. They warn that, if direct work is to be offered, it must be focused, sufficiently intensive and of a high standard.

> Too much of the child preparation work was underdeveloped, the aims and methods were poorly formulated and the practitioners lacked the confidence to carry out this task. Clearly, if the work is to be undertaken by mainstream child care workers, they need better training and supervision, legitimation of the task and allocation of proper time to do it. (p.47)

There is a linked issue here, which is the lack of training and opportunity to practise the skills of direct work with children that many practitioners can identify both from their initial and subsequent training. The training needs of workers in this respect have also been the concern of many child protection inquiry reports. To some extent, the curriculum and assessed modules within the Post Qualifying Award in Child Care have attempted with some success to address the problem (General Social Care Council 2001). Concern about skills in direct work are not new. Crompton, writing in 1990, suggested that 'Direct work with children has been integral to the approach of workers in many fields for at least 20 years' (p.8) and she identifies some of the concerns that workers had then, and still have. These are:

- The discomfort caused in the worker by really listening to a child's needs, fears and worries, especially when knowing that their own professional actions can contribute to more possible distress.

- Fear of damaging a child by clumsy interventions and therefore preferring to seek 'an expert'.

- A feeling of being ill prepared by training for the professional role.

However, Crompton goes on to argue that:

Working directly with children is essential. This is made doubly apparent when things go wrong, as in Cleveland in 1988. Such work can be effective only if adults really listen to children, however difficult and uncomfortable this may be, and all workers should receive training preparation and continuing support... Direct work with children is done every day by ordinary people in ordinary agencies. (p.9)

Training and supervision

In spite of Crompton's optimism, there is no doubt that direct work of any sort requires workers to be both trained and supervised. Where therapeutic work is involved, workers need to understand the impact that such work may have on them and ensure that skilled supervision is available to them from individuals who understand child development and concepts such as transference and counter-transference. It is important that workers understand their own inner worlds and the impact the child's emotional pain may have had on them. This also applies to any situation in which children are in need. As Simmonds suggests:

> The dilemma for workers engaging in direct work with children is that the relationship between worker and child – the means by which any work is done – is also capable of evoking a range of feelings, some of which will be associated with other relationships, particularly relationships with parental figures. These feelings can, in turn, become re-enacted in the relationship between worker and child in such a way as to seriously distort that relationship. In some cases, this can threaten to confirm for both worker and child the hopelessness of ever attempting to make a trusting and significant relationship. (1992, p.17)

Once these feelings have been recognised, they can be used to help understand children's experiences and how they have shaped their development. They form part of the evidence which informs professional decision-making.

Direct work – a challenge for workers

The challenge for professionals working with children and families is to recognise that safeguarding and promoting the welfare of children are essential elements of their statutory role (s11 Children Act 2004). Such a role cannot be carried out without an understanding of the effects of life events on children's development. Workers also have to accept the responsibilities of engaging with children and strive to develop the necessary skills for building a working relationship with them. Furthermore, it involves recognition of the boundaries between different professionals. All workers should be able to talk to children but some may feel that they are not trained or experienced enough to engage in therapeutic work with children who are undergoing transitions or those whose behaviour warrants a more specialist approach. This might mean planning a multi-disciplinary approach, identifying with whom a child has the most rapport, knows, trusts and chooses to talk.

In cases where safeguarding is a priority, it is now recognised that there is a place for ongoing direct work alongside the gathering of evidence through more formal interviewing carried out by designated professionals in preparation for court proceedings (Home Office *et al.* 2002). If anything, children's development may be more damaged by not responding to their distress on the grounds this will corrupt any evidence in a criminal court case. Communication with children and their families aimed at identifying and meeting needs or planning to safeguard children are the bedrock of practice and process in children and families' work (Seden 2000).

Some direct work is universal across all settings. Practitioners in all settings need to be able to:

- listen to children and elicit their thoughts, feelings, wishes and views

- talk with and engage with children to build a working relationship for partnership work

- talk to children and give information about events in their lives

- engage in work which helps children with processes that happen to them, e.g. moving home, starting a new school, changing foster placement

- do this in a way which is appropriate to their age, ability, understanding and background

- talk sensitively with children around complex and painful issues in their lives

- interview children and young people when writing reports or collecting evidence for court.

To do this effectively a developmental understanding is essential. The evidence for these assertions comes from a research based developmental approach to understanding the needs of children, as was discussed in Chapter 1.

Understanding children's developmental needs and communicating effectively cannot remain a theoretical matter. Such work is crucial if children are to be enabled to 'move on' and develop. The application of knowledge to practice has to move beyond knowledge frameworks, legal mandates and policy directives into effective practice in the real lives of children who are growing up in situations where they need support and help to make sense of their world and the difficulties that they are facing.

How can practitioners do this?

Those working with children might want to reflect on their own position about communicating directly with children and young people and to do this with colleagues. This could be done by auditing their skills, identifying their training needs and making an action plan to improve their skills. To become more competent in this area, practitioners have to decide to take the time to gain the necessary underpinning knowledge and to practise their skills. Understanding how to communicate in the context of children's developmental needs and social circumstances is crucial (Department for Education and Skills 2005a). It cannot be seen as an option when working with children – too much work in children's services happens 'around and about' children and not directly 'with and alongside them'. In embarking on direct work with children, workers might find it helpful to observe the following principles:

- observing skilfully, looking, seeing, noticing, observing play where relevant
- talking to children about topics they are interested in, in order to build relationships
- listening to what children say very carefully
- reflecting on a child's capacity to understand and respond
- checking the child's understanding from time to time
- consulting with a child as far as possible
- being clear with a child when adults are making changes in their lives
- being honest about roles and responsibilities
- thinking about interventions that can enhance a child's developmental opportunities
- working at the child's pace as far as possible
- taking account of how a child likes to communicate
- being imaginative about methods of working
- finding therapeutic help for a child if needed
- taking an interest in the child's activities and interests.

Throughout this chapter, reference has been made to writings across a number of decades (Aldgate and Simmonds 1992; Crompton 1990; Fahlberg 1984; Oaklander 1978; Winnicott 1964). This is because face-to-face work with children and young people remains the core professional task of those with responsibility for children whose development may be or is being impaired. For reasons discussed in this chapter, direct work with children has too often been avoided, undertaken with poor skills and ill-defined purpose, or relegated in priority (the use of paid escorts for contact visits by children in foster care or in being transported to and from court appearances is one example of lost opportunities). The importance of such work cannot perhaps be better articulated than by Clare Winnicott in a lecture to the Association of Social Workers in 1963:

> To sum up, I would say that our 'face-to-face' responsibility for children involves us in three overlapping areas of work with them.
>
> First we try to reach the children, to establish communication and to construct a working relationship with them which is personal and yet structured.
>
> Having reached the child we try to look at his world with him, and to help him to sort out his feelings about it; to face the painful things and to discover good things.
>
> Then we try to consolidate the positive things in the child himself and in his world, and to help him to make the most of his life.
>
> These three areas of work add up, it seems to me, to the process of social casework with children.
>
> As a last word, I want to say that even if we are unable to help the children as much as we should like to do, we can at least attempt to prevent muddle from arising in their lives; or if it has arisen, continually make the effort to sort it out for them so that things add up and make some sort of sense and in this way we can prevent and relieve a great deal of distress. (Winnicott 1964, pp.57–58)

The combination of knowledge about children's development and the commitment, with accompanying skills, to direct work with children provides an important foundation to effective intervention in the lives of vulnerable children and to the improvement of their outcomes.

CHAPTER 14

Communicating with Children about Adverse Experiences

David Jones

The ability to communicate with children and young people is a key skill for frontline practitioners who work with children and young people. The central importance of direct work with children was emphasised in the previous chapter. Teachers, social workers with children and families, youth workers, nurses, health visitors, and child and adolescent mental health professionals communicate with children each day. Most of these conversations are either general in nature or task specific. This chapter is mainly concerned with the skills required for communicating with children and young people about difficult subjects. Such subjects may prove a challenge for adults, children or for both. Sometimes the professionals' work is centrally concerned with communicating with children about very difficult issues. Social workers in children and families assessment teams frequently address difficult and challenging issues with children when they are undertaking direct work, as part of initial or core assessments (Department of Health, Department for Education and Employment and Home Office 2000b).

For other professionals, difficult or challenging subjects arise less frequently and may not be a core aspect of their work, e.g. for teachers, who occasionally need to communicate with a child presenting with personal difficulty.

Some examples of subjects which are difficult or challenging

The following list provides some examples of subjects which might be particularly challenging for professionals or others when communicating with children and young people. The list is not exhaustive but intended to illustrate the kinds of areas which present difficulties for adults, and sometimes for children too.

1. Listening and/or obtaining information from a child:

   o Situations which involve children's experience of adverse personal events during which they may have suffered harm (e.g. child abuse and neglect).

   o Where children are knowledgeable about, or witness to, significant violence (e.g. inter-parental violence, but also other forms of family violence, including being witness to murder).

   o Understanding children's views, wishes and feelings concerning sensitive issues, e.g. contact with relatives and place of residence.

   o Evaluating a child's capacity to consent to medical investigation or treatment.

2. Imparting sensitive information, or 'telling':

   o Children who either need or want to know about their own health status, including life threatening illnesses, or those who need to know about illness in a person who is close to them.

   o Events and situations which involve shame or secrecy, either for the child or more commonly for her or his parents. Examples include illnesses such as HIV/AIDS, where there has been a history of abuse or violence within the family, or where a parent has committed a serious crime.

   o Knowledge about parentage (e.g. genetic origins in relation to the new reproductive technologies, or knowledge about genetic origins derived from DNA examination, or where birth parentage has been kept secret by carers for other reasons). This may become particularly relevant where one carer is a non-genetic parent, and where the child may reasonably expect that he or she is a genetic parent.

Why communicate with children about difficult or sensitive issues?

One reason is that studies have found that children want to. If lines of communication are not opened up with children in the type of circumstances listed above, then, later on, children wish that they could have been and that somebody had communicated with them when they were younger.

Second, children have a right to know about or understand certain matters that involve them, such as their parentage.

Third, sometimes it is necessary to enquire about the child's situation where there is a possibility that they may be suffering harm and a professional has to establish whether the child requires safeguarding. Information may also be required in order to protect a third party.

Fourth, children may need information in order to prevent future distress, harm or disadvantage. Examples include: knowledge about prior abuse or neglect to the self, e.g. children who when younger were abused and who need information about what occurred; illness; significant information about self or a loved one which would be harmful if delayed, e.g. parentage, which may result in lack of trust if withheld.

Fifth, the need for clarification. Children may in any case have some memory about a particular event, but the information communicated should be as accurate and true as possible, taking into account the limitations posed by the child's developmental level. A further important objective is to establish an accurate 'script' for the future. This is important for children's future development in many ways, including their emotional development.

Hence there is an obligation on adults to provide opportunities for children to communicate about difficult or sensitive issues. How we do so is all important. Skill and sensitivity are both necessary, and it is important that children are not coerced or otherwise pressurised, notwithstanding any urgency which the practitioner may have.

Communication

Communication means the process of imparting, transmitting, and receiving information. When considering communication between adults and children, it refers to a range of activities involved in sharing information between adults and children. It is a two-way process. Necessary preconditions include being receptive, whether through listening, hearing, or alternative means. Much material is communicated nonverbally. Even when words can be found, we convey added meaning through reliance on nonverbal techniques as well as verbal, through timing, accompanying gestures, and body language. For some children forms of language other than verbal are preferred, for example, sign or other types of augmentative communication. Practitioners require particular attributes to communicate with children effectively, especially concerning challenging topics.

What additional areas of knowledge or skill are required?

Some knowledge of the particular area which presents a difficulty or a challenge for the child and adult, for example:

- child abuse and neglect
- inter-parental conflict and domestic violence
- children's knowledge of death
- life-threatening illness either in the child or family members
- the field of divorce, post-divorce conflict
- contact and residence
- implications for child and family health of the new reproductive technologies.

Practitioners will also need to have:

- sufficient knowledge of developmental psychology, including memory, suggestibility, and language development in children
- awareness of common areas which affect children who are referred for specialised services, such as:
  - attachment and attachment disorders
  - mental health needs of looked after children
  - parental mental health and child welfare.

Further areas in which it can be helpful to understand:

- aspects of difference and disability in relation to children's communication

- the law in relation to childhood

- a systemic understanding of different disciplines which work with children and families

- psychology of violence and victimology

- the psychology of disclosure – how children communicate about personal adversity and what factors contribute to delay or sustained silence.

We now select the area of child maltreatment for more detailed consideration of communication issues. This is a common adverse event affecting children and young people and one which presents numerous challenges for practitioners, yet where good quality communication can provide the opportunity for safeguarding children and providing effective interventions for children and their families.

Child maltreatment

Overall approach

These are particular points and principles to bear in mind when communicating with children about the possibility of maltreatment.

The approach necessary for communicating effectively can be summarised in terms of those qualities most likely to lead to successful communication, while also preserving an accurate and full account, contrasted with those qualities likely to lead to a poorer outcome. Positive qualities:

- Listening to and understanding the child.

- Maintaining a non-biased approach.

- Maintaining personal neutrality about any issues raised (but not indifference).

- Managing one's personal responses to any distressing material which the child communicates.

- Adopting the perspective that it is the child or young person who is the expert, not the adult practitioner.

- Conveying genuine empathic concern, to a degree that is congruent with the child or young person's situation.

- Using open-ended and non-biased approaches to communication with the child.

- Bearing in mind that if the adult does not ask, it is unlikely that he or she will be told.

- Allowing children to recall their experiences freely.

- Operating within a context of continuing professional development and critical review of personal practice.

- Ensuring that the best way to record the exchange has been planned in advance.

In addition, when undertaking initial or core assessments (Department of Health *et al.* 2000b), the following aspects should also be added.

- Identify the aims of the work, including who has asked for the assessment and what plans have been decided upon, and why.

- Record the exchange, including both its content and duration.

- Clarify any ambiguous information arising from the child or any other adult.

- Report the content of communications afterwards, as appropriate, to the relevant agency or group of professionals, where necessary obtaining consent to do so (Department of Health *et al.* 2003).

Qualities to avoid or discourage:

- Maintaining assumptions or biased views which may negatively influence the interchange between the child and adult.

- Employing leading questions or other techniques that are prone to error.

- Using coercion or pressurising methods of enquiry.

Some preliminary considerations

Sometimes children's experiences are spontaneously communicated without prior warning. In other circumstances there is time to plan how best to conduct a session. Where this is so, areas to be considered include:

- clarification of objectives in the session
- reviewing what is already known
- reviewing consent and capacity issues
- the precise approach and necessary personnel
- the site for the session
- recording
- how the interview will be analysed (Jones 2003, pp.120–123 and 94–95).

Consent and confidentiality

It is useful to distinguish between giving consent to communicate with the child, and subsequently sharing information. Impromptu first responses to children's concerns are not pre-planned, formal interviews but immediate responses to children's presentations. Therefore, consent is either implied, because it is inferred from the circumstances in which the communication occurs, or it is not practicable to obtain it because it is necessary at the time to determine whether the child requires safeguarding. These first responses contrast with communications which are planned in advance, which do raise issues of consent. Generally, it is important to obtain informed consent from children or their parents in relation to any procedures that affect them. Similarly with younger children, they should be involved as far as possible and their assent or agreement sought, even if they lack capacity to provide consent.

If there are clear cut concerns about the child's safety, then the child should be referred to the appropriate agency (social services or police) (Department of Health *et al.* 1999). In response to the referral, social workers may undertake initial and core assessments. Before commencing an assessment, they should obtain consent from someone with parental responsibility for the child, unless to do so would place the child at risk of harm. The child's consent or, if not capable of providing it, their assent, should be sought too.

Information sharing

Generally personal information acquired during the course of working with children and families is confidential and one has to take particular care about sensitive information (Department of Health *et al.* 2003). However, information may need to be shared either with consent, or sometimes without the consent of either the person who has provided the information (a child), and/or the person about whom the information relates. Normally these exceptions to confidentiality involve circumstances where information is necessary to disclose on a 'need to know' basis so that the child's welfare may be safeguarded. This has to be proportional to the nature of the information itself and potential harm to the child involved. The Government practice guidance, *What to Do if You're Worried a Child is Being Abused* (Department of Health *et al.* 2003) outlines the legal constraints on the disclosure of confidential information, summarising the common law duty of confidence, the Human Rights Act 1998, and the Data Protection Act 1998. Broadly, professionals are not prevented by law from sharing information if either consent is given or the public interest in safeguarding the child's welfare overrides the need to keep the information confidential, or, lastly, if disclosure is required under a Court order or other legal obligation.

Direct work with children and young people

Three types of situation can be delineated:

1. First responses to those concerns which are expressed to frontline practitioners.

2. Initial assessments undertaken by practitioners, which include consideration of the possibility that the child may have suffered harm

3. As part of a core assessment, in-depth interviews with children about possible maltreatment or significant harm.

Each of these circumstances requires a different approach, as outlined below.

First responses to children's concerns

Any professional working with children can be faced with a situation where either a child wants to communicate, or the professional senses the need to respond to a child. Often the child initiates these situations unexpectedly, during the context of everyday services provided for children, such as education, primary health care and hospital care.

All practitioners working with children should make themselves available to respond to concerns expressed by children and young people. These professionals are often in a position of trust vis-à-vis children and therefore the ones to whom the child or young person turns in their search for a listening ear or for help. It is vitally important from the child's perspective that professionals convey verbally and nonverbally that they can listen and respond to children and young people. At the same time professionals should avoid overpowering or pressurising the child.

It can be difficult to decide whether the child should be seen on his or her own. Sometimes children find the presence of other children inhibiting or may find settings unhelpful, such as a head teacher's office, which is associated with discipline. Therefore practitioners such as teachers may need to find an opportunity to communicate with a child away from the main class group and consider where would be most appropriate.

Paediatricians or general practitioners normally see children with their parents. Sometimes raising the issue of the child's possible reluctance with a parent and child together can allow a parent to withdraw temporarily, if the child appears to want to communicate without the parent present. At other times it may be possible to talk with a child directly, even though the parent is, perhaps, to one side or out of the child's direct line of vision.

CHOICE OF APPROACH

A common dilemma for the practitioner is just where and how to start? This will normally depend on the manner through which concern has been raised. The range of possibilities include: something that the child has just said, physical disease or findings, or a change in the child's behaviour or emotional state.

A child's word

In these circumstances, the practitioner can invite the child to elaborate on the matter that has just caused the concern. An alternative would be to see whether the child would prefer to talk to a colleague. For example, in a school this might mean talking to a designated teacher or one with whom it is known that the child has a positive relationship.

The professionals' approach should be open ended and consist of an invitation to talk if the child so wishes. For example, children can be asked to say why they are concerned about a particular place or person (if they have just told the teacher about such a concern).

Similarly, a child might be asked to say a little more about an expressed concern or worry (for example, where a child is reluctant to be collected by a particular adult). In these situations, specific questions are avoided and the question is phrased in an open ended way, without conveying either verbal or non-verbal pre-supposition about harm.

Physical disease or findings

A doctor or health visitor can ask how a child became sore or bruised, or marked in a particular part of their body, while examining them. A similar approach can be used when a child has a sexually transmitted disease, or one which is often, but not always, transmitted through direct sexual contact.

Behavioural or emotional change

In these circumstances, the practitioner might wish to ask more about the child's emotional condition such as sadness or anxiety. Similarly, practitioners can ask directly about behaviour change, particularly where this involves violence or sexualised behaviour towards another, inviting the child to explain his or her behaviour and its recent change, while at the same time responding to the consequences of his or her actions. Maintaining the possibility of communication while at the same time attending to the child's responsibility can provide an opportunity for some children to communicate any concerns which they may have.

GENERAL CONSIDERATIONS

It can be helpful to practise potential responses to situations such as those above, discussing these with colleagues or designated or named professionals. Discussion with colleagues from other disciplines in multi-disciplinary training events can also prove useful.

First responses are very important because suggestive practice by professionals can jeopardise future responses to the child's situation. By contrast, good initial practice lays the foundation for future work and helps establish the child's trust in professionals.

The professional's role in first responses is simply to listen, note the conversation as soon as possible afterwards, and then respond appropriately.

The professional should not attempt to investigate the situation independently if concerned about the child's safety, but instead arrange referral to social services or the police as appropriate for further action.

RECORDING COMMUNICATIONS

It is important to record conversations which have raised concern about possible harm having occurred, just as soon as possible. The professional should record not only the full sequence but also the events which preceded the conversation, as well as subsequent events. Practitioners should note nonverbal elements of communication as well as verbal ones, and include, as far as possible, everything that can be recalled about what they said as well as the words of the child. Normally, these impromptu communications are not planned and, therefore, only rough jottings would be likely to be made during or immediately after. These jottings should be kept, along with any fuller record which should be completed as soon as possible after the event. These records become especially important in situations that progress to formal procedures to safeguard children.

WHAT HAPPENS NEXT?

The possibilities range from concerns about the child being allayed through to a revelation that the child's safety is seriously compromised. For other children the situation remains unclear, notwithstanding the professional's best efforts. In these latter circumstances, it is important to keep a line of communication open with the child, while perhaps also arranging for other services to help or respond to any needs for extra help that the child may have.

The professional will have to decide whether local safeguarding children procedures should be set in motion through sharing information with social services. If in doubt, advice can be sought either through colleagues or through channels set out in local procedures (Department of Health *et al.* 1999, 2003). Many professional concerns are allayed through these first responses and, following an assessment, services may be provided, but the use of the procedures is not justified.

Initial assessments

These are undertaken by social workers, in collaboration with other professionals and the child and family members (Department of Health *et al.*

2000b). When undertaking these assessments under s17 of the Children Act 1989, the child's wishes and feelings must be ascertained and given due consideration when deciding what services to provide (s53, Children Act 2004).

Initially decisions need to be made about who to see, and in what order. The child's age is likely to affect this decision. Teenagers are likely to seek greater independence in the arrangements, compared with younger children who will probably want to be seen nearby, or even with, their parent. Younger children may need more than one session in order to establish trust with an unknown professional from outside their family, if they are to communicate effectively. Similarly, disabled children are likely to expect professional adults to do things for and to them and may, therefore, require more extensive preparation to enable them to communicate their concerns freely without adult direction or prompting. Race and cultural expectations may also affect decision making. Specialist help may be required in order to communicate effectively.

The starting points, under 'First responses' above, can be developed further in initial assessments, for example by elaborating on initial comments made by children, or by exploring reasons for physical findings or changes in behavioural or emotional state.

Other approaches to initial assessment include the following:

USING GENERAL OPPORTUNITIES

There are likely to be many opportunities to raise the possibility of adverse experiences. For example, assessments often include general discussion about sleeping routines and arrangements, and with older children, issues of privacy and discussions about their living space. These provide opportunities for concerns to be expanded upon, if children wish. Similarly, discussions concerning discipline often bring out accounts of excessive punishment as well as routine disciplines. Discussion about family structure and relationships is an integral part of specialist assessments. This allows for questions about whom the child likes to spend time with, and those with whom they do not. To whom is the child close or not so close? Answers to questions such as these can be followed up with open-ended enquiry to further explore the basis for these preferences.

In general, a useful approach is to pair positive experiences with potentially negative ones. Thus, discussions might be initiated about whom the child is close to and then alternatively to whom they do not feel so close;

or 'the best thing that has happened to you', followed by 'the worst thing that has happened to you'. Similarly, the person 'you like being with' compared with the person 'you don't like being with'.

EXPLORATORY QUESTIONS

Below are suggestions for exploratory questions, which could be adapted for different aged children. They are intended to supplement the approaches already outlined. As a general principle, when questions such as these are used, it is important that, if the child responds in the affirmative, subsequent questions should consist of open-ended prompts and invitations to describe any adverse experiences in more detail. In this way the possible objections to exploratory questions are addressed, but at the same time the child is given the opportunity to raise his or her experiences with a professional, but is not pressurised.

Examples of approaches

'Has anybody done anything to you, which upset you? (await response); or made you unhappy?'

'Has any person hurt you?' (await answer) 'or touched you in a way that you didn't like?'

'Or touched you on private parts of your body?' (await answer) 'or in a sexual way?'

A circular, permission-giving question can be useful in some circumstances, such as, for example, where the possibility of victimisation or adversity seems quite strong, yet the child appears to be inhibited:

'Some children talk about being upset or hurt in some way – has anything like this happened to you?'.

RESPONDING TO CONCERNS RAISED UNEXPECTEDLY

Sometimes concern about maltreatment arises unexpectedly during the course of an assessment. The child should not be prevented from communicating but, equally, the professional should be careful not to adopt an investigating role, deferring to mandated agencies for this purpose. The child should be allowed to finish raising whatever issues he or she wishes to and then an opportunity found to refer on to relevant professionals.

ADULT SUSPICION AND VULNERABLE CHILDREN

Adults may be concerned about a child, even though the child in question has expressed no concerns. The practitioner may be able to capitalise on general situations, but exploratory questions may also be necessary in order to initiate communication about possible adversity. It is important to maintain a balance between leading the child and failing to provide the child with an opportunity for communication. Provided exploratory questions are limited to one or two, and tentatively framed, they are unlikely to lead to a false account.

WHAT NEXT?

At the end of an initial assessment, the practitioner should prepare the child for what might happen next, whether this might be no further action, provision of services, review later, or progression to a more in-depth assessment or even an investigative interview if a crime may have been committed (Home Office *et al.* 2002).

A full record should be made, together with any observations about the child's nonverbal communications.

In-depth interviews with children

In-depth interviews are undertaken by social workers or others as part of core assessments. When section 47 enquiries are initiated, the core assessment is the means by which these enquiries are carried out (Department of Health *et al.* 2003). Other professionals may undertake in-depth interviews too, when requested, in order to assist social services, or if requested to undertake an assessment in Family Proceedings. Sometimes some elements of an in-depth interview are required when adversity or possible maltreatment emerges in response to open-ended enquiry, often unexpectedly during a first assessment. Practitioners should follow the guidance set out in *Achieving Best Evidence* (Home Office *et al.* 2002), where a crime is thought to have been committed.

PLANNING

Interviews such as these require advance planning in order to establish the main purpose, specific objectives and to identify issues particular to this child and family. Specific objectives might include the child's psychological condition, or understanding the child's views, wishes, and feelings about particular persons or contact arrangements.

Planning should also cover the following:

- a review of existing information
- the specific aims and objectives of the session
- children's and parents' rights particularly with respect to consent and confidentiality
- who to interview
- who would undertake the assessment
- the approach to the child and introductions
- collecting information
- recording
- the site for the interview
- resources (with respect to age, special needs, impairments or disabilities)
- what time scale is anticipated
- analysis of any information obtained and feedback to family and other professionals.

PREPARATION

The child may need preparation, for example, to allay or address excessive fearfulness, to attend to special needs or impairments, or to respond to an older child's concerns about confidentiality and the consequence of disclosing their experiences. Other children with significant mental health problems or where children are very young may also need special preparatory time. Sometimes carers require preparation too.

A schema for undertaking in-depth interviews

1. Introductory, rapport-gaining phase.
2. Enquiry into suspected adverse experiences.
3. Further exploration.
4. Closure.

RAPPORT-GAINING PHASE

The main aims of this phase of the interview are to establish a working relationship with the child, to engage his or her interest in the session, and at the same time to place the child or young person at ease. If a preparatory session has not occurred previously, it will be necessary to deal with some of these items in this phase of the main interview. Even if there has been a successful preparatory session, the interviewer can use this phase of the interview to talk about a neutral matter in order to practise the ground rules of the interview which will follow. These include issues such as, the central ethos of, an in-depth interview is that the child is the expert, whereas the adult is not. Hence, to choose a neutral subject which the child has knowledge of, but the interviewer does not, provides an excellent opportunity for practising the style of the session which follows. Possible approaches might be:

- to discover how the child travelled to the interview

- particular interests

- activities recently participated in.

The practitioner generally avoids the areas of concern which led to the interview unless the child or young person appears to find this irritatingly slow and wants to progress more rapidly.

It may be necessary for the practitioner to explain who they are, if this has not been done at a preparatory stage. Such introductions should be brief and avoid specific reference to matters of concern. It is perhaps best to avoid identifying oneself as someone who 'protects children' or ensures they are 'safe' because this establishes a predetermined agenda for the session. Equally, it would be inappropriate for the practitioner to educate the child about correct words for parts of the body, or personal safety issues, or to pass an opinion on what adults should or should not do.

Once rapport has been established, the interviewer's aim is to encourage the child to recall freely his or her memories and perceptions of adverse experiences. The aim is to do this without introducing or suggesting any version of events that emanates from the practitioner (leading questions). Many children will be aware of the reason for the interview, either because they have previously expressed their concern, or because the broad purpose of the interview has been discussed during a preparation phase. A single, open-ended prompt from the practitioner is often sufficient to enable the child to start talking freely about areas of concern. This particularly applies to those children who have disclosed information previously (Sternberg *et al.* 1997). Some sample open-ended prompts are:

- 'Do you know why you are here today?'
- 'I want to talk now about why you are here today.'
- 'Tell me the reason you came here today.'

Clearly, if children pre-empt the practitioner and launch into an account of their concern, it would not be appropriate to stop or discourage them while they are spontaneously recounting memories. If this happens before there has been a chance to set out the ground rules for the session, these can be returned to at a later stage in the interview, if necessary (Poole and Lamb 1998).

Sometimes these straightforward approaches do not lead to the child communicating anything. In these circumstances the practitioner may feel there is sufficient concern to justify further exploration, and some means will need to be found to gently explore such concerns further, without introducing any new information.

ENQUIRY INTO SUSPECTED ADVERSE EXPERIENCES

There are circumstances when practitioners decide there is sufficient concern to talk to the child about possible adverse experiences. Examples of this include where it has been decided after a strategy meeting that the child's situation does not fulfil criteria for a joint investigation but the child has expressed concerns about an experience in his or her life (Department of Health *et al.* 1999, at paras. 5.31 and 5.32); or circumstances where there has already been an *Achieving Best Evidence* interview (Home Office *et al.* 2002), and where a decision not to press criminal charges has been made, yet where there is sufficient concern to justify further exploration. These are the grey areas, which appear to be quite common in practice. The approach that the practitioner follows depends on what kind of concerns led up to the current assessment. The following possibilities are quite frequently encountered:

- The child may have already spoken to someone about his or her concerns.
- The child may be considered to be at risk of some form of adversity or maltreatment.

- The child may have been found to have a physical condition which raises the possibility they have been exposed to adversity or maltreatment.

- Behavioural change in the child may have led to concerns expressed by parents, teachers, or some other adult.

The following are some suggested phrases for managing the transition and introducing enquiry about adverse experiences. They are organised according to the mode of presentation and the origin of concern. Within each category, possible questions to use are set out, starting with relatively open enquiries, progressing towards more direct questions.

When the child has already disclosed information of concern

'I understand something may have happened (which upset you, which scared you, which made you sad). Please tell me every detail that happened, from the beginning to the very end.'

'I understand that some things have been happening in your family (or school, another house, etc.). Tell me about them.'

'I have spoken with (your mum, your teacher, mummy) and it sounds as though a lot of things have been happening in your (family/school/etc.). Tell me about that.'

'Your (mum) said she had talked with you – about some things that had upset you. Tell me about that.'

Adult suspicion about a place or person

'Tell me about (place/person/time of incident causing concern).'

'Tell me who looks after you when your mum goes out. (Pause) What things do you like to do with (name of baby-sitter/childminder) – anything that you don't like when X comes to your house/looks after you?'

'I've been talking to (your mum) and she told me she was worried about you (at place or time of witnessed incident). Tell me everything about what happened.'

'(Your mum) told me that you (don't like it/get upset) when (Uncle John) comes to stay at your house. Tell me about that.'

At risk of harm

First, introduce general enquiry about the situation in which the child is considered to be at risk of harm. For example, initiate discussions about school when the concern relates to bullying; punishment for wrong doing where the concern is about physical abuse in the home; family relationships or household arrangements, likes and dislikes, where the concern is about possible sexual maltreatment within the household.

In other circumstances, a child may have described some adverse circumstances and the practitioner is concerned about other possible forms of adversity:

> 'You've told me that (summary of adverse events already disclosed, such as witnessing interparental violence, being bullied, and experiencing physical or sexual abuse). Has anyone (hurt, upset, or harmed) you in any other way?'
>
> or, 'Has anybody done anything else to you that you didn't think was right?'
>
> or, 'Did anything else happen to you at (place or time of already disclosed incident).'
>
> or, 'Did any other person hurt you?'
>
> 'Your (brother/name of different child about whom there is concern) has told me about some things that happened to him. Tell me what you know about that.'
>
> Then, after pause, 'and she (your mum) was worried about you'.
>
> or, 'Did anyone do something to you that you didn't think was right?'
>
> or, 'Did anything happen to you at (place or at the time of the abuse disclosed by another child)?'

Inter-parental violence

Enquire about home, in general.

> Then, 'What's the best thing about being at home?' followed by
>
> 'What's the worst thing about being at home?'
>
> 'Your mum told me that she and your dad have been arguing – getting upset. Tell me everything about that.'

'Have there been any times when your mum hit your dad, or dad hit your mum?'

'Your mum told me that she had to go to the hospital/doctor after she had an argument with your dad. Tell me everything about that time.'

Physical disease/change

'I've been talking to Doctor X. She told me that [brief reference to condition, e.g. you've had trouble going for a wee-wee, or a sore bottom, or trouble going to the toilet]' (in the case of a young child with suspicious repeated urinary tract infections).

'I've been talking to Doctor X, she told me that you've had to have some [medicine/tablets/injections] because of a problem in your bottom (e.g., for a child with unexplained sexually transmitted disease) – can you tell me everything about that?'

Behaviour change

Enquire directly about the child's symptoms (anxiety, depression, nightmares):
For example:

'I hear you've been worrying a lot. Tell me all about that.'

'I hear you've had a lot of very scary dreams. Tell me what happens when you have them.'

'You've told me you're very (depressed, worried, upset) – tell me all about that.'

Enquiry when child displays sexualised behaviour problems:

'Can you think about the time when you were (playing with/having sex with – repeat essence of presentation of sexualised behaviour) like that with Fred? – Tell me everything about that.'

Followed by:

'Have there been any other times when things like that have happened?'

or, 'Has anybody done things like that with you?'

Specifically concerning aggressive behaviour:

'I want to talk with you now about (aggressive episode). Tell me everything about that time.'

Followed by:

'Have there been other times when things like that have happened?'

'Do you know why that (aggressive episode) happened?'

'Have there been any things that have been upsetting you?'

'Has anybody done things like that to you?'

Specific questions following deliberate self-harm:

'Do you know why that happened?'

'Have any things been upsetting you?'

Follow this with general enquiry about school, friends, family members, for example:

'Sometimes young people (hurt themselves, take tablets) if they have something very upsetting which they have seen, or has happened to them and they don't know how to talk about it' – pause – 'has anything like that happened to you?'

Then, direct questions about possibility of maltreatment (see further approaches, below).

If the child says 'yes' to any direct question, then the next one should be along the lines of 'Tell me a bit more about that' or, 'I think I understand, but just help me by telling me a bit more about that.'

FURTHER APPROACHES FOR RAISING ISSUES OF CONCERN

Sometimes further sessions may be required. Providing the child is appropriately prepared and anxieties are contained, repeated interviews, per se, do not lead to inaccurate accounts. If, however, interviews are conducted inappropriately and a pre-determined 'answer' relentlessly sought, erroneous accounts can emerge. A properly conducted repeat interview, with due attention to what happens between sessions, is better than attempting to prise an account from a child in one session.

Sometimes more direct, focused questions will be appropriate in the present interview session because there are other strong indications that a child has been harmed. Examples include:

About place and time

'Has anything happened to you at [place or time of alleged incident]?'

'Did anything happen to you at [place, or actual time of abuse disclosed by another child]?'

About physical assault

'Has anyone hurt you or hit you' [pause]. 'Either another young person, or an adult?'

About domestic violence

'Have there been any times when your mum hit your dad, or dad hit mum?'

'Have you heard your mum and dad fighting?'

'Have you seen your mum hurt your dad? [pause] or your dad hurt your mum?'

'Your mum told me that she had to go to the hospital/doctor after she had an argument with your dad. Tell me everything about that time.'

About bullying

'Have you been hit or hurt by another child, either at school or on the way to and from school?'

'Have you been hurt in a sexual way by another child?' (for an older child).

About possible sexual assault

'Has anyone touched you on your body in ways that you didn't like?'

'Your mum said that you had some worries…about being touched on private parts of your body – tell me about that.'

'Has anyone touched the private parts of your body, and made you feel uncomfortable?'

'Did anyone, even a grown up who you are close to, ever touch the private parts of your body?'

'I talk to a lot of children, and sometimes to children who have been touched on private parts of their body – it can help to talk about things like that. Has anything like that ever happened to you?'

'Some children are touched on private parts of their body, sometimes by people they know very well. It can help to talk about things like that. Has anything like that ever happened to you?'

These latter two involve permission-giving statements initially, but end with a direct question. Questions of this kind are clearly potentially suggestive and would therefore only be of value if suspicion of adversity was high, and the nature of the concern being assessed was severe.

Next steps

The direction at this stage would depend upon whether professional concerns have been allayed by the sessions so far, or uncertainty continues, or alternatively, concerns are confirmed.

If professional concerns are allayed, the interview would need to be closed before the child returns home and parent or carer informed of the outcome. Arrangements for follow up should be made and possibly other plans for further assessment of the child's needs.

If concerns about adversity are confirmed by the interview, the practitioner will need to consider whether, on the basis of the information revealed, the child should have an investigative interview to gather evidence for criminal proceedings, bringing the interview to a close and making the appropriate arrangements. Alternatively, the decision may be made to clarify any details about adverse experiences, particularly if any ambiguities remain outstanding (see Jones 2003, pp.140–142).

In other situations, concerns remain unclear. Although professionally frustrating, it is preferable to close the session, without having pressurised the child, rather than to become drawn through professional anxiety into a hectoring or coercive stance. Plans can be made for a review or reassessment in the future, with time to reflect on any possible impediments to successful communications so far. Children, their parents, and other professionals would probably need advice as to how to handle any interim phase (Jones 2003, pp.139–140).

CLOSING THE INTERVIEW

This is a very important part of an in-depth session. It serves to orientate the child to the next steps and also to recognise and vindicate the child's communication and, where appropriate, expression of emotion. The practitioner should convey appreciation and empathy for the child's situation. Congratulation, personal perspectives of the professional, or promises which cannot be delivered are all inappropriate. The child should be asked if there is anything which he or she wants to know or raise. Contact numbers for future help are important, especially for older children. Some children want to know about what information will be shared with others.

The child's communications about victimisation or adversity should be considered alongside his or her overall needs and welfare status.

CHAPTER 15

Making Plans: Assessment, Intervention and Evaluating Outcomes

David Jones, Nick Hindley and Paul Ramchandani

Assessment is a key activity and provides the foundation for intervention. When children have suffered harm, it becomes of special importance because of the concern to avoid future repetition and the need to maintain safety for the child, as well as to do all possible to obtain the best outcome in terms of the child's welfare. When the government introduced its Assessment Framework (Department of Health 2000; Department of Health, Department for Education and Employment and Home Office 2000b), the primary aim was to improve the quality of assessments, which were made not only by social workers but for all those professionals working with children. It was particularly designed for those professionals determining whether a child was in need and, if so, to work out how best to assist. There was a great deal of hope at the time that the Assessment Framework would achieve this and lead on to more focused interventions. In general, the framework has been well received but there remain concerns about how to bridge the gap between gathering data, amassing information on children and their families, and delivering effective interventions (Cleaver et al. 2004). Between these two poles lies a series of decisions which are made by frontline practitioners and their managers. This chapter seeks to fill this gap and thereby to assist practitioners and their managers in promoting positive developmental outcomes for children. It will do so by first considering decision-making, then reviewing what is known about the outcomes for children after a child has been identified as having been harmed, before considering how we can use the evidence base in day to day practice.

Decision-making

We still know relatively little about how professionals actually make decisions in these situations. Some research has focused on providing cameo vignettes to frontline workers and asking them what they would do and how they would decide the next steps. This methodology has been criticised because practitioners may well say what they feel they should have done, rather than what they have actually done in similar cases. Asking people to recall what they did in real cases is complicated by the constraints of retrospective recall, but also by the expectancy effect and the desire of most professionals to present what they think they ought to have done or would have done ideally. Still more difficult is to track frontline workers in the field and ask them what they are actually doing while they are doing it. Very few practitioners thank the researcher for this degree of intrusion! Notwithstanding these difficulties, it is worth exploring decision-making in the field of health and social care further.

An obvious consideration is, was the decision right or wrong? The lay perspective on decision-making might well focus on this, as is demonstrated by the number of inquiries over the years which have followed celebrated occasions in which decision-making appears to have gone awry (Department of Health 1991a and, more recently, Cm 5730 2003). This may seem a straightforward question at first glance, but there are different ways of looking at the question of whether the decision was a correct one or not. The most common way in which we look at such decisions is with respect to whether it led subsequently to the most desirable outcomes for the child. So, in the case of significant harm to a child, a decision is said to be the 'right' one if its expected consequences turn out to be the most desirable. This is generally known as the consequentialist model of decision-making, i.e. looking ahead to the endpoint or outcome of the decision in the future.

An alternative model is to focus to a relatively greater extent on the process by which the decisions were made which led to the outcome in question. Process considerations include:

- who makes the decision

- how a decision was reached

- adequacy of information available

- timing issues.

From a moral perspective, this raises the issue of autonomy and is of particular importance in the child protection field because of concerns about the balance between decisions made by agents of the state, such as social workers or those advising them and, on the other hand, those made by parents. A greater involvement of parents in decision-making and explicit attempts to work in partnership with parents have focused upon these kinds of relationships and tensions (Shemmings and Shemmings 2001). In a similar vein, there can be conflicts and tensions between decisions made by parents on the one hand, and on those made by children under 16 years who have the capacity to understand and make their own decisions (see Appendix 3 on Information Sharing in Department of Health *et al.* 2003).

A further dimension to consider within the decision-making process might be how a decision was reached.

- Were sufficient and appropriate steps taken?

- Was sufficient information available to enable appropriate decisions to be made?

- Were the right people involved or asked their opinions or to provide information?

- Was the timing appropriate to the nature of the decision that had to be made? For example, was the decision made quickly enough or, on the other hand, too quickly for the nature of the risk of harm posed to the child in the particular case?

Another consideration is whether there was fairness in terms of the nature of the discussions and the interactions between different people.

The field of significant harm to children is undoubtedly a complex one, where a wide variety of factors and dimensions have to be taken into account. Furthermore, the evidence base upon which to make decisions is limited, and not always directly applicable to the individual case in hand. For both these reasons, the case for a consequentialist approach to examining whether a decision was the right one or not is relatively weaker and, from a moral perspective, a greater proportion of our efforts should be focused on process aspects of decision-making. Additionally, as can be seen from the brief discussion above, there are different approaches to the analysis of decision processes and, in practice, these are very often conflated without an explicit recognition or agreement as to which perspective should take prominence. In such cases, decision analysis may lurch to and fro between a consequentialist analysis to one focused on process. This is important because it is probably only through careful analysis of the decision processes that we can further define effective operational practice and have an influence over supervision undertaken for frontline workers.

Unsurprisingly, therefore, there is considerable variation across England and Wales in the outcome of our decision-making. For example, rates of child protection registration vary greatly, as do the numbers of children who are looked after by the local authority, as well as those who are adopted (Department for Education and Skills 2004a; Department for Education and Skills 2005b). While it is true that some of these differences depend upon regional differences in factors such as deprivation, even when indices of social deprivation are applied to the figures variation persists. Hence it is likely that deprivation levels affect some of the items listed above, but it has also been pointed out that the nature of local multi-disciplinary working practices also contributes to variation. Sometimes this variation can be traced to the relative weight given to different contributors, either through personality or by their professional title. Lord Laming's inquiry concerning Victoria Climbié (Cm 5730 2003) emphasised this issue in relation to the relatively high weight given to medical opinion. He concluded that there was a need for this to be subject to greater challenge than had been the case at the time of Victoria's death. In addition, we have data that even among the same type of professional, a person's own background and personal life experience can enter into the decision process too (Goodman *et al.* 2003). In this research, professionals who had personal histories of abuse and neglect in their own childhood were relatively more likely to conclude that a child had been sexually abused than their peers who had not been mistreated during childhood.

Further, Hudson (2000) has pointed to the central place of human relationships in a multi-disciplinary context, notwithstanding repeated exhortations about improving working together practices. The same theme emerges from a review of serious child abuse cases in Wales (Owers, Brandon and Black 1999). In a related vein, Lowenstein *et al.* (2001) review the evidence for the importance of feelings and emotions to the decision-making behaviour of professionals, stressing how little emphasis there has been on this dimension hitherto. It may also be presumed that the level of the professional's knowledge and skill, together with the ease of access to relevant data, affects the quality of his or her decision-making. Central to this dimension is likely to be the quality of supervision available to key professionals who are making frontline decisions about children's welfare situations. Once again this latter point was drawn to attention by Lord Laming (Cm 5730 2003) and has emerged from previous inquiry findings.

Effective supervision in this area of work comprises the following characteristics. Supervision needs to:

- be regular and easily available

- be flexible enough to adapt to the supervisee's individual needs

- be not merely legal or administrative, but also include detailed discussion of the supervisee's decision-making processes

- include the supervisee's note taking, record keeping, letters, phone calls, and communications with others

- involve actual evidence of practice, from direct notes, observations, feedback from users, fellow workers and/or referrers; perhaps involve live co-working or use of video

- be linked with clear-cut objectives for supervisee's practice.

A key component of the decision-making process is whether the practitioner uses the evidence which is available and incorporates it into what he or she does. There is an evidence base for the outcome for children after child abuse and neglect has been identified. These data are reviewed below. Even if the evidence base does not precisely match the mix of factors in an individual case, nonetheless it is important that we use the evidence base systematically, whilst at the same time recognising its limitations.

The evidence base

In this section we review the evidence on the possibility of repeat abuse and neglect as well as other types of poor outcomes such as those affecting the child's development generally, educational progress, or emotional and behavioural outcomes for children which follow initial identification that a child has been significantly harmed. It is this outcome research which is the key evidence base for those of us working in the child protection field. The work which has been done has generally divided into studies which prospectively track cases over time and those which look back retrospectively at cases which turn out to have had a poor outcome.

Prospective studies examine re-abuse rates and other child welfare outcomes after significant harm has been established. Sometimes the outcome studied is the likelihood of successful reunification of the child with his or her family, and/or the likelihood that the child will return into the care system. The net is sometimes spread wider, examining not only re-abuse and neglect but also other aspects of the child's development, emotionally, educationally and physically. Studies have looked at re-abuse and outcomes for the index child or for all of the children within the same family setting, or alternatively at whether the adults involved in harming or neglecting children have done so to a further child in a different family.

Retrospective studies look at the characteristics of cases where efforts to reunify children with their parents have proved unsuccessful and the child has been returned, or even remained within the care system. Sometimes these children are compared with those where reunification has not been attempted. There have also been studies of child deaths, in order to examine which characteristics are most commonly associated with this extreme final outcome.

Methodological considerations

There are significant methodological difficulties with existing studies. The quality of the studies which we draw upon has varied enormously. This makes interpretation of the data difficult. Nonetheless research on outcomes can be used effectively to draw out those factors which are more likely to be associated with an increased or reduced likelihood of future harm. Strictly speaking, the studies focus primarily on those factors which are associated with future harm rather than enabling us to understand how the factor in question influences the outcome for the child. That is, the studies are studies of associated factors rather than risk factors.

Assessment of studies

Jones has previously summarised the principal factors associated with re-abuse and other poor outcomes for children in the wake of significant harm (Jones 1991 and revised 1998, summarised in Chapter 4 of Department of Health, Department for Education and Employment and Home Office 2000b). Jones (1991, 1998) reviewed rates of recurrence of child maltreatment, as well as the factors associated with relatively good or less good outcomes for the child. He also reviewed available work on the characteristics of successful versus unsuccessful interventions. The main findings of these two reviews were as follows:

- Once child maltreatment had occurred, rates of recurrence lay between 20 per cent and 30 per cent. However, it was not necessarily the case that the same type of abuse recurred subsequently.

- Rates of recurrence for cases of neglect were higher than for other forms of maltreatment.

- Neglect cases were found to be very difficult to work with and generally led to a poorer outcome than other forms of maltreatment.

- A poor outcome in terms of the child's welfare befell up to one half of cases on follow up.

- Better outcome was associated with provision of services, especially those services which contained an outreach component and where partnerships with parents had been able to be forged.

- The follow up studies indicated little value in prolonged assistance being offered to resistant families.

- Furthermore, focused treatments were better than non-specific support in achieving better outcomes.

Jones (1991, 1998) also listed the characteristics of those cases in which intervention was much less likely to be successful with respect to re-abuse and/or lack of success with attempted family reunification. These were the following:

- a group of factors associated with severity (extensive harm, duration and frequency)

- mixed forms of maltreatment

- abuse with accompanying neglect or psychological maltreatment

- sadistic acts

- a group of factors connected with denial (absence of acknowledgement, lack of co-operation, inability to form a partnership and absence of outreach)

- Parental mental health (personality disorder, learning disabilities associated with mental illness, psychosis, substance misuse).

Jones then organised the factors deriving from his reviews into groups of factors associated with a better chance of successful reunification compared with those linked with a markedly reduced likelihood. The factors were listed in a table in 1991 which was updated in the light of subsequent studies (Jones 1998). They were considered using the ecological perspective on the occurrence and maintenance of child maltreatment, which was first proposed by Bronfenbrenner (1979).

A framework for understanding

This developmental/ecological framework is important to emphasise because it means that the assessment itself can be grounded within a theoretical framework concerning the nature of child maltreatment and the influences which are relevant to its recurrence. The assessment is then likely to be more comprehensive and include all areas likely to affect outcome. As discussed in Chapter 1, the ecological component of the model refers to the child's individual world as being surrounded by concentric layers of social organisation which are increasingly complex, and each of which is potentially capable of influencing the child's welfare. The first layer involves parent figures and carers, then family influences, followed by extended family, neighbourhood influences and finally those emanating from the broader social environment. At the same time, this ecological perspective on the child and his or her context should be placed within a developmental framework, in order to consider both historical influences as well as subsequent events and processes after an incidence of significant harm to a child, all considered in relation to the child's rate of growth and development. It is this theoretical approach which underpins the Assessment Framework for assessing children in need and their families (Department of Health *et al.* 2000b) and is the basis for interprofessional work where there are concerns about children (Department of Health *et al.* 2003).

In this way developmental and ecological considerations can be brought together into one model. We argue that this makes the job of assessment more comprehensive from a descriptive perspective. It does not, however, necessarily explain *how* maltreatment has occurred or may recur, but merely enables us to consider the range of factors and influences which are known to affect the likelihood of future harm.

The following groups of factors are drawn from this framework and used to organise Table 15.1, because they have been shown to have an influence both on the occurrence and likelihood for significant harm to be maintained or to recur over time:

- factors related to the original abuse or neglect
- child factors
- parent factors
- factors associated with parenting and parent/child interaction
- dynamics and relationships within the family
- factors linked to the neighbourhood and social setting in which the family live
- factors associated with the professional system and the resources which are available.

The authors of this chapter undertook an evidence-based, systematic review of studies of outcome following identification of child abuse and neglect, in order to provide the most up to date assessment of factors which pertain to the likelihood of re-abuse and other poor outcomes (Hindley, Ramchandani and Jones 2006). We reviewed many thousands of abstracts, and selected only those which met our criteria. From these 16 studies, the rate of recurrence of abuse or neglect following demonstrated incident averaged 20 per cent. The rate for recurrence within the family was 30 per cent.

The factors with the strongest association with future risk of maltreatment are indicated in italics in Table 15.1 (see page 286). The strongest associations were with:

- a prior history of maltreatment before the index case
- rapid recurrence
- neglect cases
- interparental conflict
- parental mental health problems.

In addition, there was a strong, but less powerful link with:

- parental substance/alcohol use
- family stress
- lack of social support
- younger children
- parents' own history of abuse.

Table 15.1 sets out those factors associated with an increased likelihood of future harm, contrasted with those where the likelihood is decreased following initial identification of significant harm to an index child. Factors in italics are those which withstood the rigorous inclusion criteria we used in our systematic review. The remaining factors have support from other studies which did not necessarily meet our inclusion criteria.

Table 15.1: Factors associated with future harm

Factors	Future significant harm more likely	Future significant harm less likely
Abuse	Severe physical abuse including burns/scalds *Neglect* Severe growth failure Mixed abuse *Previous maltreatment* Sexual abuse with penetration or over long duration Fabricated/induced illness Sadistic abuse	Less severe forms of abuse If severe, yet compliance and lack of denial, success still possible
Child	Developmental delay with special needs Mental health problems Very young – requiring rapid parental change	Healthy child Attributions (in sexual abuse) Later age of onset One good corrective relationship
Parent	*Personality disorder* – anti-social – sadistic – aggressive Lack of compliance Denial of problems Learning disabilities plus *mental illness* Substance abuse *Paranoid psychosis* Abuse in childhood – not recognised as a problem	Non-abusive partner Willingness to engage with services Recognition of problem Responsibility taken Mental disorder, responsive to treatment Adaptation to childhood abuse
Parenting and parent/child interaction	Disordered attachment Lack of empathy for child Poor parenting competency Own needs before child's	Normal attachment Empathy for child Competence in some areas

Continued on next page

Table 15.1 cont.

Factors	Future significant harm more likely	Future significant harm less likely
Family	Inter-parental conflict and violence	Absence of domestic violence
	Family stress	Non-abusive partner
	Power problems: poor negotiation, autonomy and affect expression	Capacity for change
		Supportive extended family
Professional	Lack of resources	Therapeutic relationship with child
	Ineptitude	Outreach to family
		Partnership with parents
Social setting	Social isolation	Social support
	Lack of social support	More local child care facilities
	Violent, unsupportive neighbourhood	Volunteer networks

Source: adapted from Jones 1991, 1998.

We next turn to how the information set out in the table above can be used in everyday practice by those making decisions about children who have been harmed.

Using the evidence base

But can we use these findings in the real world of practice? We can, but not in a precise or numerical way. The research can be used as a guide, but not to determine practice. There are several reasons for this, aside from the reservations already considered on the quality of the evidence base, above. These reasons include the following.

Limitations with actuarial approaches to assessing risk

It has not been possible to develop a reliable method for ascribing weighted scores to individual factors in order to emerge with a numerical expression of the relative risk of recurrence of abuse. We have already listed those factors which have the strongest association with future risk of recurrence, and so for some factors we can have a greater degree of confidence that if a particular factor is present, or not so strongly present, then risk of recurrence is likely to vary accordingly for the individual child. However, the confidence we can place on this link is not sufficient to allow for a reliable use of numerical scoring of relative risk. In fact, to do so at this limited stage of knowledge would be probably dangerous in itself, leading either to a false sense of confidence or pessimism as to outcome in the individual case. The evidence base, as set out above, can guide our decision-making but cannot be regarded as a short cut to be reduced to mere numbers.

A further issue limits the degree to which we can use an actuarial approach. This is the question of how individual factors interact with one another. These interactions are complex, both because there are a large number of different factors involved in most cases, but also because of subtle interactions between positive and negative factors in the individual case. For example, to what extent can parental insight ameliorate the factor of a parental tendency to explosive violence? In this particular example, we can fairly reliably say that behaviour matters more than insight with regard to impulsive violence. So, if an adult has learnt new or different forms of behavioural response to situations, which would previously have led to a violent outburst, and if this new-found behavioural difference has been repeated on a number of different occasions in different contexts, then we can begin to be more confident about future risk of harm. Insight or understanding in this situation might be one of the factors which helps a person to learn how to change his or her behaviour, accept treatment efforts etc., but does not necessarily affect the negative behaviour directly.

Another consideration is that *efficacy* of a particular approach to intervention or treatment when assessed under ideal circumstances (e.g., cases selected for pure groups of symptoms, well motivated to attend for research assessments, without accompanying problems or co-morbid conditions, or learning disabilities, and with fully trained and staffed research teams working to guidelines to deliver interventions) may or may not equate to *effectiveness* within the real world of practice. This issue has been of major interest within the field of psychotherapy outcome research (Margison *et al.* 2000), and to those studying child mental health treatments (Angold *et al.* 2000).

Qualitative assessment

Qualitative assessment of individual factors is likely to be of great importance in real world decision-making. Thus, although impulsive violence features as one risk factor in Table 15.1, the precise nature of an impulsive act, the degree to which it was context-based or entirely unpredictable, and its force or, perhaps, quality of sadistic accompanying elements, is likely to differ greatly from case to case, and be of major importance to those making decisions about children's safety.

Often, of course, we do not have the outcome data from research which matches the precise situation we face in reality. This may be because of either the complexity of the case or the particularity of the circumstances surrounding it. However, we can still make use of research findings to inform decision-making by examining one particular aspect of a multitude of factors which have contributed to each complex predicament. On their own, however, these individual factors are not good predictors of future risk of harm.

In the individual case, a single factor may override all others, notwithstanding a consideration of the range of factors as outlined above. For example, the nature of a particular blow may be so concerning that it outweighs all other considerations clinically, and may not be adequately reflected in research studies. Additionally, aspects such as the motivational intention behind harm may be relevant to decision-makers, rather than the effect of that harm on the child. Deliberate cruelty may be less responsive to intervention than misjudged discipline, yet each result in a similar looking bruise to a child's head. Thus, while Table 15.1 can assist decision-makers, it is important that it is used flexibly and that practitioners still allow other factors, which may not necessarily yet be adequately reflected in research studies, to enter into their decision-making processes about individual children.

Practitioners have to make judgements within these complex human situations, with respect to the relative importance of different factors. It is suggested here that having the factors set out and available for us provides practitioners with the basis for making these decisions, and that the recent findings help us with where we are to look for emphasis and salience, either positively or negatively, even if a precise, numerically based instrument remains elusive. It can reasonably be stated that, in the real world of practice, it is highly unlikely that an actuarial approach will take us further than the realm of guidance for a practitioner's individual decision-making, simply because of the complexity and multi-factorial nature of individual cases in the real world.

Given these observations, it seems especially important to ensure that the process is as open as possible, from an ethical as well as a practical point of view.

Openness of decision-making processes

There are several reasons why openness, with respect to decision-making, is preferable. It is clear that the consequences of decision-making are very serious in the field of child abuse and neglect. Making the wrong decision, in either direction, can be very serious for children and their families. Both children and their parents have a right to understand and be involved with the decisions that are being made about them, particularly because the results of decisions in this area are so far-reaching. There are also practical benefits to be derived from openness. First, the assessor has to think carefully about his or her own decision-making. It also enables practitioners to describe the process through which they made a decision, to their supervisors. This concentration on process potentially enables practitioners to become aware of their own personal responses and reactions to the people and situations that they are evaluating. Openness also encourages the practitioner to distinguish between amassing facts and evaluating the relative importance, positively or negatively, of the data that have been gathered. All this allows for scrutiny both by the individual practitioner, in conjunction with his or her supervisor, and by parents and outside agencies, including Courts. It is to be hoped that in this way there would be room for checks and balances, enabling challenge to any bias to be made. In addition, having a transparent process provides a framework through which to assess outcomes of intervention. It also means that the criteria for assessing change can be considered in the light of the total picture, or the overall assessment of risk of harm to the child.

Generally, open processes are more likely to lead to equitable decision-making in the highly emotive field of child maltreatment.

Implications for practice

It is clear from the discussion above that we need to take into account both the limitations and imprecision of the evidence base when making decisions in this area. Furthermore, we need to be aware that emotional factors do enter into decision-making and therefore cannot be set aside. For these reasons checks and balances must be built in. Openness is a key quality to be incorporated into practice, and this is reflected in recent case law decisions within the Family Justice system that have emphasised the need for transparency with respect to processes in decision-making (Re L 2002).

As practitioners we need to take the most logical and sensible approach and apply it as best as possible to the individual case before us. Subsequently, however, we will need to continually re-assess how the individual case unfolds over time, adjusting our evaluation of expected outcome accordingly. This implies a major move in the direction of risk management, rather than an emphasis on a risk assessment. Risk assessment, for all the reasons outlined above, is simply too imprecise and inexact to apply in this field. However, that is not to say that risk of future harm to the child cannot be managed in a sensible, logical and open manner. What follows is an approach to making decisions and planning interventions based on these considerations.

Making decisions, where a child has been significantly harmed

The following stages of decision-making are proposed, based on the foregoing considerations:

1. Data gathering.

2. Weighing relative significance.

3. Assessment of the current situation.

4. Circumstances that might alter the child's welfare.

5. Prospects for change.

6. Criteria for gauging effectiveness.

7. Time scale proposed.

8. The plan for the child (child in need plan, child protection plan or care plan, depending on status of the child).

Data gathering

This is the familiar stage for all practitioners, in which all relevant information is gathered from all the different areas which pertain to the risk of future harm to the child. It will be important to draw together both positive and potentially negative factors from each of the different areas that we have identified. Some material would derive from history taking, while other material would be available from direct observation of individuals and groups of family members interacting with one another.

Weighing relative significance

Next is the process of weighing the different factors, both positive and negative, in order to consider how much force, or influence, each has with respect to the child. A crucial aspect of this phase is to consider the potential interactions between different factors. For example, do individual factors when added up render the picture more serious than was originally evident? Do certain factors act to compensate or modify other factors? As we have already considered, there is no mathematical formula for weighting these different factors. Sometimes the nature of one factor is so overwhelmingly harmful, or perverse, that it cancels out any other, more positive considerations. More usually, however, there are factors on both sides of the equation, some of which would need to be ascribed greater weight than others. It is suggested that Table 15.1 be used to consider these factors, bearing in mind those factors that emerged from our stringent review of studies, but also taking into account qualitative aspects of the individual case, as described in the preceding section.

Assessment of the current situation

This is crucial and involves setting out the current status of the child from a welfare perspective. It involves drawing together the factors, as already discussed, and formulating a coherent evaluation of the child's situation, including but not limited to significant harm and the prospects thereof in the future. Clearly, all factors would be drawn together from each of the three sides of the Assessment Framework triangle (Department of Health *et al.* 2000b). This is where the practitioner needs to be bold and state exactly what he or she thinks about the child's situation. Very often this all-important stage is omitted, or given insufficient prominence in the practitioner's conclusions. However, the subsequent stages follow from it, and there is greater danger from avoiding a definite conclusion about the child's current welfare status than there is from making a conclusion that subsequently turns out to need revision. After all, as we have discussed above, our individual fallibility in this area must be acknowledged, implying a need to make decisions on the best information available, and in the most open way, but allowing these initial conclusions to be open to revision in the light of new information over time.

Circumstances that might alter the child's welfare

Here, the practitioner identifies those factors or circumstances that might affect the child's future welfare. Some factors may make things worse and others be reasonably predicted to improve the situation. Here we can include all proposed intervention strategies, including social work help and support, psychological treatments and so forth. Once again, we need to consider all domains within the Assessment Framework triangle and all the various strategies that might be likely to affect outcomes.

Prospects for change

In this stage we consider the likelihood for change in the situation facing the child. How does the practitioner consider that change could occur, and if so, through what mechanisms? At this stage we will need to set out alternative outcomes, linked where possible to different forms of interventions, and/or changes in future circumstances. For example, the outcome for a child with one parent may depend to a large extent on whether the parent remains with an abusive partner or not. Mental health professionals conceptualise this stage in terms of prognosis.

Criteria for gauging effectiveness

It can be very useful to set out the criteria that the practitioner is going to use to evaluate the outcome of intervention. If the desired outcome is family reunification then how will practitioner, parent, child or the Family Justice system know whether the situation has improved sufficiently from the child's perspective to permit reunification? It is also important to lay out the criteria for gauging effectiveness of the care or intervention plan in order to engage the family and encourage parental participation and involvement. Setting criteria for change early on in the process of care planning can be very empowering for parents to the extent that they are involved with and make contributions to plans about their family and children. A frequent refrain of parents who have had their children removed is to the effect that 'no one told us' what they had to achieve or what was required of them before their children were summarily removed. It can be difficult to articulate criteria and outcomes which are possible to evaluate and measure. However, notwithstanding these challenges the desired outcomes should be made explicit.

Time scale proposed

How long is a reasonable period of time within which to expect changes to be made? The key issue here is the needs of the child. The younger the child the more likely it is that the time scale would be shorter so as to enable babies and young children to be able to form alternative selective attachments to substitute caregivers, should this be required. The twin tracking initiative of concurrent planning has taken on board many of these themes, described above, with the explicit aim of reducing delay for children who are subject to care proceedings, enabling permanent plans in the direction of birth or substitute care to be made as swiftly as possible (Monck, Reynolds and Wigfall 2001). The Family Justice System's recent introduction of the protocol for child care cases represents a similar initiative from the legal perspective, again aimed at reducing delay and allowing permanent plans for children to be made as soon as possible in the wake of severe parenting problems (Family Division, Lord Chancellor's Department *et al.* 2003).

The plan for the child

In this stage all the plans for the child and his or her parents are summarised, including those for support, intervention, residence and contact arrangements. The roles and responsibilities of the different professionals and agencies will need to be specified here. Additionally, we need to record who will notice any of the changes that have been predicted to appear above, and what action will be taken in response to any changes noticed? It will, therefore, be important to know who is going to notice whether, for example, the child's language development reaches a plateau and how might this information be brought to the attention of the core members of the professional group. What is the date and time of the next review? What are the arrangements for an earlier review than anticipated?

The untreatable family?

It goes against the grain for those working in children's services to conclude that some families are beyond our abilities to facilitate change. It can even be seen as offensive to consider some families beyond help. The phrase is used here in order to draw attention to the fact that no matter what resources we have or skills we bring to bear, sometimes families seem unable to change sufficiently to render their child safe in their care. The whole notion appears discordant with the professional sense of duty and therapeutic optimism. However, it is vital to hold the concept in mind, from the perspective of the child's future welfare. The key issue is the developmental needs of the child. Sometimes one is faced with a situation where change is possible but the time scale is simply too extended for the child's needs. As we have already discussed, the situation is more urgent with babies and young children than with older children because of young children's need for security, combined with their vulnerability to damage from a physical assault. Deciding that it is time to stop efforts at reunification, for example, can be even more complicated when lack of resources colours the decision-making equation. Nonetheless, the reality is that resources will always be limited, and fair choices have to be made within the envelope of resource availability.

The explicit recognition of the fact that not all families are treatable, or even wish to be treated, is central to the concurrent planning movement (Monck *et al.* 2001). Concurrent planning allows the possibility of substitute care to be held in the minds of family members and/or professionals, including those providing specific psychological treatments, right from the beginning of the intervention process. As stated above, openness in the decision-making and care planning process from the beginning is important. It also permits the child, when older, to look back and, it is to be hoped, be able to make sense of and understand the decisions that were made over time. It is likely that this will be of major importance for the child's future identity, particularly if he or she is raised in substitute care or adopted.

Ideally, separation of parent and child can be conducted with dignity from the parent's perspective, enabling birth parents and eventually the child to negotiate better the loss involved in separation. This is a very difficult part of the process but can be extremely helpful with respect to future contact arrangements, as well as for the birth parents' attitude and approach to future pregnancies. On occasion a parent can agree to relinquish care of one child, while starting an extended process of change which eventually enables him or her to care for a future child adequately. Such situations are possible, even where the harm to the index child has been severe.

CHAPTER 16

The Developing World of the Child: Children's Perspectives

Wendy Rose

Introduction

Throughout this book we have talked about the importance of acknowledging that children are active agents in their own development. This has profound consequences for all those professionals and others who provide care and services for children. They have a responsibility to seek out children's views, to understand their perspectives and to take these fully into account when considering children's developmental issues. This has been enshrined in law for children who are deemed to be 'in need' under the Children Act 1989 in England and Wales following an amendment in section 53 of the Children Act 2004. The principles, however, apply to all children, in accord with the UN Convention on the Rights of the Child. As was discussed in Chapter 13, direct work with children by professionals in many of the public services has been sadly neglected. However, there is evidence at government level of its intention to rectify this through the planned reform of the children's workforce, recognising that a common core of skills, knowledge and competence is required in this area (Department for Education and Skills 2005a). Many advocates of children's participation and citizenship have argued (see, for example, Cairns 2001; Cairns and Brannen 2005) that taking account of children's perspectives also requires a fundamental change of ethos and culture, and a move away from an adult-driven approach to the accepted ways of dealing with issues.

It requires a conscious sharing of power and control with children and young people if more appropriate and effective policies and services are to be developed. The transforming effect when this occurs was experienced at the UN General Assembly's Special Session on Children in May 2002 (UNICEF 2002) when more than 400 children joined the high level world-wide delegates. The UN Secretary-General, Kofi Annan, opened the session by saying: 'The children in this room are witnesses to our words' (UNICEF 2002, p.3). However, as the Executive Director of UNICEF, Carol Bellamy, records:

> They were that and more, as children and young people turned business-as-usual into an extraordinary UN experience. They challenged us, informed us. The stories of their lives gave us pause. And throughout, their faith in our collective abilities to make change – and their hope – inspired us. (UNICEF 2002, p.3)

From this Special Session, the United Nations Member States pledged themselves to an ambitious set of millennium development goals to be achieved by 2015 to move nearer to a World Fit for Children (UNICEF 2002).

The children at the UN Special Session described themselves as follows:

We are the world's children.

We are the victims of exploitation and abuse.

We are street children.

We are the victims and orphans of HIV/AIDS.

We are denied good-quality education and health care.

We are victims of political, economic, cultural, religious and environmental discrimination.

We are children whose voices are not being heard: it is time we are taken into account.

We want a world fit for children, because a world fit for us is a world fit for everyone. (UNICEF 2002, p.9)

Many of the children whom we have had in mind when compiling this book would describe themselves in terms similar to those of the children and young people at the UN: victims of exploitation and abuse; denied good quality education and health care; victims of political, economic, cultural, religious and environmental discrimination. This includes children who are living away from home, children who are refugees and seeking asylum, children who are growing up with complex physical or learning disabilities. These are all children whose developmental progress has been disrupted or set back in some way and who have come to the attention of the statutory and independent services. What do such children think and feel about what has happened to them, and what help or interventions have made a difference to them? In this chapter, we explore children's perspectives on different aspects of their development and identify some of the small and large interventions that have had a beneficial impact on their developmental outcomes. We would argue that evidence of the usefulness of a developmental approach to understanding children's needs and to intervening in their lives best comes from children and young people themselves.

There is an increasingly rich source of children's perspectives as researchers have become more interested in finding out and recording children's views and opinions. A significant resource is to be found in the 24 studies evaluating the implementation of the Children Act 1989, which was commissioned by the Department of Health. Twelve of the studies included interviews with children. As Aldgate and Statham, who conducted an overview of the studies, say:

> There is a strong focus on the views of the children in need and their families whose lives have been affected by the Children Act 1989. This is appropriate in view of the Act's intentions to listen to children and work with parents to safeguard and promote children's welfare. (Department of Health 2001, p.19)

Furthermore, children's opinions are now being recorded in critical circumstances such as divorce (Butler *et al.* 2003), living in step-families (Smith 2003, 2004), being adopted (Thomas *et al.* 1999), being bullied (Oliver and Candappa 2003), or as young carers (Aldridge and Becker 2003; Gorin 2004), as well as being consulted as part of developing training materials to implement policy, such as on safeguarding children (Children's Rights Alliance for England 2003; see also consultation with children about keeping safe from harm, Morgan 2004). Perhaps most powerful is the autobiographical material children and young people have produced (for example, Fever 1994 and, written when older, Frampton 2004) or which has been compiled by organisations such as Voice for the Child in Care (Voice for the Child in Care 1998) or The Who Cares? Trust (Shaw 1998). We have drawn on many of these sources to provide the vivid illustrations of children's perspectives. However, Gorin notes in her review of children's experiences of domestic violence, parental substance misuse and parental health problems that there is still very little research 'about children's experiences of contact with professionals when there are problems at home and children remain within the household' (2004, p.79). There is a rather richer vein of research emerging about children's perspectives of care and accommodation (such as Cleaver 2000; Skuse and Ward 2003; Ward, Skuse and Munro 2005) which includes their views of services they have received.

In exploring children's views of the impact of experiences on their lives and on their developmental progression, we have adopted Michael Jacobs' (1998) framework of key themes, developed from Erikson's psychosocial model of development (1980), rather than using the developmental stages which gave shape to Part 2 of this book. These themes may be central at particular stages of development, but they also continue to appear 'in different forms throughout life' (Jacobs 1998, p.13). As such they provide a useful way of discussing children's perspectives on a range of developmental issues. Jacobs argues that these themes are relevant across the lifespan but particularly notes the significance of what happens in adolescence. At this critical period issues from early childhood are thrown into the melting pot: 'Issues about sexuality, about authority, and issues about faith, hope and integrity, all central to the period of adolescence, have appeared before in childhood, and will remain concerns throughout life' (Jacobs 1998, p.13).

The themes are conceptualised in a sufficiently broad way as to have relevance to children in a range of situations and circumstances. They will appear differently in diverse cultural situations and allow us to discuss children's views on a wide range of topics, with the aim of exploring the kinds of interventions in their lives by professionals that were helpful. It also allows us insight into the impact on children of having their developmental needs met or, in some cases, left unattended.

The three sets of themes which Jacobs identifies are:

- trust and dependency
- authority and autonomy
- co-operation and competition.

This chapter will look at each theme and some associated developmental issues in turn, and conclude with what is known about the qualities in professionals that are important to children and the interventions that make a difference to them.

Trust and dependency

In Chapter 4, we explored the significance for a newborn baby of finding a dependable other to be relied upon to meet his or her basic needs and to provide security and protection from harm. These early experiences form the foundation for the later development of relationships, as well as influencing a child's sense of self and feeling of security in the world. Jacobs (1998) argues these are continuous processes:

> Being dependent intertwined with learning independence, and attachment as well as separation, are also part of a continuous process, from birth, through weaning, through taking first steps, in going to play group and school, into adolescence and on to the many other occasions for change in adult life… (p.91)

Although the initial basic trust of a baby may lead, as the child grows and his or her world is enlarged, to more refined forms of trust (Jacobs 1998), the theme of trust and dependency continues to be significant throughout life. For some children, trust in an attachment figure or significant carer may be shaken, eroded or destroyed from an early age, for example, because of domestic conflict or violence between parents or because of mental illness or alcohol misuse. Gorin (2004) in her literature review of children's experiences of parental problems notes how children in these circumstances live in an unpredictable world and quotes a child's view from Mullender *et al.*: 'It was the worst part of my life – constantly being shouted at, frightened, living in fear. You will never know what it's like, thinking that every day could be your last' (2002, p.94).

The study by Butler *et al.* (2003) of children's experiences of their parents' divorce reveals the extent to which children are distressed by growing conflict between parents and the impact that witnessing violence has on them. A common consequence of divorce is the subsequent confusion with which children may be left, as a result of separation and loss of important relationships, and the introduction of new partners and siblings. There is a sense of the world changing irrevocably for these children and of children feeling different from their friends. As Sioned and Jenny (in Butler *et al.* 2003) describe their experiences, this comes through graphically:

> I used to hear them arguing. They always used to shout at each other and basically scream their head off at each other. Me and my brother were at the top of the stairs and we used to hear them shouting in the kitchen. It felt horrible. I felt that I was the only child that's parents were getting divorced. Every morning you could hear them shouting and every evening when you got back from school and it was non-stop arguing. (Sioned, aged 12, p.34)

> I could hear him calling her things like, 'You stupid idiot', things like that. Then my father came round and told me to go to my bedroom and he was just calling her names. In the night, he pushed her down the stairs. He used to do things like that. (Jenny, aged 8, p.35)

The places where children are told of impending parental separation may become charged with sadness for them from then onwards:

> Mum sat us down. I don't like our front room any more because we always go to the front room when something really bad is happening 'cos when Dad had a problem, we came to the front room. And that was upsetting. Then Mum sat us down and told us. So I don't particularly like the front room. (Sophie, aged 15, in Butler *et al.* 2003, p.37)

Interestingly, children and adults have different memories of being told about the separation, a third of children in the study report not having been told, although every parent reported doing so 'either severally or jointly' (Butler *et al.* p.35). Differential recall by age (younger children reporting not being told more than those aged over 12) may account partly for this but issues concerned with effective communication (or lack of it) throughout the process were found to be significant. It is evident from children's accounts that information and its communication are critical factors in children's adjustment to adverse experiences.

Children whose parent or parents are suffering from physical or mental health problems or problem alcohol or drug use may find the roles of carer and being cared for are reversed. Also reversed in such situations are the positions of trust and dependency, so that the parent may become dependent on the child/carer, having to put his or her trust in the child. Two children in Gorin's overview (2004) express what this can mean and its impact on their daily lives:

> Sometimes I help her to get dressed and undressed to go to bed, if she goes to bed before me…it's slightly embarrassing helping your mum when she hasn't exactly got clothes on. (Quoted in Dearden and Becker 1996, p.22)

> I'm frightened to leave her in case she goes into a fit or something. When we were little…she got really down and started taking overdoses and that really scared us… When she's really down she says I'm going to take an overdose… I'm frightened to leave her. (Quoted in Newton and Becker 1996, p.25)

Taking on caring responsibilities may not, however, only have negative connotations. Some children experience caring for a family member as a source of pride and a way of expressing their love. As Gorin (2004) notes: 'The strength of children's love and loyalty to their parents comes across in many children's accounts. Children and young people often want to be able to help their parents in anyway they can' (p.29) and she quotes a child from Bibby and Becker's study of young carers (2000): 'It can get difficult but it's good afterwards knowing I've helped my mum. I enjoy helping my mum. I only wish it could be a bit easier' (p.44).

For those children unable to continue living at home, this may entail varying degrees of separation from parents, brothers and sisters and other significant people in their lives, as well as multiple losses. This may include loss of friends, home, school, pets, belongings – all those things which contribute to the sense of self and a sense of security. The impact of changing homes, acquiring new families or carers and undergoing yet further moves inevitably make enormous demands on children and may have detrimental effects on their ability to trust.

In a study of children's views of care and accommodation (Skuse and Ward 2003), children's comments 'clearly expressed the anxiety that frequent change created' (p.115). Eliza, who first entered care at the age of 12 and had four placements in 15 months, followed by further moves, comments:

> I used to hate it when I either had to change social workers or change placements or something like that because it was just another thing to get used to – just settling into new families and starting all over again…fitting in with other kids that live there especially if it was their birth children…it varied how they treated you, especially when they compared you to their own, and when

they got annoyed with you because you didn't know how to take them or anything (p.115).

Rebuilding trust with adult carers after such experiences becomes a major challenge for children. We have included the reflections of an adoptive mother, who adopted Harry at the age of 2, about the longer term effects of instability on young children:

> From the experience that I've had adopting three children with special needs, all different backgrounds, different circumstances, I would like to say that I don't know whether anything can be done about it, but children don't bounce. Yes, they are resilient, but if you move a child several times before their adoption then the adoptive parents are going to have a very long struggle to get them to realise that this is where they are for good, this is where they are going to stay, because children will be very hesitant to give you their love, to trust you... It takes years. It does take years for that child to realise that they can depend on you, you are going to be here for them forever and that the adoptive parents realise these things, the children may be playing up but you must really try hard because it's difficult to read the body language...if a child's got special needs and they've been moved several times, it does take years for them to settle down. (Skuse and Ward 2003, pp.116–117)

It is not surprising that some children in care and accommodation, who have experienced early adverse circumstances, reach adolescence feeling unloved, unsafe and unimportant. Ann at 16 expressed these feelings in the following poem:

I feel

I feel lonely, I feel scared
Can someone please just tell me why
I feel unhappy, I feel pressurised
Can someone please just tell me why
I feel unloved, I feel like no one cares
Can someone please just tell me why
I feel confused, I feel insecure
Can someone please just tell me why
I feel I have no say in important things in my life
Can someone please just tell me why

(Voice for the Child in Care 1998, p.38)

A strong thread running through children's accounts of living in care and accommodation is the experience of multiple losses and, with those losses, a severance of connectedness with people and places. Where children have undergone a number of moves, this may include losing touch with important previous carers and other children in residential units or foster homes. It only serves to compound the feeling of being different and the loss of security. Joanne, in Skuse and Ward's study (2003), describes her experiences:

> There's so many kids coming in and out of children's homes, or foster homes. You can have a best friend one day, and then you can go to the shop and they've gone, and they're not allowed to tell you where they've gone, so you don't know. Cos it's local authority and you don't know who you're getting in next. (p.118)

The loss of possessions is all too common, stolen by other children, mislaid in the home or in transit, or deliberately withheld. Alison recalls:

> Every single foster home I went to, there was somebody there that stole from me. Every time... The first home I went into, when I left my grandma's and my granddad's, my scientific calculator went missing which I had to have for school, It was, like a compulsory item. A gold chain I got when I was christened, from my godparents and just tapes and bits and pieces. (Quoted in Skuse and Ward 2003, p.131)

Skuse and Ward (2003) report that a number of young people 'were upset by the fact that presents their foster carers had given them whilst they were looked after were withdrawn at the end of a placement' (p.132). Lara lost tangible memories of her foster home: 'They (foster carers) took all my photos I had of them, so I've got like no photos of them' (in Skuse and Ward 2003, p.132).

The importance of remaining connected to parents and to wider family and previous carers is underlined by children's accounts in a number of studies (for example, Cleaver 2000; Thomas et al. 1999). It is not only through contact face to face, by telephone or correspondence, but by indulging in particular activities or hanging on to special objects such as dog-eared photographs, items of clothing or toys, that children reinforce their memories of home and family (Cleaver 2000). Greg (aged 10) describes in Cleaver's study how looking at the stars helped him feel closer to his parents: 'When I look at the stars because we always used to do it on Bonfire Night or every night we were outside... We all had a game who could find the most shooting stars' (in Cleaver 2000, p.206). Mary (aged 11) in the same study had a cherished photograph and a few special items of clothes: 'These are the clothes I wear mostly because they remind me of my mum. Because they're what my mum's just bought me' (in Cleaver 2000, p.207).

Children and young people can be very clear about who are the significant people in their lives, now and in the past (Brannen *et al.* 2000; Cleaver 2000; Marsh and Peel 1999), and the value to them of facilitating and reinforcing those connections comes through strongly from their accounts. Steve (aged 14), in Thomas and Beckford's study of adopted children, describes how he and his brother John, now both adopted, keep in touch with their previous foster carers by sending cards and presents, and more recently by speaking to them on the phone:

> I've heard how they looked after me. They're quite special to me... They're still very much in the picture. I'd like to keep in touch with them... I just sort of like to know them again. Like, they still remember us. They haven't heard our voices for ages. We were just little kids' voices and [when] they actually hear our voices, feel us growing up, I just thought it would be nice to get to know them again... So we just phone them up. I enjoy phoning up... As soon as I hear [my foster mother's] voice, for some reason all the memories just flood back into my mind. I can remember things, photographs. I just see them in my head again, and I remember things. (Quoted in Thomas *et al.* 1999, p.106)

Authority and autonomy

The second set of themes around authority and autonomy, if successfully negotiated, lay the foundation 'for self esteem in terms of what might be achieved, for confident independence, and for the potentiality for the pleasure and creativity of self-expression' argues Jacobs (1998, p.99). A child's increasing capacity for coordination of movement combined with the development of language and communication allow greater exploration of the world around him or her, and greater engagement with it. At this point, choices enter into the picture – for example, to crawl this way or that way, to eat with a spoon or with fingers, to take what is offered or to refuse. The resolution of choice is all too often not dependent on the infant's wishes or desires, which introduces the issue of how adult expectations will be learned and understood. Jacobs suggests that a child's world can become puzzling, then baffling and finally mystifying when faced with often confusing and apparently paradoxical expectations in areas such as toilet training. 'It is scarcely surprising that it is difficult for a young child to comprehend in so short a time the complexities and subtleties of the rules of the adult game of life' observes Jacobs (1998, p.100).

Thus, increasing competence brings with it gradually more independence, accompanied by issues of control and their negotiation. Jacobs sums up the importance of this set of themes:

> Attitudes towards self and others over these important matters of doing, making, and acting, acquired in the early years, will be reinforced within the family in later childhood and adolescence, supported and challenged in school, and become a major influence on the way in which learning, work, and relationships with authority in particular, are faced and worked with in adult life. (1998, p.98)

For children who have experienced frequent changes of adult carers and homes, this growing mastery and acquisition of competencies may be interrupted and delayed. Sometimes, it can be the result of neglect of basic health care, such as regularly checking hearing and sight, which could be easily overcome. At other times, it can be lack of opportunity which prevents a child acquiring basic skills, such as learning to swim or to ride a bicycle. Fred Fever, in his autobiography of a childhood in Barnardo's, describes the sheer joy of mastering such skills and the impact it had for him, of feeling good and of belonging in a group of friends:

> Before moving to Sittingbourne I had never even sat on a push-bike, let alone ridden one. There I was, eleven years old, and unable to ride a bike. I had never owned a bike nor had access to one. The majority of my friends on the Manor Grove Estate had their own bikes and all of them could cycle pretty well. On days when they got their bikes out and cycled up and down the paths and pavements, I would just sit and watch. They soon saw that I was feeling a bit left out so they suggested I borrow their bikes and we could all take it in turns to ride. I had to admit then that I didn't know how to ride a bike. They immediately set to work teaching me how. After many hours, days and quite a few accidents I began to grasp the basics of cycling. Then one day I suddenly found myself cycling down the path on my own. My friends were standing at the opposite end and

as I approached them, cycling with no assistance, they began to clap and cheer. I had done it, I could ride a bike!

Betty [foster carer] owned a small green push-bike, which she used occasionally when going to visit her mother. The bike was fairly old and had very small wheels, but it was reliable. Now that I could ride a bike (just about), I approached Betty about the possibility of borrowing her bike now and again. At first, she was less than enthusiastic, but eventually she agreed, on the condition that I paid for any damage I caused and that I didn't ride on the roads. So now I could cycle around happily with my friends and I began to feel that I was a part of things. (1994, pp.91–92)

Another group of children who may have to struggle with negotiating life on a daily basis are disabled children. In the study by Connors and Stalker (2003), they found there was a different 'feel' to the perception of difficulty in disabled children's and parental accounts, the children citing much more concrete and immediate issues such as learning 'timestables, doing spelling homework, writing a story' (p.37). A further set of issues may arise from parental concern to protect their disabled children and the restrictions this may place on activities, friendships and other choices. Connors and Stalker give voice to some of the issues for older children with physical impairments 'around gaining independence, whilst still having to rely on their parents…for a high level of physical care' (2003, p.40). Lorna, aged nearly 14, talks of her struggle to challenge her mother's assumption of her as a 'little girl':

> She's got to understand that she can't rule my life any more. Because when I get older she's just going to tell me what to do but I just want to make up my own mind because she's always deciding for me, like what's best for me and sometimes I get angry. She just doesn't realise that I'm grown up now but soon I'm going to be 14 in September and I won't be a wee girl any more. (Quoted in Connors and Stalker 2003, p.41)

For children from minority ethnic groups living away from home, issues of racism, and religious or cultural needs may feature strongly in their daily negotiations with adults. Gina was 14 years old when she became looked after and came from a strictly traditional Pakistani family. She experienced overt bullying and racism in her first placement in a children's home. In her next placement, efforts were made to meet her cultural needs but 'poor communication and a lack of cultural awareness' meant these were largely unsuccessful (p.183):

> The food was difficult because of the Asian way. They found that difficult and would not get the meat that I was used to and instead gave me vegetable rubbish. Anyway they got me on the SOL (a semi-independent living scheme) so that I could get and cook my own food. I was still a kid and I really didn't enjoy cooking for myself. (Quoted in Skuse and Ward 2003, p.184)

As Jacobs (1998) asserts, issues of authority and autonomy will be either supported or challenged in school. School is a significant experience in almost all children's lives, as was discussed in Chapter 8. As we have seen, good school experiences – of achievement, enjoyment and friendships – can provide positive reinforcement of self-esteem, as well as contributing protective factors in the face of other adverse circumstances (Haggerty *et al.* 1996). There are several processes at work within the school environment, for example, the school ethos or culture, academic work, the making (and breaking) of friendships, the presence or absence of bullying, and pupil–teacher interaction. The influence of inspirational teachers is often cited as a turning point in the lives of individual young people, opening new doors and encouraging new interests. Brannen and her colleagues (2000) found that children aged 10 to 12 years old mentioned teachers performing diverse supportive roles in their lives. Harker and colleagues (2004) report that teachers were most frequently mentioned by the young people, in their follow up study of the education of looked after children, as the people fulfilling a supportive role 'both in terms of supporting academic achievement and in motivating the young people to believe in their ability' (pp.279–280). An 18-year-old responded: 'Yes my teacher. She was really good at listening to my problems and stuff when there wasn't really anyone else I could talk to about them outside of school' (Harker *et al.* 2004, p.280).

Frequent moves and changes of school may make it hard for children to begin to develop such relationships or experience the positive benefits of school. The reverse may happen and compound their existing difficulties. Christine was 11 when she went into foster care in a placement away from London, her home city (Voice for the Child in Care 1998):

> I went to school but I didn't get on. I was a Londoner, a Cockney, and I didn't fit in. I found the schoolwork hard. I kept being put in new schools halfway through the term. I did get in quite some

trouble at school and I didn't get any help. One of the foster mother's kids said she'd show me what to do. She then told her mother that I'd copied her work and I got into trouble. (Quoted in Voice for the Child in Care 1998, p.87)

Three young people in the study by Skuse and Ward (2003) insisted on remaining at the same school. Alison, who had experienced changes of school before she became looked after at 15, persuaded her social services department to keep her in the same school:

So how do you feel about the fact you didn't change school when you were in care?

Amazing. I put my foot down… Because they said, when I went to live with my P & K that they'd change school and I said 'No you can't make me change again'. I was in my final, you know, exam year and I was fed up with moving schools and having to make friends again…my foster mum used to drop me at school on her way to work and I'd catch two buses home. (Quoted in Skuse and Ward 2003, p.27)

Lara, aged 15 when she was looked after, similarly refused to move school: 'They just wanted me to and I wouldn't do that because I knew that I would have to make new friends and things like that, so that they had to supply a taxi because I wouldn't move. They didn't like it but they had to live with it' (in Skuse and Ward 2003, p.28). Eliza, against considerable odds, had achieved seven GCSEs and was studying for three A levels and, despite experiencing many different placements from the age of 12, was determined to remain at the same school:

I always said from the beginning that if I had to change school I wouldn't go – because I had always been quite bright at school so it was a pretty positive thing that I wanted to stay at my own school because I wanted to do well – but if they had put me in another school, it would have just been another change in my life that I didn't want, and luckily they agreed that the school was important to me, so they let me stay at [school name]. (Quoted in Skuse and Ward 2003, pp.27–28)

Many writers (for example, Alderson 1999) have commented that schools are not the most democratic of institutions, that they are hierarchical in character, that the consumers are considered to be the parents, and that the opportunities for exercise of choice and influence by children are severely constrained. Yet it is in this environment that key developmental issues of authority and autonomy will be forged and will play such a major part in children's lives. When children's opinions are sought, listened to and used in bringing about change, there can be dramatic results.

An example of such influence is to be found in the redesign of a struggling comprehensive school, classed as a 'special measures' school, in South London.

> The first task for Morrison [head teacher] and his deputy, Cathy Bryan, was to ask pupils to make an audit of the school – what worked and what didn't. Their comments were fascinating reading. Pupils said they would rather go home than use the school lavatories because they were so disgusting and frightening; but, if they did go home, they probably wouldn't go back to school that day. Girls felt they had no place in the playgrounds because boys took them over to play football. Computer and audio-visual equipment was locked away most of the time for fear of theft. CCTV cameras in corridors emphasised the lack of trust between pupils and teachers. As for public spaces inside the school, pupils wrote things like: 'This corridor needs to be trashed.'
>
> With the help of School Works and DRMM [architects], pupils, teachers and governors agreed to a revamped plan for the school based around a new internal public square. They wanted corridors to be abolished, decent lavatories and places to meet that would discourage bullying and allow girls and boys to be on equal terms.
>
> The result is quite remarkable. Corridors have gone. Classrooms are now reached directly from the school's covered courtyard. Lockers, designed by the architects but with pupils' input, are no longer concealed in spaces where bullies can dominate. Lavatories are well lit, well ventilated, well designed. Colours are bright...
>
> Kingsdale's success is the result of pupils, parents, teachers and governors taking their audit of the school and rethinking how they might work together. The architectural programme is an extension of this process... (*The Guardian* (2004), *G2* pp.12–13)

Being heard, being believed and being able to influence what happens are important issues to children in a range of different circumstances, such as in divorce proceedings, being looked after in care and accommodation, being bullied or subjected to abuse or exploitation, or campaigning for insulin pumps for diabetic adolescents. Children are often all too realistic about the limits to their choices and to their ability to bring about change. Eleven young people who constituted the Branksome School Group in Darlington in 2004 report on their two years' work to improve their comprehensive school, to make it more student friendly:

> We have recently begun to see the effort of our work pay off and changes have been made in our school.
>
> - Vending machines have been installed and are a success.
>
> - Lessons in the library, to help students to revise, this is an improvement.
>
> - Mentors – personal guides for students – this is a useful step.
>
> - Exam conditions are better, we don't have to wear uniforms and the fans have been fixed.
>
> - We can now wear tracksuit bottoms in PE; students have wanted this for a long time.
>
> Although most of us will be leaving school in 2 months, we hope the changes will help students moving through the school and we hope the work we have started continues. (Investing in Children Newsletter 2004, p.9)

Co-operation and competition

The third set of themes focuses on children's development of relationships, in families, in friendships, at school and in other social groups. As Jacobs puts it: 'If the first theme revolved around issues of dependency, and the second around issues of independence, the third is essentially about interdependence' (1998, p.143). He alerts us to two aspects in the development of relationships, 'whether relationships incorporate parity and equality, or whether they are fraught with rivalry and competition' (1998, p.143). These issues become particularly important when we consider those children whose formation of relationships has been disrupted by adverse circumstances. As we have seen earlier in this chapter, a child's sense of security may have been undermined and the ability to trust others severely impaired by the circumstances they have experienced, either when living at home or when away from home in care or accommodation. The opportunity to master relevant skills and competencies, and to develop a confident sense of self may also have been affected and will influence a child's capacity to develop friendships and other significant relationships. As Hedy Cleaver has shown in Chapter 7, the impact of parental or other problems within families may be ameliorated by the positive and appropriate support of the other parent or of siblings. Similarly wider family, such as grandparents, or the development of strong friendships in later childhood may also be an important source of support. However, some young people may be inhibited from finding such support and friendships curtailed, for instance, when, due to parental problems, there is embarrassment about bringing friends home (Cleaver *et al.* 1999). From their interviews with former young carers, Frank and her colleagues (Frank, Tatum and Tucker 1999) observe that 'frequently choices have to be made between accepting the demands of family life and developing other kinds of relationships outside the immediate family circle' (p.8). A process of self-exclusion may take place, whereby the young carer avoids 'making wider social contacts or developing the kind of commitments that might necessarily flow out of externally generated relationships' (Frank *et al.* 1999, p.9). The young person thus loses out on opportunities for reciprocity, shared experiences and affirmation. Former carers tell us the impact of this may last into adulthood. Three young people in the study reflect on their experience:

> You tell yourself not to be ambitious and want other things, just accept what there is and do what you can as best as you can.

> You know that caring is what you had to do, so you shunned anything outside that might distract you.

> Eventually I became nervous about going out because they all went to work and had something to talk about… I didn't want to feel different. (p.9)

Brannen and her colleagues remind us that many children have to negotiate different aspects of family change including, in some situations, parental separation and divorce, and becoming a step-family. These are 'social processes which children must make sense of, and in which children are implicated as social actors' (Brannen *et al.* 2000, p.68). Such processes often involve developing new relationships with potential parental figures, as well as step-siblings and their wider family, processes which may be fraught with anxiety, tension, anger and rivalry. These processes do not end with new family members. As the same time, children may be learning 'to negotiate new ways of engaging with their parents as a result of the advent of their new partners' (Butler *et al.* 2003, p.111). Robert, aged 13, gives a graphic description of the process of negotiating family change. He appears to be moving from the 'friendship phase' to beginning to see his mother's partner as a step-father:

> I get along with John [mother's partner] quite well and occasionally he can be strict, but I suppose it's just his way. He's used to it. He shouldn't change for me. I shouldn't have to change that much, I suppose. It's not like I treat him like a dad. I suppose I treat him like an adult that I know well, kind of like a friend, you know. I'm used to him now; and Mum, you know, kissing in front of me. Before, I used to think, 'Why in front of me?' You know, I understand now. If he had been my dad, that's how they'd be acting. I kind of think of him as that now, step-dad. I suppose I've got used to it now, thinking about it. (Quoted in Butler *et al.* 2003, p.108)

Butler *et al.* (2003) conclude, after listening to children's accounts, that in these circumstances 'new relationships cannot be hurried and if an assumption is made that a new partner can pick up where a parent left off, this is likely to be met by anger and resentment from the child' (pp.116–117).

Children demonstrate considerable resilience in negotiating family change and it is not a negative experience for all of them. Nor is the move to care or accommodation always a negative experience. Even where children were unhappy at the time and the placement process difficult, Skuse and Ward (2003) found that on reflection 15 out of 21 young people interviewed thought their placement away from home was 'a good thing' (p.198). However, as we have seen earlier in the chapter, frequent moves can disrupt the development of secure relationships with new parental figures and interfere with the all important development of friendships at school and in the wider family and local community. Skuse and Ward (2003) note that 'friendships made with other residents or foster children rarely appeared to be continued once young people had ceased to be looked after' (p.97), although there were exceptions. Rob was one who was still in contact with his closest friend whom he met whilst being looked after, despite now living hundreds of miles apart. He provides an insight into the value of continuing to be able to meet and the difficulties entailed:

> My best friend has been up to mine. I've been to his. We do see each other, we're on the phone, we're on the internet, so we do stay in touch...every other month or so I'll come down here or he'll come up to mine. But the distance does put a problem between us. (Rob,

looked after between the age of 14 and 18 years, in Skuse and Ward 2003, p.98)

Apart from factors such as placement instability, school moves and the impact of distance, Brannen and colleagues (2000), citing Hodges (1996), suggest that another important factor making friendships difficult for children in foster care may be that they are having 'to put all their energies and personal resources into building ties with their new carers and carers' families' (p.140). This may restrict the size of their friendship network. Cleaver (2000), from her study of contact for 5 to 12 year olds in foster care, concludes that ensuring continuity of schooling may play a major part in ensuring continuity of friendships (p.138).

The issues of co-operation and competition would not be complete without reference to children's experiences of bullying, which are reported as happening in the family, in residential settings, in the community or in school. La Fontaine (1991) found that 'over three-quarters of the bullying reported to [ChildLine's] Bullying Line took place at school' (p.16). The evidence is that bullying is extensive. In their major study for the Department for Education and Skills and for ChildLine, Oliver and Candappa (2003) report that over half of primary and secondary school pupils thought that bullying was 'a big problem' or 'quite a problem' in their school (p.6). Children tend to define bullying more broadly than most adult writers and to describe a more complex picture (La Fontaine 1991) and it may include intimidation by so called 'friends' within friendship groups. As one young caller to ChildLine put it: 'What hurts me so much is that she used to be my friend' (Macleod and Morris 1996, p.45).

Bullying has a negative impact on children whatever their ages and circumstances. It is of concern that many of the studies of children already living in difficult circumstances, additionally report that these children or their siblings have been experiencing bullying (see, for example, Butler *et al.* 2003; Connors and Stalker 2003; Gorin 2004; Skuse and Ward 2003), 'often adding to their general state of unhappiness' (Butler *et al.* 2003, p.169). Oliver and Candappa (2003) identify a number of possible consequences – 'loss of self-confidence, truancy, lower levels of academic attainment, increased anxiety, suicidal ideation, and attempted and actual suicide' (p.16). However, the real distress and despair can only be conveyed in the words of the children themselves. They reported 'feeling isolated, frightened, and in some cases angry about the treatment they received from bullies, but also preoccupied by it' (Macleod and Morris 1996, p.74). A small but significant group of children also discussed suicidal feelings. Jill, aged 13, describes how she feels after months of daily name-calling and threats to beat her up: 'Recently I started thinking about killing myself. I feel too scared to have a social life. I spend my days in fear in and out of school' (in Macleod and Morris 1996, p.75). The effects can be very long term, as one child said in the ChildLine study: 'It took me a long time to get my confidence back' (Macleod and Morris 1996, p.74).

In looking at pupils' responses to bullying, Oliver and Candappa (2003) found there were no tidy solutions or easy remedies identified by the children but three of the most helpful factors for dealing with bullying were friendships, avoidance strategies and learning to 'stand up for yourself' (pp.6 and 7). The researchers' key recommendations are to increase children's participation 'in formulating and implementing anti-bullying strategies', involving and consulting pupils throughout the process (p.88). Thus we return to one of the major themes that emerges from children's perspectives; that children are active agents in their own development and that this requires acknowledgement and positive action if children's development is to be supported in difficult circumstances.

Seeking help and support

In this concluding section, we look at how children find help and support in adverse circumstances; the qualities in adults, particularly professionals, that are important to them; and the help or services that make a difference. Those studies which have sought children's perspectives comment on the way they develop strategies for coping (for example, Brannen et al. 2000; Butler et al. 2003; Cleaver 2000). Butler and his colleagues observe in relation to experiences of divorce:

> We found that children were remarkably active and creative in the methods they employed to cope with difficult times. Most notably children demonstrated an impressive capacity for drawing on the resources of others around them for help... Children were usually quite clear about what kind of help they needed and capable of choosing their confidant accordingly. (2003, p.148)

Understandably, children turn most frequently for informal support to a parent or carer, relatives such as grandparents, friends and teachers (reflecting Brannen et al.'s findings, 2000). When it comes to formal support, rather less is known in circumstances such as domestic violence, parental substance misuse and parental mental health problems (Gorin 2004). Furthermore, Gorin adds, 'there are very few specialist services that exist, given the numbers of children we know are affected by these problems' (2004, p.68).

During a consultation weekend held in September 2003, contributing to the development of a national training pack (Department for Education and Skills and NSPCC 2006) to support the use of *What to Do if You're Worried a Child is Being Abused* (Department of Health *et al.* 2003), 13 children and young people were asked to rank different adults according to how much they trusted them (Children's Rights Alliance for England 2003): several adult roles were ranked as number one – 'mum, dad, foster carer, teacher and youth worker' (p.21). The children were then asked about what would make them feel they could trust an adult (Box 16.1 below).

Box 16.1: Children's and young people's conversations revealed four main groups of characteristics that help them determine whether or not they can or should trust an adult

- Being there – children and young people having the general feeling that an adult is there for them.

- Proving yourself – an adult taking the time to listen; asking appropriately; and keeping promises.

- Having the right attitude – not losing temper or trying to take over.

- Knowing what you're talking about – sharing relevant experience, and not acting as if they know more than they do (older teenagers particularly cited this as important).

(Children's Rights Alliance for England 2003, pp.21–22)

Not surprisingly, these characteristics are very similar to those qualities in professionals which are important to children summarised by Aldgate and Statham (Box 16.2) from their review of the 24 studies evaluating the

Children Act 1989 (Department of Health 2001; see also Skuse and Ward 2003):

Box 16.2: Qualities in professionals that are important to children

- reliability – keeping promises

- practical help

- the ability to give support

- time to listen and respond

- seeing children's lives in the round, not just the problems.

(Department of Health 2001, p.93)

The children were not only clear as to which professionals they found trustworthy but also why, for example:

> I personally work better with younger social workers and a bloke cos I like to do stuff that I like – golf, snooker, football, any sports really. (13-year-old boy, Children's Rights Alliance for England 2003, p.23)

> My teacher took me to places to get the help I needed ... because her work is child protection she is determined to get things done. She is trustworthy, a good teacher. She keeps things confidential – before she told the social worker, she asked me if it was alright. (13-year-old girl, Children's Rights Alliance for England 2003, p.23)

> The response from my foster carers is always honest because they have an open mind and try and look at things from my perspective as well as theirs. (17-year-old young woman, Children's Rights Alliance for England 2003, p.24)

One boy of 15 said he had never had an adult he could talk to until recently when he had a Connexions worker:

> He really helped me through a rough time…he talked me through it… He was trustworthy, he got to know me even before we got to talk about the problem. He didn't put any pressure on me…just knowing someone was there [was important] – before that I didn't have anyone to turn to, to tell confidential information to. (Quoted in Children's Rights Alliance for England 2003, p.11)

Children are also aware of the importance of attending to their developmental needs in areas such as health and education. Harker and her colleagues (2004) report that even young people appear to appreciate their social workers showing a genuine interest in their education. A 12-year-old in foster care in their study of the education of looked after children comments:

> My latest social worker really helps support me. Every time she comes she's like 'how are you getting on at school?' That's the first question she asks except for like 'how are you?' and I'm like 'oh fine' but then I have to rush upstairs and get my studies down and show her and stuff like that. She's really nice. I've had her for about a year now I suppose…all of my social workers have been good but I think she takes more interest in school. (Quoted in Harker et al. 2004, p.280)

When asked about positive interventions that make a difference, children and young people can also be very clear. As Aldgate and Statham (Department of Health 2001) conclude 'children are honest and often have very sensible views on what they see as helpful to themselves and to their families' (p.95). When consulted about improving child protection advice and support, young people came up with a long list of positive interventions under some key headings (Children's Rights Alliance for England 2003, pp.16–18):

- Help children to express themselves.
- Help children stay in control.
- Stop the harm.
- Someone to talk to.
- Give them a chance to play.
- Families matter.

- Improve physical care.

- Help children adapt...but don't change their life completely.

- Help parents too.

Children report very mixed experiences of contact with professionals, with their key concerns being 'those of being believed, professionals not talking directly to children and not acting to help them when asked' (Gorin 2004, p.70). Poor communication and professionals' lack of awareness (in areas such as cultural needs) are also recurring concerns (Skuse and Ward 2003). As we have seen, the personal qualities of the professionals are critically important to them. Aldgate and Statham argue that this means children 'need skilled, direct work and adults who are reliable and will champion their needs' (Department of Health 2001, p.94).

However, despite diverse experiences of professionals, there is a high level of consensus across studies of children's views about the services they think would help. Information is frequently mentioned – age appropriate, specific to the situation, reliable, readily available, both written and verbal, from informal and formal helpers (for example, in Butler *et al.* 2003; Department of Health 2001; Gorin 2004). Children also identify other service needs, including confidential support such as helplines and counselling, universal services such as supportive environments in schools, and specialist services such as for children with severe impairments and children coping with parental separation or parental problems. Above all children are still children and, as Gorin reports, in circumstances of parental problems 'children particularly want opportunities to get away from home and have fun and to get to know other children experiencing the same problems' (2004, p.70).

Two sets of issues have emerged from the children's perspectives of experiences that are likely to disrupt their lives and which will, therefore, have an impact on their development. First, children want to have more control over situations than they often feel they have and, second, they want to be more involved in decisions affecting them or their families. This means that wherever children live, learn, work and play, those professionals working with children and families must become much more child-centred in their approach. It means they must be prepared to develop a dialogue with children where they seek out children's ideas and opinions, listen to what they have to say and act upon their views. This is a challenge to professionals. Brannen, reflecting on her experience of involving children as experts on their own family lives in a major research study (Brannen *et al.* 2000) and subsequently in the dissemination of its findings, draws these profound conclusions:

> Taking account of children's expertise and taking children's views seriously may unsettle adult certainties about what is best for children and may make them feel less sure and less confident about their own practice. It is certainly likely to make the work of practitioners and policy makers more complex. For in order to take children's views into account, practitioners and policy makers will have to increase their engagement with children. They will need to find ways and means to engage in discussions with children and to take account of these. This ongoing process is likely to result in a greater variety of approaches whereby professionals work with children. It is certainly likely to challenge current orthodoxies namely the search for the holy grail of once and for all certainties about 'what works'. (Brannen 2003, p.12)

Afterword

In this book, we have taken a positive approach to children's development, drawing on the recent research and contemporary views on child development theory. The overarching approach has been developmental and ecological, recognising that there are factors which influence the developing child, including the child him or her self.

Foremost among these are the influences of adults close to the child. The book has stressed the importance of the part played by sensitive, committed, consistent carers who keep children safe and help them develop trust and curiosity about their world. The reciprocity of sensitive caregiving and good attachments in children are a major developmental strand. So often, views of attachment have been fixed by time and culture. We have taken the view, influenced by emerging contemporary international research, that, while carers close to the child, such as parents and extended family, will often be most important, others, such as teachers, play group leaders, youth workers and childminders all contribute to children's social and emotional development.

The ecological approach not only acknowledges the influence of people in children's homes, schools and community but also acknowledges the external environment in which children live. Children flourish where their parents have sufficient income, adequate housing and social support. They also benefit from living in neighbourhoods that are safe and foster social contacts with peers, places of faith and clubs.

Other children will also play a part in children's social and emotional development. This is a two-way process, with an individual child taking the behaviour and skills learnt from his or her main carers into relationships with other children. The child who has learnt to trust others and feels confident will convey this to other children. A child who is confident and loved will also have the resilience to cope with the playground culture of brutality and have inner strengths to combat adversity.

The book recognises that children themselves are central to their own development. One of the main themes of the book has been to emphasise children's individuality and adaptability. This is most evident in the potential for optimal developmental achievements in disabled children. We have stressed how children can adapt to different styles of parenting to ensure that adults are responsive to them. Children can influence the reactions of their caregivers from a remarkably young age, as the research on babies has shown. At older stages, especially in adolescence, the maturing child takes increasing pleasure from responsibility and self efficacy, as well as engaging in social relationships that test developing skills and emotions, and the boundaries set by their caregivers.

The book has recognised that different aspects of development are more prominent at different stages. This does not in any way diminish the unique pattern of development for an individual child. The book has taken the view that there has to be a balance between the concept of developmental progression, which recognises there is an order to developmental stages, and the development of an individual child. It is helpful to have guidelines and expectations of when and how different stages of development may occur but these must always be seen in the context of the circumstances and unique progression of an individual child.

Though looking at the development of children in general, the book has paid special attention to the needs of children whose development has been interrupted and who have come to the attention of professionals. This includes children who have been maltreated. It also includes children who have experienced separation and loss of caregivers. We have looked at the importance of responding to the impact of these events on children. The book has taken the view, evidenced by recent international research on attachment, that development is influenced but not irrevocably set by the experiences of the early years. Children can recover from events that have interrupted their development, provided that they have sensitive caregiving and are allowed to continue their development in an environment which provides physical and emotional nurture. The job of each professional is to identify his or her unique contribution to ensuring children have the best environment in which to continue any interrupted journeys.

In the course of preparing this book, we have been struck by the optimism of contemporary writers on children's development. If there is one message to convey, it is that resilience may rise from adversity, and that, with timely and appropriate help from family, friends and professionals, children can adapt to new circumstances. With this optimism in mind, it seems fitting to end the book with a quote from Rudolph Schaffer, whose evolutionary work on children's development has inspired many of us over several decades. His words challenge professionals to act positively and appropriately to promote the best possible outcomes for the developing child.

> We now know that there are survivors as well as victims, that children who miss out on particular experiences at the usual time may well make up subsequently, that healthy developments can occur in a great range of different family environments and that there are many 'right' ways of bringing up a child. We also know that the effects of stressful experiences can be minimised by suitable action, and that isolated traumatic events need not leave harmful consequences and that an individual's personality does not for ever more have to be at the mercy of past experience. We have even learned that stress, under certain circumstances, can produce beneficial results. (1998, p. 249)

Jane Aldgate, David Jones,
Wendy Rose and Carole Jeffery

APPENDIX A

Steering Group

Wendy Rose, Faculty of Health and Social Care, The Open University (Chair)

Jane Aldgate, Faculty of Health and Social Care, The Open University

Hedy Cleaver, Royal Holloway, University of London

Monica Dowling, Faculty of Health and Social Care, The Open University

Ro Gordon, NSPCC Training Centre

Jenny Gray, Department for Education and Skills

Anna Gupta, Royal Holloway, University of London

Evender Harran, NSPCC Training Centre

Enid Hendry, NSPCC Training Centre

Carole Jeffery, Faculty of Health and Social Care, The Open University

David Jones, The Park Hospital for Children, Oxfordshire Mental Healthcare NHS Trust

Janet Seden, Faculty of Health and Social Care, The Open University

APPENDIX B

Advisory Group

Jenny Gray, Department for Education and Skills (Chair)

Vic Citarella, Local Government Association

Jacqueline Crittenden, Child Psychology Service, Southwark Social Services

John Coleman, Trust for the Study of Adolescence

Pauline Coulter, The Children's Society

Sheena Doyle, The Children's Society

Naomi Eisenstadt, Sure Start, Department for Education and Skills

Lena Engel, Early Years Development and Childcare Partnership, Richmond upon Thames

David Holmes, Department for Education and Skills

Helen Jones, Department for Education and Skills

Maria Lagos, Training Organisation for the Personal Social Services (Topss)

Denise Lawes, Services for Children and Young People, Wandsworth Social Services

Shelley Lewis, Local Government Association

Margaret Lynch, Department of Health

Teresa O'Neill, School for Policy Studies, University of Bristol

Jill Pedley, Social Services Department, Nottinghamshire City Council

Melanie Phillips, Independent Consultant

Jane Powell, Obstetric Hospital, University College Hospital

Julia Ridgway, Department for Education and Skills

Sheelah Seeley, Health Visitor, Cambridge

Peter Smith, Department for Education and Skills

Sally Weeks, Barnardo's

Jan Welbury, Consultant Community Paediatrician, City Hospitals Sunderland NHS Trust

Alison Williams, National Children's Bureau

References

Ainsworth, M. and Eichberg, C. (1991) 'Effects of infant-mother attachment of mother's unresolved loss of an attachment figure, or traumatic experience.' In C.M. Parkes, J. Stevenson-Hinde and P. Marris (eds) *Attachment Across the Life Cycle.* London: Routledge.

Ainsworth, M.D.S., Blehar, M., Waters, E. and Wall, S. (1978) *Patterns of Attachment.* Hillsdale NJ: Erlbaum.

Alderson, P. (1999) 'Human rights and democracy in schools: do they mean more than "picking up litter and not killing whales?"' *International Journal of Children's Rights 7,* 185–205.

Aldgate, J. (1992) 'Work with children experiencing separation and loss.' In J. Aldgate and J. Simmonds (eds) *Direct Work with Children.* 3rd edn, London: Batsford.

Aldgate, J. and Bradley, M. (1999) *Supporting Families through Short Term Fostering.* London: The Stationery Office.

Aldgate, J. and Simmonds, J. (eds) (1992) *Direct Work with Children.* London: Batsford.

Aldridge, J. and Becker, S. (2003) *Children Caring for Parents with Mental Illness: Perspectives of Young Carers, Parents and Professionals.* Bristol: The Policy Press.

Allen-Meares, P. and Lane, B.A. (1987) 'Grounding social work practice in theory: ecosystems.' *Social Casework: The Journal of Contemporary Social Work,* November, 515–521.

Amato, P.R. and Keith, B. (1991a) 'Parental divorce and the well-being of children: A meta-analysis.' *Psychological Bulletin 110,* 26–46.

Amato, P.R. and Keith, B. (1991b) 'Parental divorce and adult well-being.' *Journal of Marriage and the Family 53,* 43–58.

Angold, A., Costello, E.J., Burns, B.J. Erkanli, A. and Farmer, E.M. (2000) 'Effectiveness of non-residential specialty mental health services for children and adolescents in the real world.' *Journal of the American Academy of Child and Adolescent Psychiatry 39,* 154–160.

Argyle, A. (1992) *The Social Psychology of Everyday Life.* London: Routledge.

Auer, G.J. (1983) 'Contact with the absent parent after separation or divorce.' *International Journal of Family Psychiatry 4,* 95–140.

Bailey, S. (2002) 'Treatment of delinquents.' In M. Rutter and E. Taylor (eds) *Child and Adolescent Psychiatry. Modern Approaches To Treatment.* 4th edn, 60, 1019–1037.

Baker, K, and Donelly, M. (2001) 'The social experiences of children with disability and the influence of environment: a framework for intervention.' *Disability & Society 16,* 1, 71–85.

Baldwin, J. (1897) *Social and Ethical Interpretations in Mental Development: A Study in Social Psychology.* New York: Macmillan.

Baldwin, S. and Hirst, M. (2002) 'Children as carers.' In J. Bradshaw (ed.) *The Well-being of Children in the UK.* London: Save the Children.

Barber, M. (1994) *Young People and their Attitudes to School.* Keele: University of Keele.

Barber, M. (1996) *The Learning Game.* London: Gollancz.

Barnardo's (2002) *Family Group Conferences: Principles and Practice Guidance* London, Barnardo's.

Baron-Cohen, S. (1994) 'Development of a theory of mind: where would we be without an intentional stance?' In M. Rutter and D. Hay (eds) *Development Through Life: A Handbook for Clinicians*. Oxford: Blackwell Scientific Publications.

Baumeister, R., Tice, D. and Hutton, D. (1989) 'Self presentational motives and personality differences in self-esteem.' *Journal of Personality 57*, 547–579.

Beck, A. and Weishaar, M. (1989) 'Cognitive therapy.' In R.J. Corsini and D. Wedding (eds) *Current Psychotherapies*. 4th edn, Itasca, IL: Peacock Publishers.

Bee, H. (1995) *The Developing Person*. 6th edn, London: Harper Row.

Bee, H. (2000) *The Developing Child*. 9th edn, Boston: Allyn and Bacon.

Beek, K.S. (2000) 'Spirituality: a development taboo.' *Development in Practice 10*, 1, 31–43.

Beek, M. and Schofield, G. (2004a) 'Providing a secure base: Tuning in to children with severe learning difficulties in long-term foster care. *Adoption and Fostering 28*, 2, 8–19.

Beek, M. and Schofield, G. (2004b) *Providing a Secure Base in Long-Term Foster Care*. London: British Agencies for Adoption and Fostering.

Beitchman, J.H., Wilson, B., Johnson, C.J., Atkinson, L., Young, A., Adlaf, E. *et al.* (2001) 'Fourteen year follow up of speech/language impaired and controlled children: psychiatric outcome.' *Journal of American Academy of Child and Adolescent Psychiatry 40*, 75–82.

Belsky, J. (1993) 'Etiology of child maltreatment: a developmental–ecological analysis.' *Psychological Bulletin 114*, 3, 413–434.

Ben-Arieh, A. (2002) 'Outcomes of programs versus monitoring well-being: a child-centred perspective.' In T. Vecchiato, A.N. Maluccio and C. Canali (eds) *Evaluation in Child and Family Services*. New York: Aldine de Gruyter.

Bentovim, A., Gorell Barnes, G. and Cooklin, A. (1982) *Family Therapy: Complementary Frameworks of Theory and Practice*, vols I and II. New York: Academic Press.

Berger, K.S (1999) *The Developing Person Through Childhood and Adolescence*. New York: Worth Publishers.

Berger, K.S. (2001) *The Developing Person Through the Life Span*. 5th edn, New York: Worth Publishers.

Berk, L. (2003) *Child Development*. 6th edn, Boston: Allyn and Bacon.

Berlin, L. and Cassidy, J. (1999) 'Relations among relationships contributions from attachment theory and research.' In J. Cassidy and P.R. Shaver (eds) *Handbook of Attachment – Theory, Research and Clinical Applications*. New York and London: The Guilford Press.

Bettelheim B. (1951) *The Uses of Enchantment*. London: Thames and Hudson.

Bettelheim, B. (1982) *The Uses of Enchantment*. Harmondsworth: Penguin.

Bettner, B. and Lew, A. (1990) *Raising Kids Who Can: Use Good Judgement, Assume Responsibility, Communicate Effectively, Respect Self and Others, Co-operate, Develop Self-esteem and Enjoy Life*. Newton Center, MA: Connexions Press.

Bibby, A. and Becker, S. (eds) (2000) *Young Carers in Their Own Words*. London: Calouste Gulbenkian Foundation.

Bilson, A. and Ross, S. (1989) *Social Work Management and Practice, Systems Principles*. London: Jessica Kingsley Publishers.

Bishop, D.V.M., North, T. and Donlan, C. (1995) 'Genetic basis of specific language impairment: evidence from a twin study.' *Developmental Medicine and Child Neurology 37*, 56–71.

Black, D. (1990) 'What do children need from parents?' *Adoption and Fostering 14*, 1, 43–50.

Booth, T. and Booth, W. (1994) *Parenting under Pressure: Mothers and Fathers with Learning Difficulties*. Buckingham: Open University Press.

Bowlby, J. (1951) *Maternal Care and Mental Health, WHO Monograph Series No.2*. Geneva: World Health Organization.

Bowlby, J. (1953) *Child Care and the Growth of Love*. Harmondsworth: Penguin Books.

Bowlby, J. (1958) 'The nature of the child's tie to its mother.' *International Journal of Psycho-Analysis 39*, 350–373

Bowlby, J. (1969) *Attachment and Loss: Vol. I Attachment*. London: Hogarth Press.

Bowlby, J. (1969/1982) *Attachment and Loss: Vol. I Attachment*. New York: Basic Books.

Bowlby, J. (1973) *Attachment and Loss: Vol. II Separation Anxiety and Anger*. New York: Basic Books.

Bowlby, J. (1988) *A Secure Base: Clinical Applications of Attachment Theory*. London: Routledge.

Boyden, J., Ling, B. and Myers, W.E. (1998) *What Works for Working Children*. Stockholm: Save the Children, Sweden.

Bradford, J. (1995) *Caring for the Whole Child*. London: The Children's Society.

Bradshaw, J. (ed.) (2001) *Poverty: The Outcomes for Children*. London: Family Policy Studies Centre.

Brannen, J. (2003) 'The use of video in research dissemination: children as experts on their own family lives.' *Childhoods in Late Modern Society*. Göteborg: Göteborg University.

Brannen, J., Heptinstall, E. and Bhopal, K. (2000) *Connecting Children*. London: Routledge/Falmer.

Brearley, J. (1991) *Counselling and Social Work*. Buckingham: Open University Press.

Bridging the Gaps, Health Care for Adolescents (2003) *Royal College of Paediatrics and Child Health*. Royal College of Psychiatrists Council Report CR114.

Brinich, P. and Shelley, C. (2002) *The Self and Personality Structure*. Buckingham: Open University Press.

Brodzinsky, D.M. (1987) 'Adjustment to adoption: a psychological perspective.' *Clinical Psychology Review 8*, 27–32.

Brodzinsky, D.M. (1990) 'A stress and coping model of adoption adjustment.' In D.M. Brodzinsky and M.D. Schechter (eds) *Psychology of Adoption*. New York: Oxford University Press.

Bronfenbrenner, U. (1979) *The Ecology of Human Development: Experiments by Nature and Design*. Cambridge, MA: Harvard University Press.

Buhrmester, D. and Furman, W. (1990) 'Perceptions of sibling relationships during middle childhood and adolescence.' *Child Development 61*, 1387–1398.

Butler, I., Scanlan, L., Robinson, M., Douglas, G. and Murch, M. (2003) *Divorcing Children – Children's Experience of Their Parents' Divorce*. London: Jessica Kingsley Publishers.

Butler-Sloss, E. (1988) *Report of the Inquiry into Child Abuse in Cleveland, 1987*. London: HMSO.

Butterworth, G. (1995) 'Origins of mind in perception and action.' In C. Moore and P.J. Dunham (eds) *Joint Attention: Its Origins and Role in Development*. Hillsdale, NJ: Erlbaum.

Byng-Hall, J. (1991) 'The application of attachment theory to understanding and treatment in therapy.' In C.M. Parkes, J. Stevenson-Hinde and P. Marris (eds) *Attachment Across the Life Cycle*. London: Routledge.

Cairns, L. (2001) 'Investing in children: Learning how to promote the rights of all children.' *Children and Society 15*, 347–360.

Cairns, L. (2004) 'Newsupdate…' *Investing in Children Newsletter 59*.

Cairns, L. and Brannen, M. (2005) 'Promoting the human rights of children and young people: the 'Investing in Children' experience.' *Adoption and Fostering 29*, 1, Spring, 78–87.

Cairns, R. and Cairns, B. (1994) *Lifelines and Risks: Pathways of Youth in our Time*. Hemel Hempstead: Harvester Wheatsheaf.

Calam, R.M. (2001) 'Normal development in adolescence.' In S. Gowers (ed) *Adolescent Psychiatry in Clinical Practice 1*, 1–29. London: Hodder.

Calam, R.M., Cox, A.D., Glasgow, D.V., Jimmieson, P. and Groth Larson, S. (2000) 'Assessment and therapy with children. Can computers help?' *Child Clinical Psychology and Psychiatry 5*, 3, 329–343.

Calam, R.M., Cox, A.D., Glasgow, D.V., Jimmieson, P. and Groth Larsen, S. (2005) *In My Shoes: A Computerised Assisted Interview for Communicating with Children and Vulnerable Adults.* Manchester: University of Manchester, Department of Psychology.

Campbell, R., Cuninghame, C., Mooney, S., Nevison, C., Pettitt, B. and Rodgers, P. (1998) *Children's Perspectives on Work.* London: Save the Children.

Cantos, A.L., Gries, L.T. and Slis, V. (1997) 'Behavioral correlates of parental visiting during family foster care.' *Child Welfare 76*, 2, 309–329.

Caplan, G. (1964) *Principles of Preventive Psychiatry.* New York: Basic Books.

Cassidy, J. (1999) 'The nature of the child's ties.' In J. Cassidy and P.R. Shaver (eds) *Handbook of Attachment – Theory, Research and Clinical Applications.* New York and London: The Guilford Press.

Cassidy, J. and Shaver, P.R. (eds) (1999) *Handbook of Attachment – Theory, Research and Clinical Applications.* New York and London: The Guilford Press.

Changing Minds (2002) A multimedia CD Rom about mental health, for students 13–17 years old and their teachers. Royal College of Psychiatrists. ISBN 1901242927.

Chester, R. (1977) 'The one-parent family: deviant or variant?' In R. Chester and J. Peel (eds) *Equalities and Inequalities in Family Life.* London: Academic Press.

ChildLine (1996) *Children and Racism.* London: ChildLine.

ChildLine (1997) *Beyond The Limit: Children Who Live With Parental Alcohol Misuse.* London: ChildLine.

Children's Rights Alliance for England (2003) *Let Them Have Their Childhood Again.* A report from a young people's consultation weekend, 27–28 September 2003, contributing to *What to Do if You're Worried a Child is Being Abused* National Training Pack. Website: www.acpc.gov.uk.

Cicchetti, D. and Lynch, M. (1993) 'Towards an ecological transactional model of community violence and child maltreatment: consequences for children's development.' *Psychiatry 56*, 1, 96–118.

Cicchetti, D. and Rizley, R. (1981) 'Developmental perspectives on the etiology, intergenerational transmission and sequelae of child maltreatment.' *New Directions for Child Development 11*, 31–55.

Cleaver, H. (1991) *Vulnerable Children in Schools.* Aldershot: Dartmouth.

Cleaver, H. (2000) *Fostering Family Contact.* London: The Stationery Office.

Cleaver, H. and Freeman, P. (1995) *Parental Perspectives in Cases of Suspected Child Abuse.* London: HMSO.

Cleaver, H. and Freeman, P. (1996) 'Child abuse which involves wider kin and family friends.' In P. Bibby (ed) *Organised Abuse: The Current Debate.* London: Arena.

Cleaver, H. and Nicholson, D. (2003) *Learning Disabled Parents and the Framework for the Assessment of Children in Need and their Families.* Interim report to the Department of Health. London: London University, Royal Holloway College

Cleaver, H., Unell, I. and Aldgate, J. (1999) *Children's Needs – Parenting Capacity: The Impact of Parental Mental Illness, Problem Alcohol and Drug Use, and Domestic Violence on Children's Development.* London: The Stationery Office.

Cleaver, H. and Walker, S. with Meadows, P. (2004) *Assessing Children's Needs and Circumstances: The Impact of the Assessment Framework.* London: Jessica Kingsley Publishers.

Cm 5730 (2003) *The Victoria Climbié Inquiry.* London: The Stationery Office.

Coard, B. (1971) *How the West Indian Child is made Educationally Sub-Normal in the British School System.* London: New Beacon.

Coleman, J. (1978) 'Current contradictions in adolescent theory.' *Journal of Youth and Adolescence* 7, 1–11.

Coleman, J. and Schofield, J. (2003) *Key Data on Adolescence.* Brighton. Trust for Study of Adolescence: TSA Publishing Ltd.

Coleman, J.C. and Hendry, L.B. (1999) *The Nature of Adolescence. Adolescence and Society.* 3rd edn, London: Routledge.

Coleridge, P. (1993) *Disability Liberation and Development.* Oxford: Oxfam.

Collins, W.A. (1984) *Development during Middle Childhood.* Washington: National Academy Press.

Compton, B.R. and Galaway, B. (1989) *Social Work Processes.* Pacific Grove: Brookes Cole.

Connors, C. and Stalker, K. (2003) *The Views and Experiences of Disabled Children and their Siblings. A Positive Outlook.* London: Jessica Kingsley Publishers.

Cooklin, A. (2004) *Being Seen and Heard. The Needs of Children of Parents with Mental Illness.* CD Rom – ISBN 1904671101, London: Gaskell Publications.

Cooley, C. (1902) *Human Nature and the Social Order.* New York: Charles Scribner's Sons.

Corby, B. (2000) *Child Abuse.* Buckingham: Open University Press.

Coulshed, V. (1991) *Social Work Practice: An Introduction.* London: Macmillan.

Coulshed, V. and Orme, J. (eds) (1998) *Social Work Practice: An Introduction.* Basingstoke: Macmillan.

Courtney, A. (2000) 'Loss and grief in adoption: The impact of contact.' *Adoption and Fostering 24,* 33–44.

Crittenden, P.M. (1985) 'Social networks, quality of child rearing and child development.' *Child Development 56,* 129–313.

Crittenden, P.M. (1995) 'Attachment and psychopathology.' In S. Goldberg, R. Muir and J. Kerr (eds) *Attachment Theory: Social, Developmental and Clinical Perspectives.* Hillsdale NJ: Analytic Press.

Crompton, M. (1990) *Attending to Children: Direct Work in Social and Health Care.* London: Arnold.

Crompton, M. (1992) *Children and Counselling.* London: Arnold.

Crompton, M. (ed.) (1996) *Children, Spirituality and Religion.* London: CCETSW.

Crompton, M. (1998) *Children, Spirituality, Religion and Social Work.* Aldershot: Ashgate.

Dallos, R. and McLaughlin, E. (1993) *Social Problems and the Family.* London: Sage and The Open University.

Daly, K.J. (1993) 'Reshaping fatherhood: finding the models.' *Journal of Family Issues 14,* 510–530.

Damon, W. and Hart, D. (1988) *Self Understanding in Childhood and Adolescence.* New York: Cambridge University Press.

Daniel, B. and Wassell, S. (2002) *Assessing and Promoting Resilience in Vulnerable Children.* London: Jessica Kingsley Publishers.

Daniel, B., Wassell, S. and Gilligan, R. (1999) *Child Development for Child Care and Child Protection Workers.* London: Jessica Kingsley Publishers.

Davies, C., Brechin, A. and Gomm, R. (2000) (eds) *Using Evidence in Health and Social Care.* London: Sage.

de Shazer, S. (1985) *Keys to Solution in Brief Therapy.* London: Norton.

de Winter, M. (1997) *Children as Fellow Citizens – Participation and Commitment.* Oxford: Radcliffe Medical Press.

Dearden, C. and Becker, S. (1996) *Young Carers at the Crossroads: An Evaluation of the Nottingham Young Carers' Project.* Loughborough: Loughborough University, Young Carers Research Group.

Demo, D. and Savin-Williams, R. (1992) 'Self-concept stability and change during adolescence.' In R. Lipka and T. Brinthaupt (eds) *Self-Perspectives Across the Life Span.* Albany: State University of New York Press.

Department for Education and Skills (2004a) *Children Looked After by Local Authority. Year Ending 31 March 2003 Volume 1: Commentary and National Tables.* London: The Stationery Office.

Department for Education and Skills (2004b) *Every Child Matters: Next Steps.* London: Department for Education and Skills.

Department for Education and Skills (2004c) *Removing Barriers to Achievement. The Government's Strategy for SEN.* London: Department for Education and Skills.

Department for Education and Skills (2005a) *Common Core of Skills and Knowledge for the Children's Workforce.* London: Department for Education and Skills.

Department for Education and Skills (2005b) *Referrals, Assessments, and Children and Young People on Child Protection Registers, England – Year Ending 31 March 2004.* London: Department for Education and Skills.

Department for Education and Skills (2005c) *The Common Assessment Framework.* London: The Stationery Office.

Department for Education and Skills and NSPCC (2006) *Safeguarding Children: A Shared Responsibility.* London: Department for Education and Skills.

Department of Health (1985) *Social Work Decisions in Child Care.* London: HMSO.

Department of Health (1990) *The Care of Children: Principles and Practice in Regulations and Guidance.* London: HMSO.

Department of Health (1991a) *Child Abuse. A Study of Inquiry Reports 1980–9.* London: HMSO.

Department of Health (1991b) *The Children Act 1989 Guidance and Regulations. Vol 6 Children with Disabilities.* London: HMSO.

Department of Health (1995) *Child Protection: Messages from Research.* London: HMSO.

Department of Health (1996) *Focus on Teenagers: Research into Practice.* London: HMSO.

Department of Health (1998) *Caring for Children Away from Home: Messages from Research.* Chichester: Wiley.

Department of Health (2000) *Assessing Children in Need and their Families: Practice Guidance.* London: The Stationary Office.

Department of Health (2001) *The Children Act Now: Messages from Research.* London: The Stationary Office.

Department of Health (2002) *The Integrated Children's System.* London: Depatment of Health.

Department of Health, Cox, A. and Bentovim, A. (2000a) *The Family Pack of Questionnaires and Scales.* London: The Stationary Office.

Department of Health, Department for Education and Employment and Home Office (2000b) *Framework for the Assessment of Children in Need and their Families.* London: The Stationery Office.

Department of Health, Home Office and Department for Education and Employment (1999) *Working Together to Safeguard Children. A Guide to Interagency Working to Safeguard and Promote the Welfare of Children.* London: The Stationery Office.

Department of Health, Home Office, Department for Education and Skills, Department for Culture, Media and Sports, Office of the Deputy Prime Minister and Lord Chancellor's Department (2003) *What to Do if You're Worried a Child is Being Abused.* London: Department of Health.

Derdeyn, A.P. (1977) 'Child abuse and neglect: the rights of parents and the needs of their children.' *American Journal of Orthopsychiatry 47,* 377–387.

Doel, M. and Marsh, P. (1992) *Task Centred Social Work.* Aldershot: Arena.

Douglas, J.W.B. (1964) *The Home and the School.* London: McGibbon and Kee.

Dowling, M. (1992) *Young Disabled People's Experiences of Social Services and Education.* London: London Borough of Hounslow.

Dowling, M. (1996) *A Qualitative Study of Children and Families: Experiences of Community Care.* Surrey: Surrey Social Services Department.

Dowling, M. (2001) 'Families with children with disabilities – Inequalities and the social model.' *Disability and Society 16,* 1, 21–35.

Downes, C. (1992) *Separation Revisited: Adolescents in Foster Family Care.* Aldershot: Ashgate.

Doyle, A.B. and Aboud, F.E. (1995) A longitudinal study of white children's racial prejudice as a social cognitive development. *Merrill-Palmer Quarterly 41,* 209–228.

Dunn, J. (1984) *Brothers and Sisters.* London: Fontana.

Dunn, J. (1988) *The Beginnings of Social Understanding.* Oxford: Blackwell.

Dunn, J. (1991) 'Young children's understanding of other people.' In M. Woodhead, D. Faulkner and K. Littleton (eds) *Cultural Worlds of Early Childhood.* London: Routledge and The Open University.

Dunn, J. (1993) *Young Children's Close Relationships: Beyond Attachment.* London: Sage.

Dunn, J. (2002) 'The adjustment of children in stepfamilies: Lessons from community studies.' *Child and Adolescent Mental Health 7,* 4, 154–161.

Dunn, J., Slomkowski, C., Beardsall, L. and Rende, R. (1995) 'Adjustment in middle childhood and early adolescence: Links with earlier and contemporary sibling relationships.' *Journal of Child Psychology and Psychiatry 35,* 491–504.

Dutt, R. and Phillips, M. (2000) 'The assessment of black children in need and their families.' In Department of Health, *Assessing Children in Need and their Families.* London: The Stationery Office.

Dweck, C. (1999) *Self-Theories: Their Role in Motivation, Personality and Development.* Philadelphia: Psychology Press.

Dwivedi, K.N. (ed.) (2002) *Meeting the Needs of Ethnic Minority Children.* 2nd edn, London: Jessica Kingsley Publishers.

Elkind, D. (1967) 'Egocentrism in adolescence.' *Child Development 38,* 1025–1034.

Emler, N. (2001) *Self-esteem: The Costs and Causes of Low Self-worth.* York: Joseph Rowntree Foundation.

Epstein, L. (1988) *Helping People: The Task Centred Approach.* 2nd edn, Columbus OH: C.E. Merrill.

Erickson, G.D. and Hogan, T. (1972) *Family Therapy: An Introduction to Theory and Technique.* Belmont: Wadsworth.

Erikson, E.H (1950) *Childhood and Society.* 2nd edn, New York: Norton

Erikson, E.H (1965) *Childhood and Society.* Harmondsworth: Penguin.

Erikson, E.H (1968) *Identity Youth and Crisis.* New York: Norton.

Erikson, E.H. (1980) *Identity and the Life Cycle.* New York: Norton.

Fahlberg, V. (1982) *Child Development.* London: British Association for Adoption and Fostering.

Fahlberg, V. (1984) 'The child who is stuck.' In M. Adcock and R. White (eds) *Working with Parents.* London: British Agencies for Adoption and Fostering.

Fahlberg, V.I. (1994) *A Child's Journey through Placement.* London: British Agencies for Adoption and Fostering.

Fairbairn, W.R.D. (1952) *Psychoanalytic Studies of the Personality.* London: Routledge and Kegan Paul.

Falkov, A. (2002) 'Addressing family needs when a parent is mentally ill.' In H. Ward and W. Rose (eds) *Approaches to Needs Assessment in Children's Services.* London: Jessica Kingsley Publishers.

Family Division, Lord Chancellor's Department, Department of Health, Association of Directors of Social Services, CAFCASS, Solicitors Family Law Association, Court Service Justices Clerks' Society, Association of Lawyers for Children, Royal Courts of Justice, Association of Justices' Chief Executives, Welsh Assembly Government, Family Law Bar Association, Magistrates Association, and The Law Society (2003) *Protocol for Judicial Case Management in Public Law Children Act Cases.* London: Lord Chancellor's Department.

Fever, F. (1994) *Who Cares?* London: Warner Books.

Flavell, J.H. (1985) *Cognitive Development.* Englewood Cliffs, NJ: Prentice Hall.

Foley, P., Roche, J. and Tucker, S. (2001) 'Children in society: contemporary theory, policy and practice.' In W. Stainton Rogers, D. Hevey, J. Roche and E. Ash (eds) *Child Abuse and Neglect: Facing the Challenges.* Basingstoke: Palgrave and The Open University.

Fonagy, P., Steele, H., Steele, M., Moran, G.S. and Higgett, A. (1991) 'The capacity for understanding mental states: the reflective self in parent and child and its significance for security of attachment.' *Infant Mental Health Journal 13,* 200–217.

Fox, N.A., Kimmerly, N.L. and Schafer, W.D. (1991) 'Attachment to mother/attachment to father: a meta-analysis.' *Child Development 62,* 210–225.

Frampton, P. (2004) *The Golly in The Cupboard.* Manchester: Tamic.

Frank, J., Tatum, C. and Tucker, S. (1999) *On Small Shoulders. Learning from the Experiences of Former Young Carers.* London: The Children's Society.

Fraser, S., Lewis, V., Ding, S., Kellett, M. and Robinson, C. (2003) *Doing Research with Children and Young People.* London: Sage.

Freud, A. (1966) *The Ego and the Mechanisms of Defense.* New York: International Universities Press Inc.

Freundlich, M. (1998) 'Supply and demand: the forces shaping the future of infant adoption.' *Adoption Quarterly 2,* 13–46.

Gardner, F. (1998) 'Observational studies of parent-child interaction and behaviour problems: their implications for parenting interventions.' In A. Buchanan and B.L. Hudson (eds) *Parenting, Schooling and Children's Behaviour.* Aldershot: Ashgate.

Gebhardt, S. (2004) *Why Love Matters: How Affection Shapes a Baby's Brain.* Hove: Brunner-Routledge.

General Social Care Council (2001) *Social Work Education – Post Qualifying Training Council.* July. London: General Social Care Council.

George, C. (1996) 'A representational perspective of child abuse and prevention: Internal working models of attachment and caregiving.' *Child Abuse and Neglect 20,* 5, 411–424.

George, C. and Solomon, J. (1999) 'Attachment and caregiving – the caregiving behavioural system.' In J. Cassidy and P.R. Shaver (eds) *Handbook of Attachment – Theory, Research and Clinical Applications.* New York and London: The Guilford Press.

Gergen, K. and Gergen, M.M. (1988) 'Narrative and the self as relationship.' In L. Berkowitz (ed.) *Advances in Experimental Social Psychology 21*. New York: Academic Press.

Gibbons, J., Gallagher, B., Bell, C. and Gordon, D. (1995) *Development After Physical Abuse in Early Childhood*. London: HMSO.

Gilligan, R. (1998) 'The importance of schools and teachers in child welfare.' *Child and Family Social Work 3*, 13–25.

Gilligan, R. (2000) *Promoting Resilience: A Resource Guide on Working with Children in the Care System*. London: British Agencies for Adoption and Fostering.

Gilligan, R. (2001) 'Promoting positive outcomes for children in need.' In J. Howarth (ed.) *The Child's World*. London: Jessica Kingsley Publishers.

Glancy J. (2004) 'Please miss, can I have detention?' by Jonathan Glancey, 19 July, *G2* 12–13.

Glaser, D. (2000) 'Child abuse and neglect and the brain: a review.' *Journal of Child Psychology and Psychiatry 41*, 77–116.

Glaser, D. and Balbernie, R. (2001) 'Early experience, attachment and the brain.' In R. Gordon and E. Harran (eds) *Fragile: Handle with Care*. London: National Society for the Prevention of Cruelty to Children.

Gleeson, C., Robinson, M. and Neal, R. (2002) 'A review of teenagers' perceived needs and access to primary healthcare – implications for school health services.' *Primary Health Care Research and Development 3*, 184–193.

Goffman, I. (1959) *The Presentation of Self in Everyday Life* Garden City, NY: Doubleday.

Golan, N. (1981) *Passing Through Transitions*. London: Collier-Macmillan.

Goode, W.J. (1992) 'World changes in divorce patterns.' In L.J. Weitzman and M. Maclean (eds) *Economic Consequences of Divorce*. Oxford: Clarendon Press.

Goodman, G., Batterman-Faunce, J., Schaaf, J. *et al.* (2003) 'Nearly four years after an event: children's eye witness memory and adults' perception of children's accuracy.' *Child Abuse and Neglect 269*, 849–884.

Goodman, R. (1998) 'Longitudinal stability of psychiatric problems in children with hemiplegia.' *Journal of Child Psychology and Psychiatry 39*, 345–354.

Goodman, R. and Graham, P. (1996) 'Psychiatric problems in children with hemiplegia: cross sectional epidemiological survey.' *British Medical Journal 312*, 1065–1069.

Goodman, R., Gledhill, J. and Ford, T. (2003) 'Child psychiatric disorder and relative age within the school year: cross-sectional survey of a large population sample.' *British Medical Journal 327*, 472–475.

Gopnik, A., Meltzoff, A. and Kuhl, P. (1999) *How Babies Think*. London: Weidenfeld and Nicholson.

Gorin, S. (2004) *Understanding What Children Say: Children's Experiences of Domestic Violence, Parental Substance Misuse and Parental Health Problems*. Report for the Joseph Rowntree Foundation. London: National Children's Bureau.

Gorell Barnes, G. (1994) 'Family therapy.' In M. Rutter, E. Taylor and L. Hersov (eds) *Child and Adolescent Psychiatry: Modern Approaches*. 3rd edn, London: Blackwell.

Gowers, S.G. (2004) 'Assessing adolescent mental health.' In S. Bailey and M. Dolan (eds) *Adolescent Forensic Psychiatry*, 1, 3–13. London: Hodder.

Graffam Walker, A. (1999) *Handbook on Questioning Children: A Linguistic Perspective*. Washington, DC: ABA Center on Children and the Law.

Green, J. (2003) 'Concepts of child attachment.' Paper given at the President's Interdisciplinary Conference, Dartington Hall, 12–14 September, published in The Rt. Hon Lord Justice Thorpe and J. Cadbury (eds) (2004) *Hearing the Children*. London: Jordans.

Green, J.M., Stanley, C., Smith, V. and Goldwyn, R. (2000) 'A new method of evaluating attachment representations on young school age children – the Manchester Child Attachment Story Task.' *Attachment and Human Development 2*, 1, 42–64.

Greenwich Asian Women's Project (1996) *Annual Report.* London: Greenwich Asian Women's Project.

Grigsby, K. (1994) 'Maintaining attachment relationships among children in care.' *Families in Society 75*, 269–276.

Grigorenko, E.L., Wood, F.B., Meyer, M.S., Hart, L.A., Speed, W.C., Shuster, A. and Pauls, D.L. (1997) 'Susceptibility Loci for Distinct Components of Developmental Dyslexia on Chromosomes 6 and 16'. *American Journal of Human Genetics, 60*, 27–39.

Hagerman, R.J. (1999) 'Foetal alcohol syndrome.' *Neurodevelopmental Disorders, Diagnosis and Treatment,* 3–61. Oxford: Oxford University Press.

Haggerty, R.J., Sherrod, L.R., Garmezy, N. and Rutter, M. (eds) (1996) *Stress, Risk and Resilience in Children and Adolescents.* Cambridge: Cambridge University Press.

Halsey, A.H., Heath, A. and Ridge, J.M. (1980) *Origins and Destinations.* Oxford: Clarendon Press.

Hardiker, P. and Barker, M. (1991) 'Towards social theory for social work.' In J. Lishman (ed.) *Handbook of Theory for Practice Teachers in Social Work.* London: Jessica Kingsley Publishers.

Harker, R.M., Dobel-Ober, D., Akhurst, S., Berridge, D. and Sinclair, R. (2004) 'Who takes care of education 18 months on? A follow-up study of looked after children's perceptions of support for educational progress.' *Child and Family Social Work 9*, 273–284.

Harris, T. and Bifulco, A. (1991) 'Loss of parent in childhood, attachment style, and depression in adulthood.' In C.M. Parkes, J. Stevenson-Hinde and P. Marris (eds) *Attachment Across the Life Cycle.* London: Routledge.

Harter, S. (1999) *The Construction of the Self: A Developmental Perspective.* New York: The Guilford Press.

Harter, S., Waters, P.L., Whitesell, N.R and Kastelic, D. (1998) 'Identification and the self-system – level of voice among female and male high school students: relational context, support, and gender orientation.' *Developmental Psychology 34*, 5, 892–992.

Hartmann, H. (1958) *Ego Psychology and the Problem of Adaptation.* New York: International Universities Press.

Hartup, W.W. (1992) 'Friendships and their developmental significance'. In H. McGurk (ed) *Childhood Social Development: Contemporary Perspectives.* Hillsdale, NJ: Lawrence Erlbaum.

Haskey, J. (1990) 'Children in families broken by divorce.' *Population 61*, 34–42. London: HMSO.

Hawkins, P. and Shohet, R. (2000) *Supervision in the Helping Professions.* Buckingham: Open University Press.

Hawton, K., Kingsbury, K., Steinhardt, K., James, A. and Fagg, J. (1999) 'Repetition of deliberate self-harm by adolescents: the role of psychological factors.' *Journal of Adolescence 22*, 369–378.

Hay, D. (1995) 'Children and God.' *Tablet 74*, 1270–1.

Herbert, M. (1981) *Behavioural Treatment of Problem Children. A Practice Manual.* London: Academic Press.

Herbert, M. (1989) *Discipline.* London: Blackwell.

Herbert, M. (1997) *Working with Children and the Children Act.* Leicester: BPS Books.

Hesse, E. (1999) 'The adult attachment interview: historical and current perspectives.' In J. Cassidy and P.R. Shaver (eds) *Handbook of Attachment – Theory, Research and Clinical Applications.* New York and London: The Guilford Press.

Hindley, N., Ramchandani, P.G. and Jones, D.P.H. (2006) 'Risk factors for recurrences of maltreatment: a systematic review.' *Archives of Disease in Childhood 91*, 744–752.

Hobbs, S. and Mackechnie, J. (1997) *Child Employment in Britain: A Social and Psychological Analysis.* London: The Stationery Office.

Hodges, J. (1996) 'The natural history of early attachment' In B. Bernstein and J. Brannen (eds) *Children, Research and Policy.* London: Taylor and Francis.

Hodges, J., Steele, M., Hillman, S. and Henderson, K. (2003) 'Mental representations and defences in severely maltreated children: A story stem battery and rating system for clinical assessment and research applications.' In R. Emde, D. Wolf and D. Oppenheim (eds) *Revealing the Inner World of the Child.* Chicago: University of Chicago Press.

Hogan, D.M. (1998) 'Annotation: the psychological development and welfare of children of opiate and cocaine users – review and research needs.' *Journal of Child Psychology and Psychiatry 39*, 609–619.

Holman, R. (1981) *Kids at the Door.* Oxford: Blackwell.

Holman, R. (2000) *Kids at the Door Revisited.* Lyme Regis: Russell House Publishing.

Home Office, Lord Chancellor's Department, Crown Prosecution Service, Department of Health and National Assembly for Wales (2002) *Achieving Best Evidence in Criminal Proceedings: Guidance for Vulnerable or Intimidated Witnesses, Including Children.* London: Home Office.

Howe, D. (1987) *An Introduction to Social Work Theory.* Aldershot: Wildwood House.

Howe, D. (1995) *Attachment Theory for Social Work Practice.* Basingstoke: MacMillan.

Howe, D. (2001) 'Attachment.' In J. Horwath (ed.) *The Child's World – Assessing Children in Need.* London: Jessica Kingsley Publishers.

Howe, D., Brandon, M., Hinings, D. and Schofield, G. (1999) *Attachment Theory, Child Maltreatment and Family Support: A Practice and Assessment Model.* Basingstoke: Macmillan.

Howes, C. (1999) 'Attachment relationships in the context of multiple carers.' In J. Cassidy and P.R. Shaver (eds) *Handbook of Attachment – Theory, Research and Clinical Applications.* New York and London: The Guilford Press.

Hudson, B. (2000) 'Interagency collaboration – a sceptical view.' In A. Brechin, H. Brown and M. Eby (eds) *Critical Practice in Health and Social Care.* London: Sage.

Hudson, B.L. (1991) 'Behavioural social work.' In J. Lishman (ed.) *Handbook of Theory for Practice Teachers in Social Work.* London: Jessica Kingsley Publishers.

Hudson, B.L. and MacDonald, G.M. (1986) *Behavioural Social Work: an Introduction.* London: Routledge.

Hunt, J. (2001) *Friends and Family Care – A Scoping Paper for the Department of Health.* London: The Stationery Office.

Hutton. A. and Sugden. K. (2006) *'Say it your own way' – including children's voices in assessment: A guide and resources.* London: Barnardo's.

Hutton, J. (2000) 'Foreword.' In Department of Health, Department for Education and Employment and Home Office *Framework for the Assessment of Children in Need and their Families.* London: The Stationery Office.

Ingersoll, B.D. (1997) 'Psychiatric disorders among adopted children: a review and commentary.' *Adoption Quarterly 1*, 57–73.

Investing in Children (2004) Newsletter 59, Jan–Feb 2004. Durham: Investing in Children.

Ironside, V. (1994) *The Huge Bag of Worries.* Edinburgh: Children 1st.

Jack, G. (1997) 'An ecological approach to social work with children and families.' *Child & Family Social Work 2*, 109–120.

Jack, G. (2000) 'Ecological influences on parenting and child development.' *British Journal of Social Work 30*, 703–20.

Jack, G. (2001) 'Ecological perspectives in assessing children and their families.' In J. Horwath (ed.) *The Child's World.* London: Jessica Kingsley Publishers.

Jack, G. and Gill, O. (2003) *The Missing Side of the Triangle,* London: Barnardo's.

Jack, G. and Jack, D. (2000) 'Ecological social work: the application of a systems model of development in context.' In P. Stepney and D. Ford (eds) *Social Work Models, Methods and Theories: A Framework for Practice.* Lyme Regis: Russell House Publishing.

Jack, G. and Jordan, B. (1999) 'Social capital and child welfare.' *Children and Society 13*, 242–256.

Jackson, S. and Sachdev, D. (2001) *Better Education, Better Futures.* Ilford: Barnardo's.

Jacobs, M. (1998) *The Presenting Past.* Maidenhead: Open University Press.

James, O. (2002) *They F*** You Up – How to Survive Family Life.* London: Bloomsbury.

James, W. (1890) *Principles of Psychology.* Chicago: Encyclopaedia Britannica.

Jeffries, R. (2002) Personal communication to the author by email, 1.10.02.

Jewett, C.L. (1982) *Helping Children Cope with Separation and Loss.* Harvard, MA: Harvard Common Press.

Jewett, C. (1984) *Helping Children Cope with Separation and Loss.* London: British Agencies for Adoption and Fostering.

Johnson, P., Wilkinson, W.K. and McNeil, K. (1995) 'The impact of parental divorce on the attainment of the developmental tasks of young adulthood.' *Contemporary Family Therapy 17*, 2, 249–264.

Joliffe, F., Patel, S., Sparks, Y. and Reardon, K. (1995) *Child Employment in Greenwich.* London: London Borough of Greenwich.

Jolly, H. (1981) *The Book of Child Care.* London: Sphere.

Jones, A. (1997) *Messages from Inspection and Child Protection Inspections, 1992–6.* London: Department of Health. [2]

Jones, D.P.H. (1991) 'The effectiveness of intervention and the significant harm criteria.' In M. Adcock, R. White and A. Hollows (eds) *Significant Harm.* Croydon: Significant Publications Ltd.

Jones, D.P.H. (1998) 'The effectiveness of intervention.' In M. Adcock and R. White (eds) *Significant Harm: Its Management and Outcome.* 2nd edn, Croydon: Significant Publications Ltd.

Jones, D.P.H. (2001) 'The assessment of parental capacity.' In J. Horwath (ed) *The Child's World.* London: Jessica Kingsley Publishers.

Jones, D.P.H. (2003) *Communicating with Vulnerable Children: A Guide for Practitioners.* London: Gaskell.

Jones, D.P.H. and Ramchandani, P. (1999) *Child Sexual Abuse – Informing Practice from Research.* Oxford: Radcliffe Medical Press.

Kadushin, A. (1997) *Supervision in Social Work.* New York: Columbia University Press.

Karr, M. (1995) *The Liars' Club.* London: Penguin Books.

Kelly, J.G. (1974) 'Toward a psychology of healthiness.' Icabod Spencer Lecture, Union College, Schenectady, NY: May.

Kemonian, R. and Leiderman, P.H. (1986) 'Infant attachment to mother and child caretaker in an East African community.' *International Journal of Behavioral Development 9*, 455–469.

Klee, H, Jackson, M. and Lewis, S. (2002) *Drug Misuse and Motherhood.* London: Routledge.

Kluth, P. (2003) *You're Going to Love this Kid – Teaching Students with Autism in the Inclusive Classroom.* London: Jessica Kingsley Publishers.

Kohlberg, L. (1969) 'Stages and sequence: the cognitive-developmental approach to socialization.' In D.A. Goslin (ed.) *Handbook of Socialization Theory and Research*. Chicago: Rand McNally.

Kohlberg, L. (1970) 'Moral development and the education of adolescents.' In R. Purnell (ed.) *Adolescents and the American High School*. New York: Holt, Rinehart and Winston.

Kohlberg, L. (1976) 'Moral stages and moralisation: the cognitive–developmental approach'. In T. Lickona (ed.) *Moral Development and Behavior: Theory, Research, and Social Issues*. New York: Holt.

Kohlberg L. (1981) *The Philosophy of Moral Development*. San Francisco: Harper & Row.

Kohlberg, L. (ed.) (1984) *The Psychology of Moral Development, Vol. 2*. San Francisco: Harper and Row.

Kohn, A. (1993) *Punished by Rewards*. Boston: Houghton Mifflin Company.

Kroeger, J. (1996) *Identity in Adolescence: The Balance Between Self and Other*. 2nd edn, London: Routledge.

Kroll, B. and Taylor, A. (2003) *Parental Substance Misuse and Child Welfare*. London: Jessica Kingsley Publishers.

Kundani, H. (1998) 'The sanction of last resort.' *Voluntary Voice 129*. London: LVSC.

La Fontaine, J. (1991) *Bullying. The Child's View*. London: Calouste Gulbenkian Foundation.

Lancaster, Y.P. (2003) *Listening to Young Children Resource Pack*. Maidenhead: Open University Press.

Lansdown, G. (2001) 'Children's welfare and children's rights.' In P. Foley, J. Roche and S. Tucker (eds) *Children in Society*. Basingstoke: Palgrave and The Open University.

Lau, M. (1984) 'Transcultural issues in family therapy.' *Journal of Family Therapy 6*, 91–112.

Lawton, D. (1998) *The Number and Characteristics of Families with More Than One Disabled Child*. York: University of York, Social Policy Research Unit.

Laybourn, A. (1994) *The Only Child: Myths and Reality*. London: HMSO.

Leach, P. (1991) *Babyhood: Infant Development from Birth*. Harmondsworth: Penguin.

Leitch, D. (1986) *Family Secrets: A Writer's Research for his Parents*. New York: Delacorte Press.

Lewis, M. and Brooks-Gunn, J. (1979) *Social Cognition and the Acquisition of Self*. New York: Plenum.

Lewis, S. (2002) 'Concepts of motherhood.' In H. Klee, M. Jackson and S. Lewis (eds) *Drug Misuse and Motherhood*. London: Routledge.

Lewis, S. and O'Brian, M. (1987) *Reassessing Fatherhood. New Observations on Fatherhood and the Modern Family*. London: Sage.

Lifton, B. (1994) *Journey of the Adopted Self: A Quest for Wholeness*. New York: Basic Books.

Lindsay-Hartz, J., De Rivera, J. and Mascolo, M. (1995) 'Differentiating guilt and shame and their effects on motivation.' In J. Tangney and K. Fischer (eds) *Self-Conscious Emotions: The Psychology of Shame, Guilt, Embarrassment and Pride*. New York: The Guilford Press.

Lishman, J. (ed.) (1991) *Handbook of Theory for Practice Teachers in Social Work*. London: Jessica Kingsley Publishers.

Littner, N. (1975) 'The importance of the natural parent to the child in placement.' *Child Welfare 54*, 175–181.

Lorion, R.P. (2000) 'Theoretical and evaluation issues in the promotion of wellness and the protection of "well enough".' In D. Cicchetti, J. Rappaport, I. Sandler and R.P. Weissberg (eds) *The Promotion of Wellness in Children and Adolescents*. Washington DC: Child Welfare League of America.

Lovinger, J. (1976) *Ego Development: Conceptions and Theories.* San Francisco: Jossey-Bass Publishers.

Lowenstein, G., Weber, E., Hsee, C. and Welch, N. (2001) 'Risk as feelings.' *Psychological Bulletin 127*, 267–86.

Lyons-Ruth, K. (1996) 'Attachment relationships among children with aggressive behaviour problems: The role of disorganised early attachment patterns.' *Journal of Consulting and Clinical Psychology 64*, 64–73.

Mackechnie, J., Lindsay, S. and Hobbs, S. (1994) *Still Forgotten: Child Employment in Dumfries and Galloway.* Glasgow: Scottish Low Pay Unit.

Macleod, M. and Morris, S. (1996) *Why Me? Children Talking to ChildLine About Bullying.* London: ChildLine.

Main, M. (1991) 'Metacognitive knowledge, metacognitive monitoring, and singular (coherent) vs. multiple (incoherent) model of attachment.' In C.M. Parkes, J. Stevenson-Hinde and P. Marris (eds) *Attachment Across the Life Cycle.* London: Tavistock.

Main, M. and Goldwyn, R. (1984–94) *Adult Attachment Scoring and Classification System.* Unpublished scoring manual. Berkeley: Department of Psychology, University of California.

Malos, E. and Hague, G. (1997) 'Women, housing, homelessness and domestic violence.' *Women's Studies International Forum 20*, 3.

Marchant, R. (2001) 'The assessment of children with complex needs.' In J. Horwath (ed) *The Child's World.* London: Jessica Kingsley Publishers.

Marchant, R. and Jones, M. (2000) 'Assessing the needs of disabled children and their families.' In Department of Health *Assessing Children in Need and their Families: Practice Guidance.* London: The Stationery Office.

Marchant, R. and Jones, M. (2001) 'Protecting babies with special needs.' In R. Gordon and E. Harran (eds) *Fragile Handle With Care: Protecting Babies From Harm.* Leicester: NSPCC.

Margison, F., Barkham, M., Evans, C., McGrath, G., Mellor-Clark, J., Audin, K. and Connell, J. (2000) 'Measurement and psychotherapy, evidence based practice and practice based evidence.' *British Journal of Psychiatry 177*, 123–130.

Marsh, P. and Crow, G. (1997) *Family Group Conferences in Child Welfare: Working Together for Children, Young People and Families.* Oxford: Blackwell.

Marsh, P. and Peel, M. (1999) *Leaving Care in Partnership: Family Involvement with Care Leavers.* London: The Stationery Office.

Maslow, A.H. (1943) 'A theory of human motivation.' *Psychological Review 50*, 370–378.

Masson, J., Harrison, C. and Pavlovic, A. (eds) (1999) *Lost and Found: Making and Remaking Working Partnerships with Parents of Children in the Care System.* Aldershot: Ashgate/Arena.

Masten, A. and Coatsworth, D. (1998) 'Development of competence in favourable and unfavourable environments.' *American Psychologist*, February, 205–220.

McWey, L. (2000) 'I promise to act better if you let me see my family: attachment theory and foster care visitation.' *Journal of Family Social Work 5*, 91–105.

Mead, G. (1934) *Mind, Self and Society from the Standpoint of a Social Behaviourist.* Chicago: University of Chicago Press.

Meggitt, C. and Sunderland, G. (2000) *Child Development. An Illustrated Guide (Birth to 8 Years).* Oxford: Heinemann Educational Publishers.

Middleton, J.A. (2001) 'Practitioner review: Psychological sequelae of head injury in children and adolescents.' *Journal of Child Psychology and Psychiatry 42*, 165–180.

Middleton, L. (1999) *Disabled Children Challenging Social Exclusion.* Oxford: Blackwell.

Middleton, S., Shropshire, J. and Croden, N. (1998) 'Earning your keep' Children's work and contributions to family budgets.' In B. Pettitt (ed.) *Children and Work in the UK*. London: Child Poverty Action Group.

Moffitt, T.E. and Caspi, A. (1998) 'Implications of violence between intimate partners for child psychologists and psychiatrists.' *Journal of Child Psychology and Psychiatry 39*, 2, 137–144.

Monck, E., Reynolds, J. and Wigfall, V. (2001) 'Concurrent planning in the adoption of children under eight years.' *Adoption and Fostering 25*, 67–68.

Morgan, R. (2004) *Safe from Harm*. Children's Views Report. Newcastle: Office of the Children's Rights Director, Commission for Social Care Inspection. Website www.rights4me.org.uk.

Morris, J. (1999) *Accessing Human Rights: Disabled Children and the Children Act*. London: Barnardo's.

Morrison, J. and Anders, T. (1999) *Interviewing Children and Adolescents*. London: The Guilford Press.

Morrison, T. (1999) *Staff Supervision in Social Care*. Brighton: Pavilion.

Moss, P. and Petrie, P. (1996) *Time for a New Approach: A Discussion Paper*. London: Thomas Coram Research Unit.

Mullender, A., Hague, G., Umme, I., Kelly, L., Malos, E. and Regan, L. (2002) *Children's Perspectives on Domestic Violence*. London: Sage.

Murray, L. and Andrews, L. (2000) *The Social Baby*. Richmond: CP Publishing.

Mussen, P.H., Conger, J.J., Kagan, J. and Huston, A.C. (1990) *Child Development and Personality*. 7th edn, New York: Harper Collins.

National Statistics/Department for Education and Skills Bulletin (2005) *Statistics of Education: Care Leavers 2003–2004 England*. Issue 01/05.

NCH Action for Children (1994) *The Hidden Victims. Children and Domestic Violence*. London: NCH Action for Children.

Nelson, E., Heath, A., Madden, P., Cooper, L., Dinwiddie, S., Bucholz, K. *et al.* (2002) 'Association between self-reported childhood sexual abuse and adverse psychosocial outcomes.' *Archives of General Psychiatry 59*, 139–145.

Newton, B. and Becker, S. (1996) *Young Carers in Southwark. The Hidden Face of Community Care*. Loughborough: Loughborough University.

Noller, P. and Callan, V. (1991) *The Adolescent in the Family*. London: Routledge.

NSPCC and Triangle (2004) *All Join In* video/DVD. London: NSPCC.

NSPCC in association with Chailey Heritage and Department of Health (1997) *Turning Points: A Resource Pack for Communicating with Children*. London: NSPCC.

Nye, R. (1996) 'Spiritual development.' In CCETSW, *Children Religion and Spirituality*. London: CCETSW.

O'Connor, T., Rutter, M., Beckett, C., Keaveney, L., Kreppner, J. and the English and Romanian Adoptees Study Team (2000) 'The effects of global privation on cognitive competence – extension and longitudinal follow up.' *Child Development 71*, 376–390.

Oaklander, V. (1978) *Windows to our Children*. London: Real People Press.

Oakley, A. (1974) *House Wife*. London: Penguin.

Office for National Statistics (2003) *Social Trends 32*. London: Office for National Statistics.

Oliver, C. and Candappa, M. (2003) *Tackling Bullying: Listening to the Views of Children and Young People*. London: Department for Education and Skills.

Oppenheim, C. and Harker, L. (1996) *Poverty: The Facts*. London: Child Poverty Action Group.

Orme, N. (2001) *Medieval Children*. Newhaven: Yale University Press.

Owers, M., Brandon, M. and Black, J. (1999) *Learning How to Make Children Safer: An Analysis for the Welsh Office of Serious Child Abuse Cases in Wales.* Norwich: University of East Anglia, Centre for Research on the Child and Family.

Owusu-Bempah, K. (1993) 'Parental information and children's behavior.' Unpublished manuscript. Leicester: University of Leicester, School of Social Work.

Owusu-Bempah, K. (1995) 'Information about the absent parent as a factor in the well-being of children of single-parent families.' *International Social Work 38*, 253–257.

Owusu-Bempah, K. and Howitt, D. (1997) 'Socio-genealogical connectedness, attachment theory, and childcare practice.' *Child and Family Social Work 2*, 199–207.

Owusu-Bempah, K. and Howitt, D. (2000a) 'Socio-genealogical connectedness: on the role of gender and same-gender parenting in mitigating the effects of parental divorce.' *Child and Family Social Work 5*, 107–116.

Owusu-Bempah, K. and Howitt, D. (2000b) *Psychology beyond Western Perspectives.* Leicester: BPS Books.

Oyserman, D. and Martois, H.R. (1990) 'Possible selves and delinquency.' *Journal of Personality and Social Psychology 59*, 112–115.

Pannor, R., Sorosky, A. and Baran, A. (1974) 'Opening the sealed record in adoption: the need of continuity.' *Journal of Jewish Communial Service 51*, 188–196.

Parke, R.D. and Asher, S.R. (1983) 'Social and personality development.' *Annual Review of Psychology 34*, 465.

Parker, R.M., Ward, H., Jackson, S., Aldgate, J. and Wedge, P. (eds) (1991) *Looking After Children: Assessing Outcomes in Child Care.* London: HMSO.

Payne, M. (1992) *Modern Social Work Theory: A Critical Introduction.* London: Macmillan.

Pearson, J., Cohn, D.A., Cowan, P.A. and Cowan, C.P. (1994) 'Earned- and continuous-security in adult attachment: Relation to depressive symptomology and parenting style.' *Development and Psychopathology 6*, 359–373.

Petito, L.A. and Marentette, P.F. (1991) 'Babbling in the manual mode: Evidence for the ontogeny of language.' *Science 251*, 1493–1496.

Pettitt, B. (1998) (ed) *Children and Work in the UK.* London: Child Poverty Action Group.

Phelps, J.L., Belsky, J. and Crnic, K. (1998) 'Earned-security, daily stress, and parenting: A comparison of five alternative models.' *Development and Psychopathology 10*, 21–38.

Phinney, J. and Devich-Navarro, M. (1997) 'Variations in bi-cultural identification among African-American and Mexican-American adolescents.' *Journal of Research on Adolescence 7*, 3–32.

Phinney, J. and Rosenthal, D. (1992) 'Ethnic identity in adolescence process, context and outcome.' In G. Adams, T. Gillotta and R. Montemayor (eds) *Adolescent Identity Formation.* London: Sage.

Piaget, J. (1932) *The Moral Judgement of the Child.* London: Routledge and Kegan Paul.

Piaget, J. (1952) *The Origins of Intelligence in Children.* New York: International Universities Press.

Piaget, J. (1965) *The Moral Judgement of the Child.* Harmondsworth: Penguin.

Piaget, J. and Inhelder, B. (1969) *The Psychology of the Child.* London: Routledge and Kegan Paul.

Pierson, J. (2002) *Tackling Social Exclusion.* London: Routledge.

Pike, A. and Atzaba-Poria, N. (2003) 'Do sibling and friend relationships share the same temperamental origins? A twin study.' *Journal of Child Psychology and Psychiatry 44*, 4, 598–611.

Pond, C. and Searle, A. (1991) *The Hidden Army: Children at Work in the 1990s.* London: Low Pay Unit.

Poole, D. and Lamb, M. (1998) *Investigative Interviews of Children: A Guide for Helping Professionals.* Washington DC: American Psychological Association.

Prilleltensky, I. and Nelson, G. (2002) 'Promoting child and family wellness: priorities for psychological and social interventions.' *Journal of Community and Applied Social Psychology 10,* 85–105.

Pringle, M.L. Kellmer (1980) *The Needs of Children: A Personal Perspective: Prepared for the Department of Health and Social Security.* London: Hutchinson.

Pringle, M.L. Kellmer, Butler, N. and Davie, R. (1966) *11000 Seven-Year Olds.* London: Longman.

Pugh, G., De'Ath, E. and Smith, C. (1994) *Confident Parents, Confident Children.* London: National Children's Bureau.

Pullman, P. (2004) 'Opinion.' *Guardian Education,* 30 March, 27.

Quarles, C.S. and Brodie, J.H. (1998) 'Primary care of international adoptees.' *American Family Physician: the American Academy of Family Physicians,* December, 58(9), 2025–2032.

Quinton, D. (1994) 'Cultural and community influences.' In M. Rutter and D.F. Hay (eds) *Development Through Life, A Handbook for Clinicians.* Oxford: Blackwell Science.

Quinton, D. (2004) *Supporting Parents: Messages from Research.* London: Jessica Kingsley Publishers.

Quinton, D., Rushton, A., Dance, C. and Mayes, D. (1998) *Joining New Families. A Study of Adoption and Fostering in Middle Childhood.* Chichester Wiley.

Quinton, D. and Rutter, M. (1985) 'Family pathology and child psychiatric disorder: A four-year prospective study.' In A.R. Nicol (ed.) *Longitudinal Studies in Child Psychology and Psychiatry.* London: John Wiley and Sons Ltd.

Quinton, D. and Rutter, M. (1988) *Parenting Breakdown: The Making and Breaking of Intergenerational Links.* Aldershot: Avebury.

Rashid, S.P. (1996) 'Attachment through a cultural lens.' In D. Howe (ed.) *Attachment and Loss in Child and Family Social Work.* Aldershot: Broomfield.

Reid, W.J. and Epstein, L. (1976) *Task-centred Practice.* New York: Columbia University Press.

Reid, W.J. and Shyne, A.W. (1969) *Brief and Extended Casework.* New York Columbia University Press.

Re L (Care: Assessment: Fair Trial) (2002) 2 Family Reports 730.

Remafedi, G. (1987) 'Male homosexuality: the adolescent's perspectives.' *Paediatrics 79,* 331–337.

Richards, M. and Wadsworth, M. (2004) 'Long term effects of early adversity on cognitive function.' *Archives of Disease in Childhood 89,* 922–927.

Robbins, D. (2001) 'Assessment in child protection and family support.' In Department of Health *Studies Informing the Framework for the Assessment of Children in Need and their Families.* London: The Stationery Office.

Robertson, J. (1952) *A Two-year-old Goes to Hospital* (film: 16mm: 45 minutes; sound). Distributors: Tavistock Child Development Research Unit, London; New York University Film Library; United Nations, Geneva.

Roche, H. and Perlesz, M. (2000) 'A legitimate choice and voice: the experience of adult adoptees who have chosen to search for their biological families.' *Adoption & Fostering 24,* 8–19.

Rogers C.R. (1961) *On Becoming a Person.* Boston: Houghton Mifflin.

Roll, J. (1992) *Lone-parent Families in the European Community: The 1992 Report to the European Commission.* London: European Family and Social Policy Unit.

Rose, W. and Aldgate, J. (2000) 'Knowledge underpinning the Assessment Framework.' In Department of Health *Assessing Children in Need and Their Families: Practice Guidance.* London: The Stationery Office.

Rosenberg, M. (1965) *Society and the Adolescent Self Image.* Princeton, NJ: Princeton University Press.

Rosenberg, M. (1979) *Conceiving the Self.* New York: Basic Books.

Ross, C.E. and Mirowsky, J. (1999) 'Parental divorce, life-course disruption, and adult depression.' *Journal of Marriage and the Family 61,* 1034–1045.

Rovee-Collier, C. (1999) 'The development of infant memory.' *Current Directions in Psychological Science 8,* 80–85.

Rowe, J. (1980) 'Fostering in the 1970s and beyond.' In J. Triseliotis (ed.) *New Developments in Foster Care and Adoption.* London: Routledge.

Rowe, J. and Lambert, L. (1973) *Children Who Wait.* London: Association of British Adoption and Fostering Agencies.

Rushton, A., Quinton, D., Dance, C. and Mayes, D. (1997/8) 'Preparation for permanent placement, evaluating direct work with older children.' *Adoption and Fostering 21,* 4, 41–48.

Rustin, M. and Rustin, M. (2001) *Narratives of Love and Loss: Studies in Modern Children's Fiction.* London: Karnac.

Rutter, M. (1974) 'Dimensions of parenthood: some myths and some suggestions.' In Department of Health and Social Security *The Family in Society: Dimensions of Parenthood.* London: HMSO.

Rutter, M. (1976) 'Isle of Wight Study, 1964–1974.' *Psychological Medicine 6,* 313–332.

Rutter, M. (1981) *Maternal Deprivation Reassessed.* 2nd edn, Harmondsworth: Penguin.

Rutter, M. (1985) 'Resilience in the face of adversity: protective factors and resilience to psychiatric disorder.' *British Journal of Psychiatry 147,* 163–182.

Rutter, M. (1989) 'Intergenerational continuities and discontinuities in serious parenting difficulties.' In D. Cicchetti and V. Carlson (eds) *Child Maltreatment: Theory and Research on the Causes and Consequences of Child Abuse and Neglect.* Cambridge: Cambridge University Press.

Rutter, M. (1990) 'Psychosocial resilience and protective mechanisms.' In J. Rolf *et al. Risk and Protective Factors in the Development of Psychopathology.* Cambridge: Cambridge University Press.

Rutter, M. (1991) 'Nature, nurture and psychopathology: a new look at an old topic.' *Development and Psychopathology 3,* 125–136.

Rutter, M. (1992) 'Nature, nurture and psychopathology: a new look at an old topic.' In B. Tizard and V. Varma (eds) (2000) *Vulnerability and Resilience in Human Development.* London: Jessica Kingsley Publishers.

Rutter, M. (ed.) (1995) *Psychosocial Disturbances in Young People: Challenges for Prevention.* Cambridge: Cambridge University Press.

Rutter, M. (2001) 'Recovery and deficit in profound early deprivation.' In P. Selman (ed.) *Intercountry Adoption, Developments, Trends and Perspectives.* London: British Agencies for Adoption and Fostering.

Rutter, M. (2005) 'How the environment affects mental health.' *British Journal of Psychiatry 186,* 4–6.

Rutter, M. and Hay, D.F. (eds) (1994) *Development Through Life – A Handbook for Clinicians.* Oxford: Blackwell Science.

Rutter, M. and Quinton, D. (1984) 'Long term followup of women institutionalised in childhood: factors promoting good functioning in social life.' *British Journal of Developmental Psychology 2*, 191–204.

Rutter, M. and Rutter, M. (1993) *Developing Minds: Challenge and Continuity Across the Life Span.* Harmondsworth: Penguin.

Rutter, M., Korn, S. and Birch, H.G. (1963) 'Genetic and environmental factors in the development of "primary reaction patterns".' *British Journal of Social and Clinical Psychology 2*, 161–173.

Rutter, M., Graham, P. and Yule, W. (1970) *A Neuropsychiatric Study in Childhood: Clinics in Developmental Medicine,* 35/36 SIMP/Heinemann, London.

Rutter, M., Giller, H. and Hagell, A. (1998) *Antisocial Behaviour by Young People.* Cambridge: Cambridge University Press.

Rutter, M., Taylor, E. and Hersov, L. (eds) (1994) *Child and Adolescent Psychiatry. Modern Approaches.* 3rd edn, London: Blackwell.

Ryan, M. (2000) *Working with Fathers.* Oxford: Radcliffe Medical Press

Safran, J.D. and Segal, Z.V. (1990) *Interpersonal Process in Cognitive Therapy.* New York: Basic Books.

Saleebey, D. (1997) *The Strengths Perspective in Social Work Practice.* New York: Longman.

Saradjian, J. with Hanks, H. (1997) *Women Who Sexually Abuse Children: From Research to Clinical Practice.* Chichester: Wiley.

Save the Children and The Refugee Council (2001) *In Safe Hands.* London: Save the Children.

Schaffer, H.R. (1977) *Mothering.* London: Fontana.

Schaffer, H.R. (1990) *Making Decisions about Children, Psychological Questions and Answers.* Oxford: Blackwell.

Schaffer, H.R. (1992) 'Early experience and the parent-child relationship: genetic and environmental interactions as developmental determinants.' In B Tizard and V. Varma (2000) *Vulnerability and Resilience in Human Development.* London: Jessica Kingsley Publishers.

Schaffer, H.R. (1996) *Social Development.* Oxford: Blackwell.

Schaffer, H.R. (1998) *Making Decisions about Children.* 2nd edn, Oxford: Basil Blackwell.

Schechter, M.D. and Bertocci, D. (1990) 'The meaning of the search.' In D.M. Brodzinsky and M.D. Schechter (eds) *The Psychology of Adoption.* Oxford: Oxford University Press.

Schofield, G. (1998a) 'Inner and outer worlds: a psychosocial framework for child and family social work.' *Child and Family Social Work 3*, 57–67.

Schofield, G. (1998b) 'Making sense of the ascertainable wishes and feelings of insecurely attached children.' *Child and Family Law Quarterly 10*, 4, 363–376.

Schofield, G. (2005) 'The voice of the child in Family, placement decision making.' *Adoption and Fostering 29*, 1, 29–44.

Schofield, G. and Beek, M. (forthcoming) *Attachment Handbook for Foster Care and Adoption.* London: British Agencies for Adoption and Fostering.

Schofield, G., Beek, M. and Sargent, K. with Thoburn, J. (2000) *Growing up in Foster Care.* London: British Agencies for Adoption and Fostering.

Seden, J. (1995) 'The Children Act and religious persuasion.' *Adoption & Fostering 9*, 2, 7–15.

Seden, J. (1998) 'The spiritual needs of children.' *Practice 10*, 4, 57–67.

Seden, J. (2000) *Counselling Skills in Social Work Practice.* Buckingham: Open University Press.

Seden, J. (2002a) 'Parenting and Harry Potter: a social care perspective.' *Children and Society 16*, 5, 295–305.

Seden, J. (2002b) 'Underpinning theories for the assessment of children's needs.' In H. Ward and W. Rose (eds) *Approaches to Needs Assessment in Children's Services*. London: Jessica Kingsley Publishers.

Sendak, M. (1963) *Where the Wild Things Are*. New York: Harper & Row.

Shants, H. (1964) 'Genealogical bewilderment in children with substitute parents.' *British Journal of Medical Psychology 37*, 133–141.

Shaw, C. (1998) *Remember My Messages...* London: The Who Cares? Trust.

Sheldon B. (1995) *Cognitive Behaviour Therapy, Theory, Practice and Philosophy*. London: Routledge.

Shemmings, Y. and Shemmings, D. (2001) 'Empowering children and family members to participate in the assessment process.' In J. Horwath (ed.) *The Child's World: Assessing Children in Need*. London: Jessica Kingsley Publishers.

Sheppard, M.J. and Uhry, J.K. (1993) 'Reading disorder.' *Child and Adolescent Psychiatric Clinics of North America 2*, 193–208.

Sheridan, M.D. (1997) *From Birth to Five*. London: Routledge.

Siegler, R., Deloache, J. and Eisenberg, N. (2003) *How Children Develop*. New York: Worth; Basingstoke: Palgrave Macmillan.

Simmonds, J. (1992) 'Social work with children: developing a framework for responsible practice.' In J. Aldgate and J. Simmonds (eds) *Direct Work with Children*. London: Batsford.

Simons, R.L., Lin, K., Gordon, L.C., Conger, R.D. and Lorenz, F.O. (1999) 'Explaining the higher incidence of adjustment problems among children of divorce compared with those in two-parent families.' *Journal of Marriage and the Family 61*, 1020–1033.

Sinclair, I., Gibbs, I. and Wilson, K. (2000) *Supporting Foster Placements, Report 2*. York: Social Work Research and Development Unit.

Sinclair, I., Gibbs, I., Baker, C. and Wilson, K. (2003) *What Happens to Foster Children?* York: Social Work Research and Development Unit.

Skuse, T. and Ward, H. (2003) *Outcomes for Looked After Children: Children's Views of Care and Accommodation*. An Interim Report for the Department of Health. Loughborough: Loughborough University, Centre for Child and Family Research.

Smith, M. (2003) 'New stepfamilies – A descriptive study of a largely unseen group.' *Child and Family Law Quarterly 15*, 2, 185–198.

Smith, M. (2004) 'Relationships of children in stepfamilies with their non-resident fathers.' *Family Matters 67*, 28–35.

Smith, M., Robertson, J., Dixon, J., Quigley, M. and Whitehead, E. (2002) *A Study of Step Children and Step Parenting*. London: Thomas Coram Research Unit.

Snow, K. (1990) 'Building memories: the ontogeny of autobiography.' In D. Cicchetti and M. Beeghly (eds) *The Self in Transition: Infancy to Childhood*. Chicago: University of Chicago Press.

Solomon, J. and George, C. (1996) 'Defining the caregiving system: towards a theory of caregiving.' *Infant Mental Health Journal 17*, 3,183–197.

Solomon, J. and George, C. (1999) 'The measurement of attachment security in infancy and childhood.' In J. Cassidy and P. Shaver (eds) *Handbook of Attachment: Theory, Research, and Clinical Applications*. New York: The Guilford Press.

Spock. B. (1999) *Baby and Child Care*. New York: Schuster.

Spufford, F. (2002) *The Child that Books Built: A Memoir of Childhood and Reading*. London: Faber and Faber.

Stainton Rogers, R. (1992) 'The social construction of childhood.' In W. Stainton-Rogers, W. Hevey, J. Roche and E. Ash (eds) *Child Abuse and Neglect: Facing the Challenge.* 2nd edn, London: Batsford.

Steele, M. (2003) *Attachment Theory and Research: Recent Advances and Implications for Adoption and Foster Care.* Paper given at the President's Interdisciplinary Conference, Dartington Hall, 12–14 September, published in The Rt. Hon Lord Justice Thorpe and J. Cadbury (eds) (2004) *Hearing the Children.* London: Jordans.

Steinberg, L., Fegley, S. and Dorenbusch, S.M. (1993) 'Negative impact of part time work on adolescent adjustment.' *Developmental Psychology 29,* 171–180.

Sternberg, K., Lamb, M., Hershkowitz, I., Yudilevitch, L., Orbach, Y., Esplin, P. and Hovav, M. (1997) 'Effects of introductory style on children's abilities to describe experiences of sexual abuse.' *Child Abuse and Neglect 21,* 1133–1146.

Sternberg, R. (1999) *Cognitive Psychology.* 2nd edn, New York: Harcourt Brace Publishers.

Stevenson, C.J., Blackburn, P. and Pharoah, P.O.D. (1999) 'A longitudinal study of behaviour disorders in low birth weight infants.' *Archives of Diseases in Child Foetal Neonatology 81,* F5-F9.

Stevenson, J. (2001) 'The significance of genetic variation for abnormal behavioural development.' In J. Green and W. Ule (eds) *Research and Innovation on the Road to Modern Child Psychiatry 1.* London: Gaskell Publications.

Stevenson, O. (1968) 'Reception into care – its meaning for all concerned.' In R.J.N. Tod (ed.) *Children in Care.* London: Longmans.

Stevenson, O. (1998) *Neglected Children: Issues and Dilemmas.* Oxford: Blackwell.

Stratton, K.R., Howe, C.J. and Battaglia, F.C. (1996) *Foetal Alcohol Syndrome: Diagnosis, Epidemiology, Prevention and Treatment.* Washington, DC: National Academy Press.

Stroud, J. (1997) 'Mental disorder and the homicide of children.' *Social Work and Social Services Review: An International Journal of Applied Research 6,* 3, 149–162.

Swadi, H. (1994) 'Parenting capacity and substance misuse: an assessment scheme.' *Association of Child Psychology and Psychiatry Review and Newsletter 16,* 237–245.

Tager-Flusberg, H. (1999) 'Language development in atypical children.' In M. Barrett (ed.) *The Development of Language.* Hove: Psychology Press Ltd.

Thelen, E. and Smith, L.B. (1994) *A Dynamic Systems Approach to the Development of Cognition and Action.* Cambridge, MA MIT Press.

Thomas, A. and Chess, S. (1977) *Temperament and Development.* New York: New York University Press and Brunner/Mazel.

Thomas, A., Chess, S. and Birch, H. (1968) *Temperament and Behavioural Disorders in Childhood.* New York: New York University Press.

Thomas, A, Chess, S., Birch, H.G., Hertzig, M.E. and Korn, S. (1963) *Behavioural Individuality in Early Childhood.* New York: New York University Press.

Thomas, C. and Beckford, V., with Lowe, N. and Murch, M. (1999) *Adopted Children Speaking.* London: British Agencies for Adoption and Fostering.

Thompson, R. (1995) *Preventing Child Maltreatment through Social Support.* California: Sage Publications.

Tomlinson, S. (1982) *A Sociology of Special Education.* London: Routledge.

Triseliotis, J. (1973) *In Search of Origins.* London: Routledge and Kegan.

Triseliotis, J. (2000) 'Intercountry adoption: Global trade or gift?' *Adoption and Fostering 24,* 45–54.

Triseliotis, J., Shireman, J. and Hundleby, M. (1997) *Adoption: Theory, Policy and Practice.* London: Cassell.

Trowell, J. and Bower, M. (1996) *The Emotional Needs of Young Children and Their Families.* London: Routledge.

Trowell, J., Hodges, S. and Leighton-Lang, J. (1977) 'The work of a family centre.' *Child Abuse Review 6,* 357–369.

Tunstill, J. and Aldgate, J. (2000) *Services for Children in Need: From Policy to Practice.* London: The Stationery Office.

Turnell, A. and Edwards, S. (1999) *Signs of Safety: A Solution and Safety Oriented Approach to Child Protection Casework.* London: Norton.

UN Convention on the Rights of the Child (1989) *Article 12.*

UNICEF (2002) *A World Fit for Children.* New York: UNICEF.

Utting, D., Rose, W. and Pugh, G. (2002) *Better Results for Children and Families. Involving Communities in Planning Services Based on Outcomes.* London: National Council for Voluntary Child Care Organizations.

van IJzendoorn, M.H. and Bakermans-Kranenburg, M.J. (1996) 'Attachment representations in mothers, fathers, adolescents, and clinical groups: a meta-analytic search for normative data.' *Journal of Consulting and Clinical Psychology 64,* 8–21.

van IJzendoorn, M.H. and Sagi, A. (1999) 'Cross-cultural patterns of attachment, universal and contextual dimensions.' In J. Cassidy and P.R. Shaver (eds) *Handbook of Attachment – Theory, Research and Clinical Applications.* New York: The Guilford Press.

van IJzendoorn, M.H., Goldber, S., Kroonenberg, P. and Frankel, O. (1992) 'The relative effects of material and child problems on the quality of attachment: a meta analysis of attachment in clinical samples.' *Child Development 63,* 840–858.

Vasta, R., Marshall, M.M. and Miller, S.A. (1999) *Child Psychology: The Modern Science.* New York: John Wiley and Sons.

Velleman, R. (1992) *Counselling for Alcohol Problems.* London: Sage.

Velleman, R. (1993) *Alcohol and the Family.* London: Institute of Alcohol Studies.

Velleman, R. and Orford, J. (1999) *Risk and Resilience: Adults who were the Children of Problem Drinkers.* Amsterdam: Harward Academic Publishers.

Voice for the Child in Care (1998) *Shout to be Heard.* London: Voice for the Child in Care.

Vygotsky, L.S. (1962) *Thought and Language.* Cambridge: Wiley.

Vygotsky, L.S. (1978) *Mind in Society: The Development of Higher Mental Processes.* Cambridge, MA: Harvard University Press.

Wallander, J.L. and Varni, J.W. (1998) 'Effects of paediatric chronic physical disorders on child and family adjustment.' *Journal of Child Psychology and Psychiatry 39,* 29–46.

Walby, C. and Symons, B. (1990) *Who am I? Identity, Adoption and Human Fertilisation.* London: British Association for Adoption and Fostering.

Walrond-Skinner, S. (1976) *Family Therapy, the Treatment of Natural Systems.* London: Routledge and Kegan Paul.

Ward, H., Skuse, T. and Munro, E.R. (2005) 'The best of times, the worst of times: young people's views of care and accommodation.' *Adoption and Fostering 29,* 1, 8–17.

Webster-Stratton, C. (1992) *The Incredible Years.* Toronto: Umbrelia Press.

Webster-Stratton, C. (1999) 'Advancing videotape parent training: a comparison study.' *Journal of Consulting and Clinical Psychology 62,* 583–93.

Webster-Stratton, C. and Taylor, T.K. (1998) 'Adopting and implementing empirically supported interventions: a recipe for success.' In A. Buchanan and B. Hudson (eds) *Parenting, Schoolgoing and Children's Behaviour*. Aldershot: Ashgate.

Weisglas-Kuperus, N., Koot, H.M., Baerts, W., Fetter, W.P. and Saver, P J. (1993) 'Behaviour problems of very low birth weight children.' *Developmental Medicine and Child Neurology 35*, 406–416.

Werner, E. (1990) 'Protective factors and individual resilience.' In S. Meisels and J. Shonkoff (eds) *Handbook of Early Childhood Intervention*. Cambridge: Cambridge University Press.

Werner, E.E. and Smith, R.S. (1992) *Overcoming the Odds: High Risk Children from Birth to Adulthood*. Ithaca and London: Cornell University Press.

Williams, J. and Stith, M. (1974) *Middle Childhood, Behaviour and Development*. Oxford: Macmillan.

Winnicott, C. (1964) *Child Care and Social Work*. Welwyn: The Codicote Press.

Winnicott, D.W. (1960) 'The theory of the parent-infant relationship.' *International Journal of Psycho-Analysis 41*, 585–595.

Winnicott, D.W. (1964) *The Child, the Family and the Outside World*. London: Penguin.

Winnicott D.W. (1985) *Home is Where We Start From*. Harmondsworth: Penguin.

Winnicott, D.W. (1988) *Human Nature*. London: Free Association Books.

Woodhead, M. (1990) 'Psychological and cultural construction of children's needs.' In A. James and A. Prout (eds) *Constructing and Reconstructing Childhood*. London: Falmer Press.

Woodhead, M. (1999) 'Reconstructing developmental psychology – some first steps.' *Children and Society 13*, 3–19.

Young, M. and Willmott, P. (1957) *Family and Kinship in East London*. Harmondsworth: Penguin.

Zahn-Waxler, C., Radke-Yarrow, M., Wagner, E. and Chapman, M. (1992) 'Development of concern for others.' *Child Development 28*, 126–136.

List of contributors

Jane Aldgate is Professor of Social Care at The Open University. She is also Honorary Professor of Social Work at Queens University Belfast.

Susan Bailey is Professor of Child and Adolescent Forensic Mental Health at the University of Central Lancashire and Chair of the Faculty of Child and Adolescent Psychiatry at the Royal College of Psychiatrists.

Hedy Cleaver is Professorial Research Fellow based at Royal Holloway, University of London.

Brigid Daniel is Professor in Child Care and Protection in the Department of Social Work at the University of Dundee.

Monica Dowling, formerly Senior Lecturer at Royal Holloway, University of London, is now Professor of Social Work at The Open University.

Anna Gupta is Lecturer in Social Work (Child Care) at Royal Holloway, University of London and a Children's Guardian.

Nick Hindley is Consultant Child and Adolescent Forensic Psychiatrist at the Warneford Hospital, Oxford.

Carole Jeffery is Senior Course Manager in the Faculty of Health and Society Care at The Open University.

David P.H. Jones is Consultant Child and Family Psychiatrist and Senior Lecturer at the Park Hospital for Children, Oxford.

Kwame Owusu-Bempah is Reader in Psychology at the School of Social Work, University of Leicester.

Marian Perkins is Consultant Child and Adolescent Neuropsychiatrist at the Park Hospital, Oxford.

David Quinton is Emeritus Professor in Psychosocial Development at the University of Bristol.

Paul Ramchandani works at the University of Oxford, where he is a research fellow and an Honorary Consultant Child and Adolescent Psychiatrist.

Wendy Rose is Senior Research Fellow at The Open University. She was formerly Assistant Chief Inspector (Children's Services) at the Department of Health.

Gillian Schofield is Co-Director of the Centre for Research on the Child and Family at the University of East Anglia. She is Chair of the BAAF Research Advisory Group Committee and a member of the Family Justice Council Interdisciplinary Family Law Committee.

Janet Seden is Senior Lecturer in the Faculty of Health and Social Care at The Open University.

Subject Index

Author Index

Lightning Source UK Ltd.
Milton Keynes UK
UKOW06f0612170915

258781UK00001B/101/P